TEEN PROGRAMS WITH PUNCH

TEEN PROGRAMS WITH PUNCH

A Month-by-Month Guide

Valerie A. Ott

Libraries Unlimited Professional Guides for Young Adult Librarians Series
C. Allen Nichols and Mary Anne Nichols, Series Editors

A Member of the Greenwood Publishing Group

Westport, Connecticut • London

Library of Congress Cataloging-in-Publication Data

Ott, Valerie A.
  Teen programs with punch : a month-by-month guide / by Valerie A. Ott.
      p.   cm.—(Libraries Unlimited professional guides for young adult librarians series,
  ISSN 1532-5571)
    Includes bibliographical references and index.
    ISBN 1-59158-293-8 (pbk. : alk. paper)
    1. Young adults' libraries—Activity programs—United States.   2. Libraries
  and teenagers—United States.   3. Teenagers—Books and reading—United
  States.   I. Title.   II. Series: Libraries Unlimited professional guides for young adult
  librarians.
  Z718.5.O88 2006
  027.62'6—dc22   2006012775

British Library Cataloguing in Publication Data is available.

Library of Congress Catalog Card Number: 2006012775
ISBN: 1-59158-293-8
ISSN: 1532-5571

First published in 2006

Libraries Unlimited, 88 Post Road West, Westport, CT 06881
A Member of the Greenwood Publishing Group, Inc.
www.lu.com

Printed in the United States of America

The paper used in this book complies with the
Permanent Paper Standard issued by the National
Information Standards Organization (Z39.48–1984).

10 9 8 7 6 5 4 3 2 1

The publisher has done its best to make sure the instructions and/or recipes in this book
are correct. However, users should apply judgment and experience when preparing
recipes, especially parents and teachers working with young people. The publisher
accepts no responsibility for the outcome of any recipe included in this volume.

For my husband

As this journey ends, I look forward to the next.

I love you.

CONTENTS

Contents

SERIES FOREWORD

We firmly believe in young adult library services and advocate for teens whenever we can. We are proud of our association with Libraries Unlimited and Greenwood Publishing Group and grateful for their acknowledgment of the need for additional resources for teen-serving librarians. We intend for this series to fill those needs, providing useful and practical handbooks for library staff. Readers will find some theory and philosophical musings, but for the most part, this series will focus on real-life library issues with answers and suggestions for frontline librarians.

Our passion for young adult librarian services continues to reach new peaks. As we travel to present workshops on the various facets of working with teens in public libraries, we are encouraged by the desire of librarians everywhere to learn what they can do in their libraries to make teens welcome. This is a positive sign since too often libraries choose to ignore this underserved group of patrons. We hope you find this series to be a useful tool in fostering your own enthusiasm for teens.

C. Allen Nichols
Mary Anne Nichols
Series Editors

ACKNOWLEDGMENTS

If there is one thing I have learned throughout my years serving as a teen services librarian, it is that my colleagues are some of the most generous, enthusiastic, and creative individuals in our profession. I was inspired time and time again during the writing of this book as I attended conferences and shared in lively discussions about library service to teens. That said, many times program ideas take on a life of their own, traveling from state to state and from library to library. Sometimes, their origins are lost along the way and they take on the flavor of each library's community. Although most of the program ideas in this book are original and of my own creation, some are amalgams of ideas I've gleaned from dedicated librarians and teachers, or adapted from workshops I have attended over the years. Wherever possible, I have given credit to the individuals or libraries who first developed the program, or to the authors of books containing an activity that spawned a whole program idea. I would especially like to thank the amazing teen services librarians of Ohio for their energy and inspiring dedication to teens; Marcia Kroft at the Ohio State University Extension Office of Medina County for her experience and expertise with the Real World program; May Sweet, Teen Services Associate at Wadsworth Public Library, who helped me develop many of these programs to try out on our teen guinea pigs; members of YALSA, who never tire of giving expert advice and guidance; and Dr. Carolyn Brodie of Kent State University, who first introduced me to the possibility of serving teens. Librarians cannot help but share their great ideas; I hope by sharing this book with you, your libraries will be enriched.

INTRODUCTION

By now, teen programming in public libraries is far from a new idea. Young adults have been a worthy focus of youth services for at least the past fifteen years, as evidenced by the heavy traffic on discussion lists like YA-YAAC and YALSA-BK; the amount of library Web sites that have dedicated "teen pages"; and the increasing number of libraries that have special teen areas, separate from children's and adult departments. Looking back, it's hard to say which came first: teen programming or fantastic teen literature. Certainly, since 2000, the Printz Award has helped garner some attention and respect for books written for this age group, and therefore it may not be coincidental that the spotlight has shifted to shine on teen services in libraries since then. But perhaps people like Patrick Jones and their undying advocacy for teens inspired writers to kick it up a notch. Regardless, recent years could be described as a golden age for teen services. The Young Adult Library Services Association (YALSA), in fact, has more than doubled its membership since 1994 and has enjoyed a 60 percent increase in membership just since 2000 (Yoke 2005).

Because young adult services are supported by many public libraries these days, perhaps this is a good time to reassess the reasons we do what we do. First, teens have issues. Increasing responsibilities at school or home, poor body image, mercurial friendships, sexual identity crises, and dating dilemmas are just some of the things the average teen juggles. While all of this may make teen librarians feel like they have to compete for attention, it also creates fodder for great programs. Such a wide range of social concerns provides opportunities to create programs that can truly help teenagers.

Second, most teen services librarians would agree that after many children reach their teen years, it is difficult to find them in the library. In fact, many of them may not frequent the library again until it is time to bring their own children to story time. The most recent statistics collected on how age relates to library usage are over 10 years old. Clearly, however, there is anecdotal evidence that suggests there is a gap here that teen services librarians can help bridge by creating programs of interest to young adults so that they become lifelong library users.

Finally, the quality of literature being published for young adults demands that we create programming around it. After all, libraries aim to connect people with books. Although libraries today have become more like community centers, making it easy to plan programs with the sole purpose of entertaining customers, it is important to remember our roots. Connecting young people with books is a worthy goal for any program, whether it is intended to inform, educate, or entertain.

Clearly, the reasons for offering services to teens have been well established over the years, but now you may be running out of ideas and feeling bored with the same tried-and-true programs. This month-by-month guide offers librarians fresh ideas and updated suggestions for teen programming. The programs offered in this book will go beyond traditional summer reading clubs, book discussion groups, and teen advisory councils that many librarians have already heard of, and may already employ. Rest assured, this book will offer relevant programs in an effort to enrich, educate, and enliven the lives of teenagers. Arts and crafts, educational, and purely recreational programs are included in an effort to appeal to a variety of teen tastes, recognizing that there is no such thing as a "typical teenager."

However, to address several of the social issues teens face today, many of the ideas you'll find here will be surprising, progressive, and perhaps less conventional than those written about before. These "programs with punch," which you can recognize by the 🎆 symbol preceding it, are fully fleshed out. They have complete instructions, as well as suggestions for supplemental materials, promotional ideas, and reading lists. Each program addresses the matter of cost, since budgets are always an issue. Each program description is preceded by a dollar-sign symbol, denoting the approximate costs your library will incur to provide these programs for your local teens. The key is as follows: $ = $0–25; $$ = $25–50; $$$ = $50–100; $$$$ = over $100.

Each chapter also indicates which grade levels would work best as the targeted audience. Finally, each chapter contains three quick and easy program ideas for librarians to employ when time and resources are in short supply. It is certainly understandable that these types of programs are often needed because of tightening budgets and a shortage of staff.

You may find it refreshing to note that the programs detailed in this book always have a connection to reading and information literacy. Included with each program is a Collection Connection section containing lists of fiction and nonfiction titles to supplement the programs. You'll find that an effort has been made to include the publication information for in-print versions of each book.

Entertaining the teens in our libraries is a worthy goal, and some of the ideas contained in this book can easily be watered down to serve this purpose alone. I think you will find, however, that all of these programs have loftier aspirations—to inspire, inform, encourage, and empower teens. What place is better equipped to achieve these goals than a library?

REFERENCE

Yoke, B. (2005, September 20). "Re: dues increase article." E-mail to C. Allen Nichols.

Chapter 1

JANUARY

The new year is a time for resolutions and good intentions. Just like adults, teens often promise to make a long list of self-improvements come January. *Resolution One: Eat Healthier.* "Veg Out" is a program designed to encourage teens who want to be vegetarians to think about the reasons why this choice appeals to them. Then, recipes and diet suggestions will help them keep their resolutions to swear off meat. *Resolution Two: Pursue My Dream.* "Get Reel" is an amateur film contest for teens who dream of becoming the next Sophia Coppola or Steven Spielberg. *Resolution Three: Learn Something New.* Goth teens are an often-misunderstood group. By planning a "Goth Gathering," the community's—or at least your library's—perception of this group of teens is bound to change.

GOTH GATHERING ($) (GRADES 9–12)

You've seen them around the library, often sporting oversized black clothing and Doc Martens, with jet-black hair, heavy eye makeup, and various piercings. Who are these teens, and why do they look like that? According to Nancy Kilpatrick's invaluable book *The Goth Bible: A Compendium for the Darkly Inclined*, defining goth as a subculture made up of morbidly artistic people does not do justice to those who embrace this lifestyle. Like any other subset of people, no one definition sums up all of the individual tastes and beliefs of persons belonging to this group. That said, Kilpatrick does a wonderful job of revealing some commonalities shared by goths in saying, "Goth is a way of being that embraces what the normal world shuns" (Kilpatrick 2004). She goes on to explain that goths tend to welcome or accept the darker, more morose side of life rather than turning away from it as many people do. Furthermore, Kilpatrick explains, "Romance is at the heart of what it means to be goth, and consequently tragedy is always a sigh away. . . . Every goth is an individual first and foremost. . . . Yet lurking within such independence is the intense need for community." This need for community is certainly understandable in light of the fact that goths are often considered to be on the fringe, or—to get in the spirit of things—in the shadows, of mainstream society. Goth teens, therefore, are likely even more in need of a welcoming atmosphere given the harsh realities of life in the average American high school.

This program is packaged as an informal get-together for goth teens to discuss the music, fashion, and trends of the goth scene. Fortunately, the program will also position your library as an accepting gathering place for an often-misunderstood group to talk about social acceptance and community education issues. As you get to know them, some of the teens may even be able to offer suggestions of materials to purchase for your library's collection that would appeal to this group.

How

Since this program is meant to be an informal get-together rather than one filled with activities or formally led discussions, there are very few step-by-step instructions to offer here. Fortunately, this makes for a fairly hands-off program requiring few supplies and incurring little cost. Since goth culture is often misunderstood and categorized as a devil-worshiping cult of drug addicts, however, I strongly suggest familiarizing yourself with many aspects of goth culture before inviting these teens to a program. That way, if any concerns arise in the community, you'll have some facts to set minds at ease. (In fact, most goths do not drink alcohol or take drugs, and while some may identify with Satan, most do not worship him.) In addition to Kilpatrick's previously quoted book—which is a fabulous resource—some other sources to consult in preparation for this program are listed below. (These are written to educate a mainstream audience. As such, they are not duplicated in the list of nonfiction titles that would appeal to goth teens, provided in the Collection Connection section below.)

- *21st Century Goth*—Mick Mercer
- *Goth: Identity, Style and Subculture*—Paul Hodkinson
- *Goth Chic: A Connoisseur's Guide to Dark Culture*—Gavin Baddeley
- *What Is Goth?*—Voltaire

So how do you hook goth teens? The easiest way to find an audience for this program is to get to know a goth teen who regularly uses the library, in an effort to further familiarize yourself with the goth scene in your community. Another way to find goths is to visit www.goth.net for a listing of events and venues in your area. Once you have established a connection to this group of teens, the program will be easier to promote through the strategic placement of flyers and good ol' word of mouth. To entice people to show up at the initial gathering, put a dark spin on things. For instance, you could plan the program on January 19 in commemoration of Edgar Allan Poe's birth.

Once a group of goth teens have started regularly gathering at your library, you may consider holding more planned activities. Some ideas include starting a discussion about the latest additions to the library's graphic novel collection, including series like *Gloom-Cookie* or *Courtney Crumrin*; showing movies like *The Crow, Sleepy Hollow,* or *The House of Usher*; having a macabre picnic in a neighboring cemetery; or serving a Victorian-style afternoon tea complete with black roses and a silver tea service. Invite the participants to either bring their own music to these gatherings, or make suggestions as to what materials they would like to see in your library. This would also be an opportune time to highlight materials (such as the books listed at the end of the chapter) of which they may not be aware, but would find interesting.

Finally, once you have gained the teens' trust, encourage them to discuss concerns they may have regarding the community's perceptions of goth culture. Although they may not be troubled by mainstream society's misconceptions, dialogue about such issues will help them define what they love about goth culture and, in turn, think of the library as a place to share their unique perspective.

Time, Cost, and Supplies

Initially, this program can be held virtually free of cost, except for any supplies you may need to promote it. Hopefully, though, goth teens will soon begin to gather more regularly at your library and you may decide to plan activities for them, at which point items such as refreshments may need to be purchased. As previously mentioned, you should read up on goth culture to familiarize yourself with the styles, music, and tastes of goth teens. Beyond that, you do not have to spend a lot of time preparing for the initial get-together. A couple of hours should be all you need to pick a dark theme for the gathering, design some promotional materials, gather some melancholic books and props, and make contact with your audience.

Promotion

Make sure to utilize the Internet to promote this program. Many goths, as previously mentioned, are solitary by nature and tend to gravitate to online methods of information gathering. Therefore, publicize the date and time of your initial "goth gathering" on Web site forums and chat rooms for goths. Also, after doing some research, you should be able to pinpoint some popular goth venues or hangouts in or near your community where you could drop off or post flyers promoting the event. As for the promotional flyer itself, use dark colors—say, black—and embellish it with intricate gothic crosses and Victorian lettering.

Collection Connection

Fiction

Abarat—Clive Barker (Joanna Cotler, 2002)

The Bell Jar—Sylvia Plath (Perennial, 1999)

Blood and Chocolate—Annette Curtis Klause (Delacorte, 1997)

The Blue Girl—Charles deLint (Viking, 2004)

Carmilla—J. Sheridan Le Fanu (Wildside Press, 2005)

The Celestial Railroad and Other Stories—Nathaniel Hawthorne (Signet Classics, 1963)

The China Garden—Liz Berry (Farrar, Straus and Giroux, 1996)

The Complete Stories and Poems of Edgar Allan Poe—Edgar Allan Poe (Doubleday, 1966)*

Coraline—Neil Gaiman (HarperCollins, 2002)

Courtney Crumrin series—Ted Naifeh (Oni Press)**

The Crow series—James O'Barr (Kitchen Sink Press)**

Darkangel series—Meredith Pierce (Magic Carpet Books)

The Diary of Ellen Rimbauer: My Life at Rose Red—Joyce Reardon (Hyperion, 2001)

Dracula—Bram Stoker (Signet Classics, 1997)

Emily the Strange series—Cosmic Debris (Dark Horse Comics)**

The Exorcist—William Peter Blatty (Harper Torch, 2000)

Frankenstein—Mary Shelley (Pocket Books, 2004)

Ghost Stories of Edith Wharton—Edith Wharton (Scribner, 1997)

Gloom Cookie series—Serena Valentino (SLG Publishing)**

Gothic: Ten Original Dark Tales—Deborah Noyes (Candlewick, 2004)

Great and Terrible Beauty—Libba Bray (Delacorte, 2003)

Green Angel—Alice Hoffman (Scholastic, 2003)

Grimms' Fairy Tales—Johnny Gruelle (Bantam, 2000)

The Haunting of Hill House—Shirley Jackson (Penguin, 1984)

The Hollow Kingdom—Clare Dunkle (Henry Holt, 2003)

In the Forests of the Night—Amelia Atwater-Rhodes (Delacorte, 1999)*

The Italian—Ann Radcliffe (Penguin Classics, 2001)

Jane Eyre—Charlotte Bronte (Penguin Classics, 2003)

Lenore series—Roman Dirge (SLG Publishing)**

The Melancholy Death of Oyster Boy and Other Stories—Tim Burton (Harper Entertainment, 1997)*

Mina—Marie Kiraly (Berkley Publishing Group, 1996)

Moondog series—Henry Garfield (Simon Pulse)

The Picture of Dorian Gray—Oscar Wilde (Modern Library, 1998)

Sandman series—Neil Gaiman (DC Comics)*

Seer series—Linda Joy Singleton (Llewellyn Publications)

*Denotes authors who commonly write about goth themes.
**Denotes a graphic novel series.

Shutterbox series—Rikki Simons (Tokyopop)**

Silver Kiss—Annette Curtis Klause (Delacorte, 1990)

Sunshine—Robin McKinley (Berkley Publishing Group, 2003)

Sweetblood—Pete Hautman (Simon and Schuster, 2003)

Tam Lin—Pamela Dean (Tor Books, 1991)

Thirsty—M. T. Anderson (Candlewick, 1997)

Tithe: A Modern Faerie Tale—Holly Black (Simon and Schuster, 2002)

The Turn of the Screw—Henry James (Bantam Classics, 1981)

Under the Glass Moon series—Ko Ya Seong (TokyoPop)**

Vampire Chronicles series—Anne Rice (Ballantine Books)*

Vampire High—Douglas Rees (Delacorte, 2003)

Vampire Princess Miyu series—Narumi Kakinauchi (Studio Ironcat)**

The Vampire's Beautiful Daughter—S. P. Somtow (Atheneum, 1997)

War for the Oaks—Emma Bull (Ace Books, 1987)

Weetsie Bat—Francesca Lia Block (HarperCollins, 1989)

Wuthering Heights—Emily Brontë (Penguin Classics, 2002)

The Yellow Wallpaper—Charlotte Perkins Gilman (Dover Publications, 1997)

Nonfiction

The Goth Bible: A Compendium for the Darkly Inclined—Nancy Kilpatrick (St. Martin's Griffin, 2004)

Journals—Kurt Cobain (Riverhead Books, 2002)

Paint It Black: A Guide to Gothic Homemaking—Voltaire (Weiser Books, 2005)

Touching from a Distance—Deborah Curtis (Faber and Faber, 1996)

VEG OUT ($$$) (GRADES 6–12)

It is difficult to find the accurate number of teen vegetarians in this country, but according to a news report, the number of teenagers who called themselves vegetarians rose 30 percent between the years 1998 and 2003 (Cleveland News Channel 5 2003). Estimates of the number of vegetarians aged 8 to 17 in the United States range from 1 to 2 percent, which equals about 500,000 to 1 million adolescents (Vegetarian Resource Group

2000). Furthermore, Teen Research Unlimited reports that 25 percent of teenagers polled believe vegetarianism to be "cool" (Glenn 2003).

With so many teens admiring the vegetarian lifestyle, it becomes very important to make sure they are aware of crucial nutritional information before adopting this eating habit. This program is a hands-on and interactive way for teen library customers to learn about the proper way to become a vegetarian through discussing reasons for adopting this lifestyle, learning about foods that provide a healthy and balanced diet, and making recipes.

How

The format of this program is pretty simple. Before beginning the fun of concocting some veggie recipes, some basic information about vegetarianism should be presented to the participants. You can do this yourself, but if you are uncomfortable providing health advice, ask a dietician or a representative from a local health food store to provide their expertise. If you choose to present the information yourself, consult current sources for information first. Several nonfiction book titles are provided in the Collection Connection section of this program, or you could try these Web sites:

A Guide to Healthy Vegetarian Eating
www.keepkidshealthy.com/nutrition/healthy_vegetarian_eating.html

Is a Vegetarian Diet Right for Me?
www.kidshealth.org/teen/nutrition/diets/vegetarian.html

Vegetarianism in Teens
www.pamf.org/teen/health/nutrition/veggieteens.html

The Vegetarian Resource Group
www.vrg.org

Vegetarianteen: An Online Magazine
www.vegetarianteen.com

First, ask the teens at your program why they are, or want to be, vegetarians. There are many reasons why people choose this lifestyle, and since it is sometimes difficult to maintain, it is important for the teens to think about their reasons for making this choice. Teens who just consider vegetarianism "cool" are making this choice for the wrong reason, and are unlikely to stick to it. Some people choose to become vegetarians simply because vegetarian food is often cheaper than a diet that includes meat.

Others are motivated by ethical concerns such as the treatment of animals, and the environmental and world hunger problems associated with raising grain for livestock consumption. Still others choose vegetarianism on the grounds that it may result in health benefits such as a decreased risk of high cholesterol and certain types of cancer. These are all sound reasons for teens to cite for choosing vegetarian eating habits.

Next, explain to the teens the different types of vegetarianism and encourage them to think about which form fits best with their reasoning to change their eating habits. Some vegetarians choose to cut only red meat from their diets. While this is not a true form of vegetarianism, it is often a way for carnivores to wean themselves away from meat. True vegetarians do not eat any meat whatsoever, including poultry and fish. An ovo vegetarian eats eggs; a lacto vegetarian eats dairy products; and a lacto-ovo vegetarian eats both. Vegans, on the other hand, eat no animal products at all, including honey and gelatin-based foods.

Finally, spend some time explaining which nutrients are lost when meat, dairy products, and eggs are eliminated from a diet. Stress the need to carefully plan meals that include iron, calcium, proteins, vitamin D, vitamin B_{12}, and zinc, since these are the nutrients often missing from vegetarian diets. Specific foods and other suggestions for achieving a balanced diet can be found in any of the resources listed in this section. To make this portion of the program a bit more interactive, use this matching quiz (Veggie Quiz, page 9). Award a prize such as a vegetarian cookbook, a recipe box, or a gift certificate to a local restaurant known for its veggie cuisine, to the teen who gets the most correct answers.

At this point, be sure to hand out or direct teens to resources that they can consult at their leisure, then open up the discussion to see if they have questions about other topics such as how to order at a restaurant, healthy fast-food options, and what to do if a family member doesn't support the choice to become vegetarian. Again, answers to many of these questions can be found in the print sources mentioned at the end of this section, but there is a wealth of Internet sources dedicated to specific topics related to vegetarianism as well:

Dining Out

Happy Cow
www.happycow.net

How to Order at a Restaurant as a Vegetarian
www.ehow.com/how_5335_order-restaurant-vegetarian.html

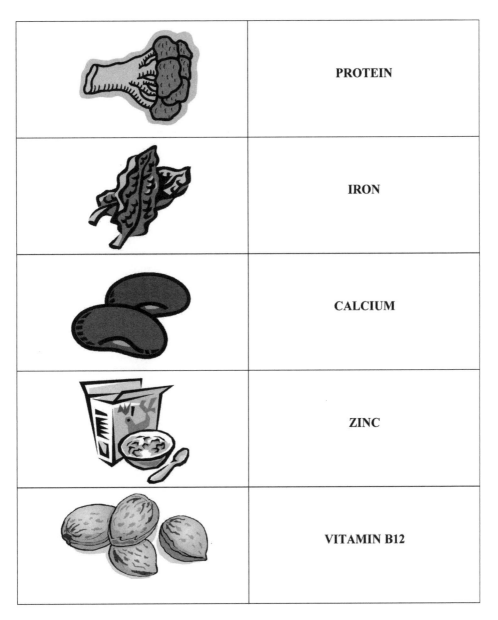

	PROTEIN
	IRON
	CALCIUM
	ZINC
	VITAMIN B12

Vegetarian Options in Fast Food Restaurants
www.vegetarian-restaurants.net/OtherInfo/FastFoodRest.htm

VegDining
www.vegdining.com/Home.cfm

Family Support

Talking to Your Parents
www.vegsoc.org/youth/packs/student-parents.html

Two Daughters: One Veg . . . One Not
www.vegetarianbaby.com/articles/twodaughters.shtml

Veggie Teens in Need of Support
www.vegfamily.com/vegan-teens/veggie-teens-support.htm

Finally, invite the teens to partake in a mini cooking class that will introduce them to the simple and tasty recipes given below. Each of these recipes will make enough for approximately twelve small, taste-test-sized portions.

Santa Fe Salad

1 c. cooked brown rice

½ c. black beans

½ c. cooked corn

¼ c. chopped yellow pepper

½ c. chopped tomato

½ c. shredded cheddar cheese (this can be substituted for soy cheese if you wish to make this recipe vegan)

4 T. olive oil

juice from one lime

1 clove of minced garlic

1 tsp. cumin

1 bag of baby spinach

Mix together first six ingredients. Whisk together next four and pour over relish mixture. Pile on top of spinach leaves.

Toasted Peanut Butter and Banana Sandwiches

8 slices of whole wheat bread

8 T. peanut butter

3–4 bananas, sliced

Toast bread, and immediately top each piece with about a table-spoon of peanut butter while the bread is still warm. Place banana slices between slices of bread. Cut each sandwich into three sections.

Tropical Fruit Smoothie

12 oz. soft silken tofu

1 banana

2 c. orange juice, chilled

1 8-oz. can of crushed pineapple, chilled

1 tsp. vanilla extract

1 T. honey

Mix all ingredients in a blender until smooth.

Chocolate Mousse

12 oz. soft silken tofu

12 oz. semisweet chocolate chips

2 tsp. vanilla extract

1 pinch salt

½ of a 12-oz. tub of whipped topping

Melt chocolate chips in the microwave. Mix tofu, vanilla, and salt in a blender until smooth, then pour in melted chocolate and blend again. Pour into a bowl and fold in whipped topping. Chill for about an hour or until set. Serve with graham crackers.

If you have a large group of teens participating, the easiest thing to do is to set up four stations—one for each of the recipes—with the necessary tools and ingredients. Before beginning this portion of the program, though, make sure to ask the teens if any of them have known food al-lergies. Then, after the teens have finished making the recipes at their assigned stations, invite the entire group to tour from table to table sampling each dish. Print the recipes on index cards so the participants can take them home.

Time, Cost, and Supplies

Allot just two hours or so to prepare for this program, most of which will be spent shopping for the recipe ingredients listed here:

1 14-oz. box of brown rice

can of black beans

bag or box of frozen corn

1 yellow pepper

1 medium-size tomato

2 c. of shredded cheddar cheese or soy cheese

olive oil

1 lime

1 bulb of garlic

cumin

1 bag of baby spinach

loaf of whole wheat bread

small jar of peanut butter

bunch of 6–8 bananas

2 12-oz. packages of soft silken tofu

1 quart of orange juice

8-oz. can of crushed pineapple

vanilla extract

honey

12-oz. bag of semi-sweet chocolate chips

salt

12-oz. tub of whipped topping

1 box of graham crackers

index cards

These ingredients will cost about $50 unless you are willing to bring some of them from home. Since it's likely that you already have some of the more common ingredients such as olive oil, salt, vanilla extract, honey, and even cumin, it would really keep costs down to contribute these items to the program—especially since the quantities required are so small. Another option would be to ask a local grocery store to donate a gift certificate so that you can purchase what you need with that. Also, it is not necessary to make all four recipes; the program will be enjoyable— and more cost-effective—if you choose only two or three of them. Additionally, you will need to gather the necessary kitchen tools to make the recipes:

- one large mixing bowl
- whisk
- several knives
- cutting board
- set of measuring spoons
- set of measuring cups
- toaster oven or electric griddle
- spatula
- can opener
- two blenders
- microwave oven

It's very likely that you'll be able to bring most of these items from home, or borrow some from a coworker. Your library is likely to have some of the tools, such as a microwave.

Promotion

Logical places to promote this program include health food and grocery stores; schools—particularly family and consumer science or health classes; and hospitals. Within the library, publicize the program with a display that's a feast for the eyes. Under the heading "Veg Out," arrange cooking supplies like bowls, tongs, plates, and measuring cups on top of a red and white checkered tablecloth. Consider stacking books inside some of the bowls along with artificial fruits and vegetables. Flyers should invite teens to the program by promising a hands-on cooking class that will prove that there is life beyond veggie burgers for vegetarian wannabes.

Collection Connection

Nonfiction

Everything You Need to Know about Being a Vegan—Stefanie Iris Weiss (Rosen Publishing Group, 1999)

Everything You Need to Know about Being a Vegetarian—Kim Serafin (Rosen Publishing Group, 1999)

I'm a Vegetarian: Amazing Facts and Ideas for Healthy Vegetarians—Ellen Schwartz (Tundra Books, 2002)

Jumbo Vegetarian Cookbook—Judi Gillies (Kids Can Press, 2002)

Munchie Madness: Vegetarian Meals for Teens—Dorothy Bates (Book Publishing Company, 2001)

The Starving Students' Vegetarian Cookbook—Dede Hall (Warner Books, 2001)

A Teen's Guide to Going Vegetarian—Judy Krizmanic (Puffin, 1994)

The Teen's Vegetarian Cookbook—Judy Krizmanic (Puffin, 1999)

Vegetables Rock! A Complete Guide for Teenage Vegetarians—Stephanie Pierson (Bantam, 1999)

Vegetarianism for Teens—Jane Duden (LifeMatters, 2001)

The Young Vegetarian's Companion—Jan Parr (Franklin Watts, 1996)

GET REEL ($$$$) (GRADES 9–12)

America's love affair with movies does not seem to have ceased since movies were first introduced in silent form in the early 1900s. For decades, movies have captivated audiences and provided an escape from everyday life. The medium is unique in that it provides filmmakers an opportunity to create something stimulating for our eyes, ears, and hearts all at once. Since the advent of video editing software for personal computers, as well as digital video cameras, it has become much easier for young film enthusiasts to create their own short films unhindered by pricey studio fees or complicated equipment. Amateur film contests and festivals are not a brand new programming idea for public libraries—particularly in California—but instructions for how to run one are difficult to find. This section, therefore, provides directions and suggestions for holding a successful amateur film contest.

How

There are two main tasks involved in running this program: soliciting submissions and planning the awards ceremony. Before starting this venture alone, however, contact your area arts council or film society to see if they are interested in partnering with your library on the project. By doing so, you may be able to secure a little extra funding, as well as a pool of experts who could serve as knowledgeable judges. First, determine whether or not your film contest will have a theme, or just categories like animation, comedy, drama, horror, and documentary. Next, decide on the criteria for submissions to ensure that the contestants have followed the same set of rules, making it a fair contest. For instance, since this is a contest for teens, you should set an age range for participants. If, though, there are film students in your area who attend a local community college or university, you may want to consider accepting entries for slightly older, but still amateur, filmmakers. Allowing college students to participate may ensure a larger number of entries. If this is the route you take, it will be necessary to judge entries in beginner and experienced categories since those with some college training are likely to have an advantage over younger contestants. Otherwise, prizes could just be awarded to the best of each category (e.g., best comedy, best documentary, etc.), and then overall prizes could be given for audience favorite, best actor, best actress, and special effects. Depending on how much funding you have for prizes, you could also include categories like best set, best screenplay, and best musical soundtrack. It is also important to specify that entries should be in either VHS or DVD format, and should be no longer than ten to fifteen minutes. Finally, ensure that the films' contents are suitable for public viewing by accepting PG or PG-13 submissions only.

Since making a short film takes a substantial amount of time, plan to have the screening and awards ceremony two to three months after you begin accepting entries. This should allow enough time for interested teens to create something for the contest after hearing about it. The awards ceremony will be a golden opportunity to invite local press and government officials to witness firsthand the cultural and developmental impact your library has on teenagers. Therefore, plan to make this event a special one.

First of all, invite guests to dress for a red-carpet evening in order to add an air of sophistication and importance to the screening and awards ceremony. As the audience begins to arrive, have teen volunteers serve them sparkling white grape juice in plastic champagne flutes, and simple hors d'oeuvres like cheese and cracker canapés or fruit. To make guests feel even more glamorous, purchase a few yards of red velvet and tack it down at the entryway to your program. Then, ask a few more teen volunteers to pose as paparazzi, snapping pictures of participants as they arrive. Play songs like "Hooray for Hollywood" or "Puttin' on the Ritz," or recognizable movie themes to enhance the atmosphere even more. As the starting time draws near, dim the lights and have two teenaged emcees welcome everyone to the event. Next, show each film in its entirety if possible. Since eligible entries had to have a time limit, it should be possible to show about a dozen ten-minute entries in the time it would take to show one feature-length film. Since this portion of the event should really not stretch longer than two hours, make sure to reserve the right to show clips from each film if you receive more than twelve entries. After the films have been shown, have the emcees open sealed envelopes to announce the winners in each category. A variety of ideas for prizes includes cash; imitation Oscar statuettes (available at novelty stores); gift certificates to movie theaters or for video rentals, or to a camera store for filmmaking supplies; or the Scene It?® board game (www.sceneit.com). If you do go the route of partnering with a local arts council or film society and, down the road, this contest enjoys some success and longevity, you may even be able to offer scholarship money for attendance at a film school.

Last, but not least, give your community ample opportunity to view the hard work and talent of these budding filmmakers by planning an encore presentation of the winning films at your library, or other branches of your library system, on subsequent nights. Or contact your local cable affiliate to see if they would be willing to air the winning films on television. Finally, keep in mind that after two or three years' worth of successful teen film contests, you should have enough material to hold a mini film festival as a way of promoting and building excitement for future contests.

Time, Cost, and Supplies

For this contest to really be successful, a fair amount of time should be spent contacting potential partners (see below). Then, spend the month or two after the promotional campaign has been launched to line up teen volunteers for the screening and awards ceremony and purchase any food and supplies for that event. At this time, it will also be important to line up a panel of judges. If you are unable to find sponsors or partners for this program, it's entirely possible to hold it anyway; the prizes may just have to be less expensive. Here is a list of supplies you will need:

- a few yards of red velvet
- plastic champagne flutes
- sparkling white grape juice
- cheese
- crackers
- fruit
- a few serving trays
- two small boxes of toothpicks
- cocktail napkins
- movie projector
- DVD and/or VCR
- movie screen
- microphone
- prizes

Because prizes are offered, this program will still be one of the more expensive ones described in this book, depending on how many categories you decide to judge and how many entries you receive. Of course, partnering with other agencies or organizations could reduce the costs significantly—especially if those entities agree to donate or purchase the prizes, leaving you more room to provide fancier hors d'oeuvres or decorations.

Promotion

Obviously, it would be pretty hard to have any kind of contest without at least a few films to screen, so spend a fair amount of time adequately promoting this opportunity to the appropriate audiences. In other words, this is a program for which it is necessary to seek out an audience; simply promoting the contest in-house will probably not be enough of an effort to ensure success. Therefore, attempt to blanket the community with printed promotional pieces. As previously mentioned, contact local arts councils or film societies to seek a partnership or, at the very least, to gain an avenue for promotion. Check with universities and community colleges to see if there are film studies classes that you could target. Seek out small movie houses that specialize in indie films, and don't forget to pay some attention to theater companies since many actors harbor the dream to direct!

For in-house promotion, under the phrase "Lights, Camera, Action!" design a large, black-and-white director's clapboard, to display the title of the contest, "Get Reel." Along the bottom of the clapboard, label three spaces "Date," "Scene," and "Time" to convey the particulars of the screening and awards ceremony. Make sure to stack plenty of entry forms nearby, along with some independent or award-winning films and several of the titles listed in the Collection Connection section below. You may also choose to make bookmarks listing the rules and other pertinent information about the contest, as well as Web sites teens can visit to gain some inspiration. Three such sites are the Online Student Short Film Festival (www.studentfilms.com), Independent Film (www.indiefilmpage.com), and Independent Film at the Internet Movie Database (http://indie.imdb.com).

Finally, all major entertainment awards have nicknames, so with a nod to Oscar, Emmy, and Grammy, consider naming your contest to lend some panache to the event. In lieu of the generic contest name "Get Reel," use this name on all printed promotional pieces, in press releases, and on the library's Web site to help "brand" the contest and make it more recognizable.

Collection Connection

Nonfiction

American Film: An A–Z Guide—Peter Kramer (Franklin Watts, 2003)

Attack of the Killer Video Book: Tips and Tricks for Young Directors—Mark Shulman (Annick Press, 2004)

Before Hollywood: From Shadow Play to the Silver Screen—Paul Clee (Clarion Books, 2005)

A Brief Guide for the High School Moviemaker—Alex Kerr (Alex Kerr, 2003)

Filmmakers—Andy Koopmans (Lucent Books, 2005)

Filmmaking for Dummies—Bryan Michael Stoller (John Wiley, 2003)

Girl Director: A How-to Guide for the First-Time, Flat-Broke Film and Video Maker—Andrea Richards (Ten Speed Press, 2005)

Pure Imagination: The Making of Willy Wonka and the Chocolate Factory—Mel Stuart (St. Martin's Press, 2002)

Reel Adventures: The Savvy Teens' Guide to Great Movies—John Lekich (Annick Press, 2002)

Ten American Movie Directors: The Men Behind the Camera—Anne E. Hill (Enslow Publishers, 2003)

Ultimate Girls' Movie Survival Guide: What to Rent, Who to Watch, How to Deal—Andrea Sarvady (Simon Spotlight Entertainment, 2004)

When Time Is Short and Money Is Tight...

Gourmet Coffee and Hot Tea Month—Set an area of the library up "café-style"; serve gourmet coffees (don't forget the whipped cream) and flavored teas along with assorted pastries; play music, and just allow the teens to socialize in a coffeehouse setting.

International Creativity Month—Gather together as many art supplies as you can find, and just let the teens express themselves through collage, painting, origami, and so on.

Celebrate the Chinese New Year with egg rolls, a kung fu movie, and information about the Chinese zodiac.

REFERENCES

Cleveland News Channel 5 (2003). Survey: Teen vegetarianism on rise. Experts say parents need to make sure kids are getting nutrients. Retrieved May 18, 2005, from NewsNet5 Web site: http://www.newsnet5.com/connectingwithkids/2172807/detail/html/index.html.

Glenn, K. (2003, May 23). Teen vegetarians. *Parade Classroom*. Retrieved May 18, 2005, from http://www.paradeclassroom.com/DL/TG/TG_03232003.pdf.

Kilpatrick, N. (2004). *The goth bible: A compendium for the darkly inclined*. New York: St. Martin's.

Vegetarian Resource Group (2000). How many teens are vegetarian? How many kids don't eat meat? Retrieved May 18, 2005, from the Vegetarian Resource Group Press Releases Web site: http://www.vrg.org/press/2000novteen.htm.

Chapter 2

◆◇◆ ◆◇◆ ◆◇◆

FEBRUARY

February is a short month, but for much of the country it drags along slowly due to the dreary weather. You can help teens beat the blahs with two of the programs featured in this chapter. "In Your Dreams" introduces teens to the idea of dream analysis, which could help them tap into their inner psyches. Then, after discovering something new about themselves, teens will be ready to channel their creative energy at the "Redo Your Room" program, which will help them create a freshened-up space that reflects who they are. With all of these changes taking place, why not challenge teens to take a look at the way they treat their gay and lesbian classmates at an "Intolerance Forum"? Chances are, some straight teens' way of thinking and behaving toward their GLBTQ counterparts could use some changing, too.

INTOLERANCE FORUM ($) (GRADES 9–12)

As a young adult librarian, I have always aimed to make sure that every teen who visits the library where I work feels welcome. That's why

I was dismayed one day when I heard a group of teens not-so-subtly whisper about a young man on my teen advisory council as he walked by them. I had always been fairly certain "Brian" was gay, and from the look on his face when he heard the whispers, I at least knew he was questioning his sexuality and had been on the receiving end of harassment before. Later, when he asked me about David Levithan's book *Boy Meets Boy*, I was happy to know that he at least felt comfortable around me, and I began to wonder what else the library could do to assist gay, lesbian, bisexual, transgender, and queer or questioning (GLBTQ) teens.

Thankfully, over the years, publishers have offered an increasing number of books featuring GLBTQ protagonists. Michael Cart, in an article entitled "Gay and Lesbian Literature Comes of Age," says that "the annual publication rate of novels with GLBTQ content has grown from an average of a single book in the 1970s to 4 in the 1980s, and from 7 in the 1990s to almost 12 in the first 5 years of the twenty-first century" (Cart 2005). At least now libraries can offer a wider variety of fiction and nonfiction for our teenaged GLBTQ customers. Resources like "Beyond Picket Fences: What Gay/Queer/LGBTQ Teens Want from the Library" (Linville 2004) and The Library Worker's Guide to Lesbian, Gay, Bisexual and Transgender Resources (library.cudenver.edu/libq/) help librarians further identify what services to provide to GLBTQ teens.

Clearly, libraries have come a long way in providing resources and services to the GLBTQ community, but, unfortunately, intolerance still exists. According to the United States Federal Bureau of Investigation's annual publication *Hate Crime Statistics*, there were 1,464 victims of anti-homosexual or anti-bisexual hate crimes in 2003 (Federal Bureau of Investigation 2004). Forty-two percent of these were victims of violent acts such as murder, rape, and aggravated assault. Unfortunately, this statistic has held pretty steady over the years. In 1996, the FBI reported 1,243 such victims, 41 percent of whom were victims of violent acts (Federal Bureau of Investigation 1996).

In the face of these sobering statistics, what can libraries do to make a difference? As librarians it is our obligation to share resources with our customers, but this becomes critical when those resources can help cultivate understanding and acceptance within our communities. Perhaps, in this case, it would be responsible of libraries to not only stock their shelves with information that fosters tolerance, but also actively disseminate it. Therefore, this program's intended audience is not GLTBQ teens (although they will likely have an interest in it), but rather the teen community at large, including parents and teachers.

How

In 1998, 21-year-old Matthew Shepard was brutally beaten, then tied to a post and left to die simply because he was gay. *The Laramie Project*, written by Moises Kaufman, is a play about the citizens of Laramie, Wyoming—where this crime took place—and their reactions to Matthew's death. Kaufman later made his play into a film by the same name. There are two ways to use this work in order to jump-start a discussion about homophobia. First, you could recruit some teens to act out scenes from the play, or simply read the scenes as part of a reader's theater. This would certainly involve teens in the program in a more hands-on way, but it may be difficult to find volunteers brave enough for the task. Check with drama classes or local theater companies to see if anyone is interested, then gain permission to use the play by downloading a form from the Dramatists Play Service (www.dramatists.com/text/npalinks.html). Alternatively, you could simply choose to show the entire film. Or, to cut down on length, it might be a good idea to show several clips instead. Since the work is mostly made up of "interviews" with actors portraying Matthew's friends, acquaintances, and other citizens of Laramie, it would be fairly easy to pick and choose the testimonials you feel are most powerful. (See Chapter 6 for a discussion about movie licenses.)

Afterward, facilitate a discussion about *The Laramie Project* in an effort to draw out the intolerance issues in your own community. There are several organizations that aim to educate teens about tolerance in order to end hate crimes. Some that specifically address GLBTQ issues are:

Gay, Lesbian and Straight Education Network
www.glsen.org

GenderYOUTH
www.gpac.org/youth

Mix It Up
www.tolerance.org/teens/index/jsp

The National Association of School Psychologists Work Group on Gay, Lesbian, and Bisexual Issues
www.nasponline.org/advocacy/glb.html

Safe Schools Coalition
www.safeschoolscoalition.org

Consulting these Web sites will help you choose the right words for discussing this topic. But for a subject this sensitive, it may be wise to ask a school psychologist, a well-liked and trusted teacher, or the school's principal to lead the forum. Or consider asking members of your local schools' Gay Straight Alliance (if there is one) or PFLAG (Parents and Friends of Lesbians and Gays) to help facilitate the discussion. Before beginning, have the audience set some ground rules to promote productive dialogue in an unthreatening environment. Here are some discussion questions to consider:

- Do you think Laramie is a town different from any other? How is it similar to where we live?
- Where does homophobia come from?
- Is there ever a good reason to feel homophobic?
- Does homophobia exist at this school or in this community? If so, what does it look like?
- Do you know any "out" GLBTQ teens? If so, how are they treated?
- What stereotypes are associated with the GLBTQ community? Do the "out" teens you know exhibit or refute these stereotypes?
- What steps could be taken to prevent what happened in Laramie from happening here?

At the conclusion of the forum, encourage the participants to think about how their own words and actions may contribute to the hostility that often surrounds their GLBTQ classmates. Take time to highlight the books in the Collection Connection section below; they may elucidate some of the issues GLBTQ teens have to face, heightening straight teens' level of acceptance.

Time, Cost, and Supplies

Executing this program is uncomplicated, and basically free of cost. Due to the sensitive nature of the topic, however, take extra care while preparing for the forum to ensure that it is handled properly. Consider consulting with someone from the mental health field, or, as previously suggested, a school psychologist. Again, though, a program such as this could be considered controversial in some communities, so be sure to consult with your library's administration and your local school's administration to determine the protocol for handling possible challenges. Other than printing costs for promotional pieces, there are no supplies or costs associated with this program (assuming you have a public performance license to show the film).

Promotion

Although you may draw an audience if your library is in an urban area, or an area that is reputably more open minded, the key to this program's success—particularly in rural areas—is to partner with local schools. Contact the guidance counselors to see if they feel a program like this would work, and consider taking the show on the road to ensure a ready-made audience. If you decide to show the film, however, make sure the school or facility hosting your program has a public performance license. Distribute flyers promoting the program at PFLAG meetings and psychologists' offices, and at parent-teacher conferences to attract concerned parents as well.

Collection Connection

Fiction

Am I Blue? Coming Out from the Silence—Marion Dane Bauer, editor (Harper Trophy, 1995)

Annie on My Mind—Nancy Garden (Farrar, Straus and Giroux, 1992)

Bermudez Triangle—Maureen Johnson (Sleuth Razorbill, 2004)

Boy Girl Boy—Ron Koertge (Harcourt Children's Books, 2005)

Boy Meets Boy—David Levithan (Knopf, 2003)

The Center of the World—Andreas Steinhofel (Delacorte, 2003)

Country Girl, City Girl—Lisa Jahn-Clough (Houghton Mifflin, 2004)

Deliver Us from Evie—M. E. Kerr (Harper Trophy, 1995)

Eight Seconds—Jean Ferris (Harcourt Children's Books, 2000)

Empress of the World—Sara Ryan (Viking, 2001)

Finding H.F.—Julia Watts (Alyson Publishing, 2001)

The Flip Side—Andrew Matthews (Delacorte, 2003)

From the Notebooks of Melanin Sun—Jacqueline Woodson (Scholastic, 1997)

Geography Club—Brent Hartinger (Harper Tempest, 2003)

Hard Love—Ellen Wittlinger (Simon and Schuster, 1999)

Keeping You a Secret—Julie Ann Peters (Megan Tingley, 2003)

Kissing Kate—Lauren Myracle (Dutton Books, 2003)

Luna—Julie Ann Peters (Megan Tingley, 2004)

My Heartbeat—Garret Freymann-Weyr (Houghton Mifflin, 2002)

Not the Only One: Lesbian and Gay Fiction for Teens—Jane Summer, editor (Alyson Publishing, 2004)

The Order of the Poison Oak—Brent Hartinger (Harper Tempest, 2005)

Orphea Proud—Sharon Dennis Wyeth (Delacorte, 2004)

Postcards from No-Man's Land—Aidan Chambers (Dutton Books, 2002)

Rainbow Boys—Alex Sanchez (Simon and Schuster, 2001)

Rainbox High—Alex Sanchez (Simon and Schuster, 2003)

The Realm of Possibility—David Levithan (Knopf, 2004)

So Hard to Say—Alex Sanchez (Simon and Schuster, 2004)

What Happened to Lani Garver?—Carol Plum-Ucci (Harcourt, 2002)

The Year They Burned the Books—Nancy Garden (Farrar, Straus and Giroux, 1999)

Nonfiction

Changing Bodies, Changing Lives—Ruth Bell (Three Rivers Press, 1998)

Free Your Mind: The Book for Gay, Lesbian and Bisexual Youth and Their Allies—Ellen Bass (Harper Paperbacks, 1996)

Girl2Girl—Norrina Rashid, editor (Diva Books, 2001)

GLBTQ: The Survival Guide for Queer and Questioning Teens—Kelly Huegel (Free Spirit Publishing, 2003)

Growing Up Gay in America—Jason Rich (Franklin Street Books, 2002)

Hear Me Out: True Stories of Teens Educating and Confronting Homophobia—Frances Rooney, editor (Second Story Press, 2005)

How I Learned to Snap—Kirk Read (Penguin, 2003)

In Your Face: Stories from the Lives of Queer Youth—Mary L. Gray (Harrington Park Press, 1999)

Pedro and Me—Judd Winnick (Henry Holt, 2000)

The Shared Heart: Portraits and Stories Celebrating Lesbian, Gay and Bisexual Young People—Adam Mastoon (William Morrow and Company, 1997)

Talking in the Dark—Billy Merrell (Push, 2003)

What if Someone I Know Is Gay? Answers to Questions about Gay and Lesbian People—Eric Marcus (Price Stearn Sloan, 2000)

IN YOUR DREAMS ($$$) (GRADES 7–10)

Do you want to run for cover when someone starts a conversation with, "I had this crazy dream last night . . ."? Chances are, you answered yes to this question. Since our dreams are often hard to translate into language and images that make sense to other people, it's often tiresome to listen to a long-winded explanation of the crazy details of someone else's dream. At the same time, however, we're often compelled to tell others about our subconscious nocturnal adventures because they're so bizarre, funny, or disturbing.

Many teens are fascinated by their own dreams, probably because they are purported to mean something significant or lead us to some insight about our psyches. Since teens are in the throws of self-discovery, it's quite logical that dream analysis would interest them, too. This program will encourage teens to become more aware of their dreams by helping them assign meaning to recurring symbols and motifs that may, in turn, help them gain insight into their psyches.

How

First, set the mood. If possible, dim the lighting in the program space and play new age music such as Enya's *A Day without Rain* softly in the background. Decorate a buffet table with white tulle woven among these heavenly treats:

Ambrosia ("food of the gods")

11-oz. can mandarin oranges, well drained

15-oz. can pineapple chunks, well drained

1 c. shredded coconut

1 c. sour cream

1 c. mini marshmallows

Mix ingredients together and chill overnight. Serves fifteen.

Orange Dream Punch

½ gal. of orange sherbet

1 (6-oz.) can frozen orange juice concentrate

2 l. of ginger ale

Place sherbet and frozen orange juice concentrate in a punch bowl. Allow to thaw for about fifteen minutes. Stir in ginger ale. Serves twenty.

Chocolate Peanut Butter Fantasies

1¾ c. white sugar

½ c. milk

½ c. butter

4 T. unsweetened cocoa powder

½ c. crunchy peanut butter

3 c. quick-cooking oats

1 tsp. vanilla extract

In a medium-sized saucepan, combine sugar, milk, butter, and cocoa. Bring to boil, and cook for one and a half minutes. Remove from heat, and stir in peanut butter, oats, and vanilla. Drop by teaspoonfuls onto wax paper. Let cool until hardened. Makes three dozen.

After the teens have arrived, briefly introduce the topic of dream analysis to them. It may be possible to find a Jungian therapist or psychology professor in your community to act as a guest speaker. If you decide to go it alone, though, any basic encyclopedia should give you enough information to familiarize the participants with the history of this practice. For instance, in ancient times dreams were considered prophetic. Later, Sigmund Freud hypothesized that dreams are the result of repressed sexual desires, while Carl Jung thought they symbolize the collective unconscious. Regardless of the many theories out there, however, many mental health professionals contend that there is a connection between our daily lives and our dreams. In other words, our dreams mean nothing unless we attach meaning to them within the context of our lives.

Dream interpretation is not an exact science, so before beginning the dream interpretation exercises, make sure the teens know that the purpose of this program is to have fun and to help them become more aware of the techniques used to analyze dreams. State that you are not an expert in this field and can only direct participants to resources that can help with dream interpretation. When you're ready to begin, have the teens recall a dream they've had, using the following questions designed to help them isolate recurring or common symbols, colors, places, and people.

- Where did the dream take place? Outdoors or inside? In a foreign or familiar place?
- Were there any objects or animals that figured predominantly in your dream? What were they?
- What people appeared in your dream?
- Did you talk to these people? If so, what was your conversation about?
- What colors were featured in the dream? What did they mean to you?
- What feelings did you have during the dream? When you awoke, did those feelings persist, or did you feel differently?

Pass out the Dream Recall Worksheet (page 30) for the teens to use as they recall their dreams, and encourage them to trust their instincts as they think about potential meanings. Again, there are many theories about why we dream, and some are based purely on physiological rather than psychological factors. For this reason, remind the teens again that there are no right or wrong answers for this exercise. The back of the worksheet provides space to jot down potential meanings for the various colors, symbols, or animals that appeared in their dreams. Using nonfiction sources such as dream dictionaries, give the teens about twenty minutes to research some potential meanings for their dreams. If you have access to the Internet in your program space, consider these Web sites:

Dream Dictionary
www.dream-dictionary.org

Dream Moods A-Z Dream Dictionary
www.dreammoods.com/dreamdictionary/

My JellyBean
www.myjellybean.com/

Soul Future Spiritual and Dream Interpretation Site
www.soulfuture.com/

Teen Dream Doctor
www.dreamdoctor.com/teen/

If time allows, ask the teens to share their findings with the group.

Dream pillows and dream journals are two easy crafts that correlate nicely with this program. At this point, invite the teens to grab a snack from the buffet table so they can eat and make their crafts at the same time. Explain that herb-filled dream pillows are often tucked inside pillowcases to aid in relaxation and deep, dream-filled slumbers. Dream journals, then, are often kept next to a person's bed so that he or she can record the details of a dream right after waking up, before the memory of it fades.

To make a dream journal, fold an 8½ by 11 piece of colored card stock in half to serve as a cover for the journal. The teens can decorate the covers any way they want. Or find clip art images not protected by copyright ahead of time, then print them out in color so the participants will only have to choose an image to cut out and glue onto their journal covers. Next, fold and insert about five to ten sheets of journal entry pages (Appendix A) that you've prepared ahead of time so that it looks like a book. Use a hole punch to make two holes near the spine of the journal, then thread a piece of raffia through the holes to secure the whole thing together. (See Chapter 10 for another use for these dream journals.)

To make a dream pillow, simply spoon some herbs into a small organza or cotton drawstring pouch and cinch it closed. These pouches are readily available at craft supply stores; alternatively, you could just purchase some material and cut it into eight-inch squares. After herbs are placed in the center of the square, ribbon or string could be used to tie up the sides. Herbs are commonly available in bulk. Lavender is probably the most common, and assists with achieving deep, relaxing sleep. Cedar and rosemary are supposed to repel bad dreams, and cloves are said to help retrieve buried memories. You could purchase one or several kinds of herbs and let the teens make their own concoctions.

Time, Cost, and Supplies

Allow approximately two hours to shop for supplies and prepare the materials such as the dream interpretation quiz (see Appendix A) and the

Dream Recall

_____
_____
_____

> Here are some questions to ask yourself as you attempt to recall a dream. Practice on a recent dream you've had, or use these exercises with the next dream you have.

1. What was the theme or story of the dream?

_____
_____
_____
_____

2. What was the location of the dream: inside, outside, familiar or unfamiliar, the place where you live or somewhere else?

_____
_____
_____

3. What were your reactions to the dream while dreaming?

_____
_____
_____
_____
_____

4. How did you feel when you woke up – happy, sad, disturbed, puzzled, etc.?

_____
_____

5. Was it easy or difficult to recall the dream? Did you remember it as a whole or as a fragment?

_____
_____

6. Who were the people in the dream?

_____
_____
_____

7. Did you interact with any animals in the dream?

_____
_____

8. Was there dialogue between you and others in the dream? What was said?

_____
_____
_____
_____
_____

9. Did the dream affect your waking emotional state?

_____
_____
_____

What does all this mean?

dream recall worksheet. The food and craft supplies you will need consist of

11-oz. can mandarin oranges

15-oz. can pineapple chunks

12-oz. bag of shredded coconut

16-oz. container of sour cream

1 bag of mini marshmallows

½ gal. of orange sherbet

6-oz. can of frozen orange juice

2 l. of ginger ale

sugar

milk

1 lb. of butter

8 oz. unsweetened cocoa powder

18-oz. jar of crunchy peanut butter

18-oz. container of quick-cooking oats

vanilla extract

colored card stock

hole punch

raffia, string, or ribbon

herbs

organza or cotton drawstring pouches, or a couple of yards of cheap material

As for costs, figure on the lower end of the $25–$50 scale if you normally get ten to fifteen teens at your program. If you think more will come, you may have to double the recipes, which will cost a bit more. All told, though, this is a pretty cheap program that has the potential to make a big impression.

Promotion

To create an ethereal feel for a display, use a light blue background covered with white clouds. Write "In Your Dreams" in freehand, cursive script over the clouds; then, nest the books and materials you want to highlight in mounds of cotton batting or white tulle. In addition, display the two crafts each participant will make at the program. Place a stack of dream interpretation quizzes next to the display and offer a copy of one of the nonfiction books listed in the Collection Connection section below as the prize in a drawing.

Collection Connection

Fiction

Angelica—Sharon Shinn (Ace Books, 2004)

Bloomability—Sharon Creech (Joanna Cotler, 1998)

A Great and Terrible Beauty—Libba Bray (Delacorte, 2003)

The Great Good Thing—Roderick Townley (Atheneum, 2001)

I Am the Messenger—Marcus Zusak (Knopf, 2005)

Kissing Kate—Lauren Myracle (Dutton, 2003)

Luna—Julie Ann Peters (Megan Tingley, 2004)

A Midsummer Night's Dream—William Shakespeare (Washington Square Press, 2004)

Mind's Eye—Paul Fleischman (Laurel Leaf, 2001)

Olive's Ocean—Kevin Henkes (Greenwillow, 2003)

One of Those Hideous Books Where the Mother Dies—Sonya Sones (Simon and Schuster, 2004)

Over and Over You—Amy McAuley (Roaring Book Press, 2005)

Pirates—Celia Rees (Bloomsbury, 2003)

Song of the Basilisk—Patricia McKillip (Ace Books, 1999)

Nonfiction

Dream Book: A Young Person's Guide to Understanding Dreams— Patricia Garfield (Rebound by Sagebrush, 2003)

Dream Catcher: A Young Person's Journal for Exploring Dreams— Patricia Garfield (Tundra Books, 2003)

Dream Power for Teens: What Your Dreams Say about Your Past, Present and Future—Rob MacGregor (Adams Media Corporation, 2005)

Dreams: Close Your Eyes, Open Your Mind—Tucker Shaw (Puffin, 2000)

Girls' Guide to Dreams—Kristi Collier-Thompson (Rebound by Sagebrush, 2003)

Naked at the Prom: The Secret Language of Dreams—Lori Reid (Ulysses Press, 2003)

Teen Dream Power: Unlock the Meaning of Your Dreams—M. J. Abadie (Bindu Books, 2003)

Teen Dreams and What They Mean—Anna Jaskolka (Quantum, 2003)

REDO YOUR ROOM ($$$$) (GRADES 7–10)

When I was about 15, my mother suggested we redecorate my bedroom. I was so excited; my room was in desperate need of a makeover because it still featured a wall full of shelves displaying my doll collection. I wanted my room to reflect who I was at 15—not 10. In her wisdom, my mother knew that "who I was" at 15 was bound to change when I turned 16, then 17, then...you get the picture. So, she suggested we use one whole wall for a bulletin board covered with fabric so I could fill it with what I wanted, but change it as I grew older. I couldn't wait to get started. As I recall, that bulletin board did change quite a bit over the years before I left for college. A Milli Vanilli poster was replaced with one of Nirvana, Greenpeace bumper stickers gave way to Amnesty International buttons, and pictures of my friends at the Freshman Ball were eventually covered with snapshots of Senior Prom. I still have all of that paraphernalia in a box in my basement, and I go through it every time I move. I just can't bring myself to throw any of it out.

Teens today, if they're lucky enough to have their own bedroom as I was, want the chance to make them their own. A teen's bedroom is usually the only space in the home that can be made to reflect his or her personality, interests, and dreams. Although parents and guardians should always be aware of what's going on in their teen's life, it's also the only room where a little privacy can be obtained for doing homework, listening to music, crying over a broken heart, or talking to friends.

Bedrooms are important to teens not just for developmental reasons such as gaining independence and defining oneself. *The Wall Street Journal* reported, "Fashion-conscious teens have a new obsession: making over the bedroom. Prodded by teen-loving retailers and inspired by some hot designers, kids are pulling together everything from Zen-themed ensembles (think bamboo) to 'hippie chic' designs with lava lamps and paisley beds" (Collins 2002). In answer to this trend, retail companies like Limited Too (www.limitedtoo.com), IKEA (www.ikea.com), Delia's (www.delias.com), and Bombay Company (www.bombaycompany.com) are designing furniture and housewares specifically for teen tastes. At the time of this writing, PBTeen (www.pbteen.com)—Pottery Barn's answer to teen decorating trends—even featured a media tie-in quiz on their Web site, promoting the movie *The Sisterhood of the Traveling Pants* and encouraging girls to take a "Sisterhood Style Quiz" to determine which character's style matches their own. How savvy is that? Finally, teens are getting in the design act on television shows like TLC's *Trading Spaces: Family* and *While You Were Out*.

This program recognizes the fact that teens need a personal sanctuary all their own. While capitalizing on teens' obsession with home décor, it also aims to help them discover a decorating style that reflects their personalities. Two easy crafts (described below) will help them turn their rooms into the space of their dreams. After all, as the editors at HGTV.com wrote, "Giving your teen a bedroom that they love helps keep them home more and gives them a sense that you are supportive of their personal style and hobbies" (HGTV n.d.).

How

First, to help the teens pinpoint what their style is, offer them the fun Style Quiz found in Appendix B. After they take the quiz, help them visualize each style with pictures of sample bedrooms. Encourage the teens to mix and match styles, or use their hobbies and interests as a jumping-off point toward creating an inspired bedroom. For example, if a teen is a member of the marching band, help him think of ways to incorporate a musical theme into his decorating scheme. Similarly, if a teen's dream is to visit Paris someday, encourage her to use this as inspiration for designing her bedroom. The books listed in the Collection Connection section below should be available to the teens for getting ideas. Catalogs from stores like IKEA, Urban Outfitters, and PBTeen would also be good to have on hand. Consider projecting pictures from some of these books and catalogs onto a screen so the teens can learn about the different styles of decorating. Just make sure to gain the publishers' permission before doing so.

Next, split the teens into two groups. Send each group to one of the two craft stations supplied with all of the necessary materials and tools. Before setting them loose, though, go over the instructions for each craft and show them a prototype that you've made before the program. Encourage them to keep their bedrooms' theme and color scheme in mind when creating each item. Instructions for each of the crafts are given below.

Magnetic Message Board

This craft will be handy for teens to tack up phone numbers, homework reminders, and keepsakes such as concert tickets or photos. For the board's surface, coat a piece of luan plywood with magnetic primer. (Have your local hardware store cut full sheets of luan down into several smaller pieces; pieces measuring 14 by 17 inches would work nicely.) After this coat dries, paint the board with a coat of white paint.

Next, a set of six magnets can be made using clear craft marbles and old magazines or, if you prefer, origami paper. If you decide to use old magazines, instruct the teens to find small images or letters to sandwich between the marble and the magnet. Since images that tiny are sometimes hard to find, tell them to look for background patterns like a field of flowers or a brick wall. Although any old magazines will work, catalogs such as Oriental Trading or U.S. Toy work well because they often feature pictures of small novelty items with fun designs like camouflage or psychedelic swirls. If you want to make this portion of the program go faster, use origami paper, which always has colorful, unique patterns on it. After the teens locate the pictures or backgrounds they think will work, tell them to place the flat side of the marble on top of each image to make sure the image is not distorted much. Have the teens cut out the images, then use a toothpick to put a dab of glue made for adhering glass or plastics on the magnet. After carefully placing the picture on top of the magnet, have them use the toothpick to put another tiny drop of glue on top of the image to adhere the marble to it. Make sure they wipe off any glue that seeps out around the edges. This same process is repeated for the next five magnets.

There are two alternatives to this craft. One idea is to use Scrabble® tiles on the message board instead of marble magnets. Have the teens glue magnets to the back of the letters that spell out their names, or decoupage pictures on top of the tiles. Another alternative is to make the message board double as a magnetic poetry board. Have the teens write words on magnetic sheets using fine-tip markers, then cut the words into small rectangles.

Cool Clock

Most teens have alarm clocks in their rooms, but they are usually more utilitarian than stylish. This craft project results in a cool clock that is more reflective of each teens' personal style. Using old magazines again, instruct the teens to find images large enough to cover an 8½ by 11 inch piece of cardboard. Magazine covers work really well because they are often the right size, and when turned into a clock, pay homage to a teen's favorite actor or band. If a teen is less interested in pop culture, however, and more interested in classical music, nature, or a specific sport, tell them to find multiple large images to make into a collage. For these participants, make sure to have a variety of magazines, not just those geared to teen interests.

Once their pictures have been selected, instruct the teens to cover the cardboard with decoupage medium using a foam brush. Have them place their images on top of the cardboard, then cover the whole project with another layer of decoupage medium. After the medium has dried, hand out clock parts and tell the teens to poke holes in one corner of the cardboard for the bolt of the gearbox to pass through. Help them assemble the hands of the clock and tighten the whole thing with the nut, then place a battery in the back. Although the clock parts themselves are very light, make sure the cardboard you supply is sturdy enough to support the battery. Finally, have the teens either draw numbers on the clock face, or use small round stickers to mark out the positions for twelve, three, six, and nine o'clock. Supply each teen with small plastic easels to prop up their finished clocks.

Time, Cost, and Supplies

The time required to plan this program depends on how crafty you are. After assessing your skills in this area, allot a correlative amount of time to purchase the craft supplies, make a prototype of each craft, and prepare the Style Quiz. The supplies you will need include the following:

¼-inch sheet luan—$11 (one 4 by 8 foot sheet should yield nine squares measuring 14 by 17 inches)

1 pint of magnetic primer—$20 (covers twenty-five square feet)

1 quart of white semigloss paint—$10

old magazines or catalogs

glue (for glass or plastic)—$3.50 a tube

toothpicks

scissors

clear craft marbles—$2.59 (bag of seventy half-sphere marbles)

½-inch round magnets—$1.99 (package of ten)

several sheets of 8½ by 11 inch cardboard

decoupage medium—$6.89 (8-oz. container)

foam brushes—$0.32 each

clock movement parts—$3.50 each

clock hands—$0.50 a set

AA batteries—$2.75 (package of four)

small round stickers

fine-tip markers

magnetic sheets (optional)

scrabble tiles (optional)

Since it is impossible for me to predict how many teens will attend your program, approximate prices have been included next to the supplies you'll most likely need to buy, to help you determine how much this program will cost. The cost code provided ($$$$) is based on fifteen teens participating. These crafts may be more sophisticated than some, but they pack a big punch and are sure to be useful and attractive features in the teens' newly redecorated rooms!

Promotion

Displaying prototypes of the two craft projects will surely grab teens' attention, but whatever you do, don't just prop these in a display in front of a solid background with staid lettering if you hope to entice would-be decorators. Instead, create a "roomscape" in your display using yards of colorful fabric, a string of paper lanterns, and props like a lava lamp and a funky picture frame. Incorporate the two craft projects into the "room" with big arrows pointing to them. If you have the space and the inclination, you could even fashion an "end table" out of cardboard boxes or milk crates so that you have a place to stack catalogs and books related to the program. Finally, ask local craft supply stores if they would be willing to display your flyers at their points of sale.

Collection Connection

Nonfiction

Change Your Room—Jane Bull (Penguin Books, 1999)

Crafty Girl: Cool Stuff—Jennifer Traig (Chronicle Books, 2001)

Groom Your Room—American Girl Library (Pleasant Company Publishing, 1997)

Have Fun with Your Room: 28 Cool Projects for Teens—Lynnette Jennings (Simon Pulse, 2001)

My Room: Teenagers in Their Bedrooms—Adrienne Salinger (Chronicle Books, 1995)

Organizing from the Inside Out for Teens: The Foolproof System for Organizing Your Room, Your Time and Your Life—Julie Morgenstern and Jessi Morgenstern-Colon (Owl Books, 2002)

Super Suite: The Ultimate Bedroom Makeover Guide for Girls—Mark Montano (Universe, 2002)

When Time Is Short and Money Is Tight...

Host an Un-Valentine's Day party complete with broken heart cookies, a mean "candy hearts" phrase contest, and unromantic Madlibs®.

As part of a passive contest, ask teens to name the official groundhog in Pennsylvania that is used to find its shadow; name the winner at a screening of *Groundhog Day*.

Host a Euchre Tournament.

REFERENCES

Cart, M. (2005). Gay and lesbian literature comes of age. *Booklist, 101*(15), 1356.

Collins, S. (2002). Teens try their hand at decorating. *Wall Street Journal*. Retrieved April 29, 2005, from http://www.realestatejournal.com/housegarden/furnishings/20021030-collins.html.

Federal Bureau of Investigation (1996). Hate crime statistics 1996. Retrieved May 1, 2005, from FBI Web site: http://www.fbi.gov/ucr/hate96.pdf.

Federal Bureau of Investigation (2004). Hate crime statistics 2003. Retrieved May 1, 2005, from FBI Web site: http://www.fbi.gov/ucr/03hc.pdf.

HGTV (n.d.). Rooms that rock: Ten teen design must-haves. Retrieved April 28, 2005, from HGTV Indoor Web site: http://www.hgtv.ca/home/articles/article98.asp.

Linville, D. (2004, August). Beyond picket fences: What gay/queer/LGBTQ teens want from the library. *VOYA*, 183–186.

Chapter 3

MARCH

Plan to save your budget this month with these three relatively cheap programs. The first program, "Swap Meet," focuses on something almost every teen enjoys. The second, "March Madness," is a program for a demographic that's often more difficult to attract: boys. These two programs are fairly lighthearted, so to round out the month, "The Experiment" will shed light on how race, religion, and gender relate to privilege and opportunity.

SWAP MEET ($) (GRADES 7–10)

I have fond memories of listening to the radio while lying on my bed as a teenager, daydreaming about my crush of the week and writing in my journal. My station of choice was the local Top-40 radio station, Kiss FM, and I always had a blank tape cued up in my tape recorder, ready to record my latest favorite songs. Those were the days before CDs, iPods, and MP3s, of course, but that didn't stop my friends and me from making and trading "mix tapes" of horrible quality with the DJ's voice heard briefly when he would cut in on songs before they were completely over. (Incidentally, that always really annoyed me.) Nowadays, teens have access to much more sophisticated ways to listen to and record their favorite music, from burning CDs to downloading from the Internet. But one thing has remained the same: teens definitely still love music, particularly anything that speaks to them, or seems to be an expression of something they feel.

Tastes in music, however, are probably more varied than ever before. Switching on your local Top-40 radio station will reveal a host of ambitious teenagers and 20-somethings singing their hearts out over the airwaves. Recording artists like Alicia Keys, Kelly Clarkson, John Mayer, and Jessica Simpson are today's faces of pop music, and the proliferation of these artists in mainstream media would lead some to erroneously believe that pop is the reigning style and teen favorite as it was in the 1950s. A quick switch of the dial, however, reveals radio stations devoted to other styles of music including country, R & B, hip-hop, and heavy metal. The variety depends, of course, on where you live but the simple fact remains that not all teens are pop music devotees; some even despise it, labeling its icons as untalented sellouts. While many teens have eclectic tastes in music, some are loyal to one particular style. Hard-core fans of Ludicris, for example, *generally* wouldn't be caught dead with a Hilary Duff CD. On the other hand, one would be hard pressed to find a 13-year-old fan of the latest boy band in the mosh pit at a headbanger's concert.

This program encourages teens to debate the merits of different musical tastes and styles, then offers an opportunity for them to swap CDs and MP3s, and sample the latest music releases.

How

Prior to the program, place signs around the room designating a table for each musical taste. The signs can represent country, R & B, hip-hop, rap, jazz, heavy metal, pop, classical, and indie music; choose which signs to make based on what tends to be popular in your city or town, but if you're not sure, use them all. Then, stack the latest CDs representing each type of music at the corresponding tables. If your library is anything like mine, popular music is often checked out and hard to get your hands on. For this reason, start reserving discs well in advance of the program to ensure you have a well-rounded representation. Or, if possible, consult with your library's audiovisual librarian to see if he or she can hang on to a few of the most recent arrivals until after your program. Another alternative is to borrow from your personal collection, or ask a music aficionado if he or she would be willing to loan a few CDs to you for use at the program.

As the teens arrive at the program, hand them each a packet of Pop Rocks® candy and instruct them to align themselves with the type of music they like the most by sitting at the table that most closely matches their tastes. Give them some time to peruse the collection of CDs placed at their tables while munching on snacks, then ask them to select the disc they feel is the best example of that musical style. One by one, play excerpts from some of the songs on each selected disc and invite the entire group to listen. For example, if the country music fans select a Dixie Chicks CD, play excerpts from two or three of the songs on that disc. Then, invite the teens to assess whether or not they'd ever buy a CD representing that musical style, by using the questionnaire given in Appendix C. Next, encourage them to debate the merits of that type of music by asking its fans to defend it, and its detractors to dis it. This should result in a lively music appreciation discussion. After five minutes or so, move on to the next musical style and repeat this process.

After the debate, allow time for the participants to swap CDs with each other. The promotion for this program should invite teens to bring CDs they don't want anymore, to exchange with someone else's castoffs. Hopefully, each participant will leave with a "new to me" CD.

Finally, pass out blank CD labels, markers, and empty jewel cases for the participants to design their own CD covers, and provide instructions for creating mixes. Art of the Mix (www.artofthemix.org) is a Web site dedicated to the art of creating mix tapes and CDs. According to this site, "Mixed tapes are a kind of creative act as well as a record of a series of decisions at a particular moment in time. It is an expression, a pastiche in which a person juxtaposes songs and sounds.... They refract and reflect a period of time, a sense of place, emotional states, [and] aesthetic sensibilities..." (Januszewski 1997). Direct the teens to this Web site for inspiration for creating their own mixes, and as a forum in which more sharing of ideas can take place. In this post-Napster age, Art of the Mix remains legal because there are no sound files available for trading on its Web site; it is solely a place where play lists are displayed and traded.

Time, Cost, and Supplies

Collecting CDs for each musical style will probably take the most time of any of the tasks associated with this program. Again, allow plenty of lead time to ensure that you have a good selection of CDs and to "preview" them before the program in order to identify which tracks might work best. Otherwise, the debate will not go very well. After this task is completed, create the signs for each station, as well as the questionnaire. The few supplies needed for this program include

blank CD labels

jewel cases

markers

Pop Rocks

snacks

a large jar

M & Ms®

If you want to include giveaways for each participant, consider posters saved from magazines, blank CDs, or gift certificates to a music store. All in all, though, this program is very cost-effective and should not take an enormous amount of time to plan.

Promotion

Assuming Eminem is still on the scene as you start to promote this program, fill a large jar with M & Ms and tape a picture of the controversial singer to the front. To entice teens to sign up for the program, ask them to guess how many "Eminems" are in the jar, and state that the best guesser must attend the "Swap Meet" to claim his or her prize. The prize you offer will depend on how much money you have to work with, but the better the prize, the more excitement you could create. An MP3 player, for example, would be very attractive for teens. If, however, your budget will not allow for such an expense, consider asking a local business to donate one, or just offer a smaller prize such as a CD case and a gift certificate to a music store. In addition to this passive contest, cover a display space with free posters from magazines, creating a montage of musical artists. Over this mosaic, create the words "Swap Meet" in a bold color. If your display resides in a secure glass case, you could use items such as a CD player or iPod to catch teens' attention. Alternatively, you could simply stack CDs and books from the list below, along with flyers describing the program and inviting teens to bring their old CDs to swap. Make sure to distribute these flyers to music stores, and send press releases to local radio stations. (Don't forget those stations located on college campuses!)

Collection Connection

Fiction

Born Blue—Han Nolan

Broken Chords—Barbara Snow Gilbert

Candy—Kevin Brooks

Cattail Moon—Jean Thesman

Cherokee Bat and the Goat Guys—Francesca Lia Block

Confessions of a Backup Dancer—Tucker Shaw

Confessions of a Teenage Drama Queen—Dyan Sheldon

Do Angels Sing the Blues?—A. C. LeMieux

Dragonsong (and sequels)—Anne McCaffrey

Fat Kid Rules the World—K. L. Going

Firmament—Tim Bowler

Glass Harmonica—Louise Marley

Guitar Girl—Sarra Manning

I Will Call It Georgie's Blues—Suzanne Newton

Mel—Liz Berry

Midnight Hour Encores—Bruce Brooks

The Mozart Season—Virginia Euwer Wolff

The Orpheus Obsession—Dakota Lane

Pepperland—Mark Delaney

Piano Man—Joyce Sweeney

Pop Princess—Rachel Cohn

Rock Star Superstar—Blake Nelson

The Song Reader—Lisa Tucker

This Lullaby—Sarah Dessen

Tribute to Another Dead Rock Star—Randy Powell

What a Song Can Do: 12 Riffs on the Power of Music—Jennifer Armstrong (editor)

Nonfiction

Angry Blonde: The Official Book—Eminem

Can't Stop Won't Stop: A History of the Hip Hop Generation—Jeff Chang

Hip Hoptionary: The Dictionary of Hip Hop Terminology—Alonzo Westbrook

Never Fade Away: The Kurt Cobain Story—Dave Thompson

The Rose That Grew from Concrete—Tupac Shakur

Shout, Sister, Shout! Ten Girl Singers Who Shaped a Century—Roxane Orgill

Tears for Water: Songbook of Poems and Lyrics—Alicia Keys

MARCH MADNESS ($$) (GRADES 7–2)

When you think of libraries, it's not common to imagine them filled with "jockish" athletic types. On the other hand, one doesn't often associate the average ESPN addict with reading. In an effort to banish all stereotypes and simply have a little fun, this program will put libraries on the map for fans of college basketball. Every March, the National Collegiate Athletic Association (NCAA) hosts a single-elimination basketball tournament for sixty-five of the best Division I college teams. As the tournament progresses from "Selection Sunday" to the "Final Four" match-ups, fans across the country fill in their own brackets with their best guesses as to which team will wind up the ultimate winner. The library's "March Madness" program will simply encourage teens who are fans of the hard court to fill out their own brackets, then gather to watch one of the big games. Lest you imagine that this program will appeal only to teenaged boys, I'd like to point out that I've known many sports-ignorant females who get into the spirit of this tournament, simply because the excitement it generates is so infectious. And, of course, there are plenty of athletic teenaged girls out there who already know about and love the NCAA tournament. That said, this is a program that most certainly will appeal to more boys than, say, the "Redo Your Room" program discussed in Chapter 2. This program, therefore, while purely for fun, has the added benefit of attracting a demographic that might normally believe the library has nothing to offer of interest to them.

How

This program is extremely simple to implement, but before kicking it off, assess your knowledge of the NCAA tournament. As a rabid college basketball fan (my father and one brother are both coaches), I felt comfortable with my knowledge to plunge right into the planning. If you don't normally follow sports, however, it would be a good idea to visit the NCAA's Web site (www.ncaasports.com/basketball/mens) to learn more about the tournament. This site also has a wealth of information about the rules of basketball, as well as blank brackets that you are welcome to print out and distribute. After brushing up on some of the basics, build anticipation and excitement by creating a giant bracket on an open wall. After the teams are announced on Selection Sunday, fill in the sixty-five team names and their corresponding seeds, or rankings, within the four bracket divisions. Then, as games are played and teams are eliminated, fill in the bracket with the advancing teams. Make blank brackets available for teens to fill out, but to prevent cheating (i.e., filling out brackets as the tournament progresses instead of all at once at the beginning), copy the brackets on a special color of paper, then make them unavailable once the tournament begins.

Select one of the games toward the end of the tournament during which to hold a "March Madness" party. Many of the games at the start of the tournament are held during the afternoon, so these probably aren't good choices as your target audience will be in school. Also, the games at the beginning of the tournament are often less exciting. Any game from the Sweet 16 on would be a suitable choice. One problem that you may encounter, however, when scheduling the party is that the game times are often stated as "to be announced" right up until the day they are aired. To pinpoint the airtime and to promote the party more effectively, contact your local cable company to see when they have blocked out time for a particular game. Since the games are televised live, you should also keep time zones in mind. For instance, a game played at seven o'clock in the evening on the East Coast is probably not going to work if your library is located in California. Once the date and time for the party have been set, the next couple of weeks should simply be spent filling in the tournament bracket and building anticipation for the big game.

The obvious activity at the March Madness party is watching the game. So, arrange for a television to be placed in a location that is easily viewable for a large group of people. As the teens arrive, have them hand in their completely filled-in tournament brackets. Let them know that the brackets will be reviewed at the end of the tournament and a prize will be awarded to whoever chooses the winning team, or at least comes the closest. As with any teen program, refreshments are key, but at a sports-themed program they're probably even more important. Define an area of the program space as the concession stand where hoagie sandwiches, pizza, chips, pretzels, popcorn, and soda are available. It would be bad form to interrupt the action on TV, but during commercial breaks and halftime, have some activities ready to keep the teens entertained. For instance, a plastic hoop and a foam or rubber ball could come in handy for a free-throw shooting contest. Or, for laughs, ask the teens to participate in a Dick Vitale sound-alike contest. During quick time-outs, you could also shout out trivia questions and throw foil-wrapped chocolate basketballs to the teens who get the answers right. Some examples of trivia questions are

- What is a diaper dandy? (Answer: a fantastic freshman)
- What is UCLA's mascot? (Answer: Bruins)
- What does PT stand for? (Answer: playing time)
- What does "on the bubble" mean? (Answer: teams that are questionable selections for the tournament are referred to as "on the bubble" or "bubble teams")
- Who was the coach of North Carolina State who won a national title in 1983, and died of cancer in 2005? (Answer: Jim Valvano)
- What is Coach K's full name? (Answer: Mike Krzyzewski)
- What is a Cinderella team? (Answer: a team that advances further in the tournament than anyone thought possible)
- What are Michigan State's team colors? (Answer: green and white)
- Where did Bobby Knight coach for most of his career? (Answer: Indiana)
- What conference is Xavier University in? (Answer: Atlantic 10)

Time, Cost, and Supplies

Although this program is kicked off a few weeks before the actual party takes place, very little work is involved along the way. Initially, an hour or so will be needed to construct the large bracket, but it just takes a few minutes after each game is played to fill in the names of the advancing teams. As the day for the party approaches, go shopping for the following items:

plastic hoop and small basketball

chocolate basketballs

paper plates and napkins

Hoagie sandwiches

chips

popcorn

pretzels

soda

On the day of the party, arrange for the delivery of some pizzas, and finalize the trivia questions you plan on using during time-outs. Most of the costs associated with this program are tied to refreshments, so the expense will vary depending on how many teens you expect to attend.

Promotion

The large tournament bracket may be all that is necessary to promote this program within the library. You could also display some of the sports-related books listed below to tie the library's collection to the theme. As previously stated, however, the target audience for this program may not consist of people who frequent the library. Therefore, it will be necessary to proactively promote this program within the community. Mail stacks of the library's brackets to basketball coaches, for instance, encouraging them to come with their teams. Post flyers in sporting-goods shops, gyms, and community centers inviting fathers and sons to "watch the big game" together at the library. If your library is located near a university, particularly one that makes regular appearances in the tournament, promotion for this program may be easier. To entice teens to participate in the bracket contest and attend the party, contact the athletic department of such a university to ask if they would be willing to donate paraphernalia, or even a signed basketball or baseball cap, to use as prizes.

Collection Connection

Fiction

Athletic Shorts—Chris Crutcher

Bat 6—Virginia Euwer Wolff

Black and White—Paul Volponi

Choosing Up Sides—John H. Ritter

Crooked Little Heart—Anne Lamott

Damage—A. M. Jenkins

Eight Seconds—Jean Ferris

Fifteen Love—Robert Corbet

A Girl Named Summer—Julie Garwood

Girls Got Game: Sports Stories and Poems—Sue Macy (editor)

Going for the Record—Julie A. Swanson

Going the Distance—Mary Jane Miller

Head above Water—S. L. Rottman

Heart of a Champion—Carl Deuker

Heat—Michael Cadnum

High Heat—Carl Deuker

Home of the Braves—David Klass

How All This Started—Pete Fromm

How I Fell in Love and Learned to Shoot Free Throws—Jon Ripslinger

Ironman—Chris Crutcher

It's a Matter of Trust—Marcia Byalick

Letters to Father Abraham—Catherine Lewis

The Luckiest Girl in the World—Steven Levenkron

The Moves Make the Man—Bruce Brooks

My Thirteenth Season—Kristi Roberts

Out of Order—A. M. Jenkins

Painting the Black—Carl Deuker

Playing without the Ball: A Novel in Four Quarters—Rich Wallace

Roughnecks—Thomas Cochran

Run for Your Life—Marilyn Levy

Rundown—Michael Cadnum

Running Loose—Chris Crutcher

Shakespeare Bats Cleanup—Ron Koertge

Slalom—S. L. Rottman

Slam!—Walter Dean Myers

Slot Machine—Chris Lynch

Some Kind of Pride—Maria Testa

The Squared Circle—James W. Bennett

Staying Fat for Sarah Byrnes—Chris Crutcher

Stotan!—Chris Crutcher

Striking Out—Will Weaver

Summerland—Michael Chabon

Tangerine—Edward Bloor

There's a Girl in My Hammerlock—Jerry Spinelli

Ultimate Sports: Short Stories by Outstanding Writers for Young Adults—Isabel Joshlin Glazer

Whistling Toilets—Randy Powell

Winning—C. S. Adler

Nonfiction

Counting Coup: A True Story of Basketball and Honor on the Little Big Horn—Larry Colton

Dreams of Glory: Poems Starring Girls—Isabel Joshlin Glaser

Friday Night Lights: A Town, a Team, and a Dream—H. G. Bissinger

Hawk: Occupation: Skateboarder—Tony Hawk

Hoop Dreams—Paul Robert Walker

Into Thin Air—Jon Krakauer

King James: Believe the Hype—Ryan Jones

Winning Sports for Girls series—Facts on File

THE EXPERIMENT ($) (GRADES 9–12)

In 1968, after the assassination of Martin Luther King, Jr., a fourth-grade school teacher named Jane Elliott began a courageous crusade against racism through a classroom experiment designed to shed light on the myth of white superiority. By separating children with brown eyes from those with blue eyes, she was able to create a microcosm in which the children exhibited the same types of behaviors African Americans experience every day. Children with green or hazel eyes were left out of the experiment, and those with brown eyes were told they were superior due to the amount of melanin in their blood. Almost immediately, the brown-eyed children began to treat the blue-eyed ones with disdain, teasing and taunting them, and gloating over the privileges they received—such as extended recess—based on their eye color. On the flip side, some of the brown-eyed children who did not normally receive high grades began to excel, seemingly due to being newly anointed as superior. "Elliott recalls, 'It was just horrifying how quickly they became what I told them they were.' Within 30 minutes, a blue-eyed girl named Carol had regressed from a 'brilliant, self-confident[,] carefree, excited little girl to a frightened, timid, uncertain little almost-person'" (Kral 2000).

That day, Elliott proved that racism is learned. From this, she hypothesized that since racism can be created, it can also be destroyed. Since then, Elliott has traveled the world as a diversity consultant, using the brown-eye / blue-eye experiment with diverse audiences, and getting the same results. Unfortunately, "Elliott says that the major difference between exercise participants today and her fourth-grade students of 30 years ago is that, now, people are 'less likely to use the word 'nigger''" (Kral 2000). We have achieved some milestones in conquering racism, but it still exists, albeit perhaps in less blatant ways. Assumptions, behaviors, and attitudes that discriminate are hard to change, but they must not be accepted or ignored.

Today's teens certainly witness discrimination in all of its ugly forms, and many of them are targets of it themselves. For instance, while Title IX mandates gender equity in organized athletics, teenaged girls most certainly still receive "flack" from their male counterparts on the playing field. In the wake of September 11, racial profiling has increased, taking its toll on the morale of Islamic teens. Further, gay bashing and homophobic attitudes continue to plague GLBTQ teens. As we all know, however, discrimination does not end with one's teen years. Opportunities are either denied or impeded for nonwhite, female, and homosexual adults as well. Therefore, while Elliott's 1968 experiment focused more exclusively on racism against African Americans, this program will shed light on several types of discrimination, including sexism and religious intolerance, in an effort to make teens more aware of their own learned attitudes and beliefs.

How

The structure of this program is simple. The teen participants will visit several "opportunity stations" set up around the program space and will make note of the treatment they receive at each station based on a code they have randomly selected. Then, a discussion about their experiences will take place during which the teens will be asked to explore their own feelings about race, gender, sexuality, and religion.

In preparation for this program, it is first necessary to ensure that you will have an audience by contacting local teachers to ask if they would be interested in involving their classes in this experiment. Social studies or psychology classes would be natural choices because this program would tie in nicely with the curriculum. English or reading classes in which novels centered on racism and discrimination are discussed would also work well, as would history classes in which the timeline of civil rights is studied.

After securing an audience, it is necessary to recruit about six volunteers to staff the opportunity stations and one to act as a police officer. The opportunity stations will consist of a probate court, a U.S. Armed Forces recruiting office, an employment agency, an airport, a college admissions office, and a real estate office. One of the seven volunteers will act as a police officer who will involve each of the participants in routine "traffic stops." Asking professionals who actually work at these places to act as your volunteers may enhance the discussion afterward in that they may have real-life anecdotes to share about their employment experiences or, perhaps, their own preconceived notions of certain clients or customers. After lining up the volunteers via phone calls or e-mails, confirm their participation a couple of weeks before the program by sending a letter asking them to arrive about a half-hour before the teens are scheduled to show up. This will allow time for you to explain their duties in more detail and thank them personally for dedicating their time. The volunteers should be made aware of the goals of the program, and of the fact that the teen participants will not know what to expect throughout its duration.

As the teens are ushered into the program space, they will randomly select a set of numbers and letters that they will then write on white labels to be adhered to their shirts. This "code" will determine how they will be treated and what opportunities they will receive at each station. The numbers and letters stand for the following:

1   Physically disabled
2   Physically able
3   Female
4   Male
5   Gay

6   Straight

7   Married

8   Single

9   Arabic descent

0   African American

Q   Caucasian

T   College educated

X   High school dropout

Y   Over 60 years old

Z   Under 60 years old

To ensure that the participants pick a set of letters and numbers that make sense (e.g., someone cannot be both married and single), make seven different buckets containing the opposing criteria. For instance, the first bucket should contain 1s and 2s, the second bucket should contain 3s and 4s, and so on. Each participant will select one number or letter from each bucket to make his or her code. An example of a code might be 2458QXZ. This person, then, is a gay, white male under the age of 60 who never finished high school. Under no circumstances should the participants be shown what their codes stand for until the end of the experiment.

After the teens have received their codes, instruct them to visit each opportunity station. The volunteers at each station will be armed with scripts that they will deliver based on each teen's code. The following sections detail what should take place at each station.

Probate Court

At this station, single teens will attempt to obtain a marriage license. The volunteer at this station should only be concerned with whether the participant's code contains a 5 or a 6. If the teen's code contains a 5, the volunteer should say, "I'm sorry, but it's illegal to grant you a marriage license in this state." Topics of discussion that may arise from the teens' experiences at this station might include gay marriage, as well as how GLBTQ teens are treated at school.

U.S. Armed Forces Recruiting Office

At this station, teens will attempt to join the armed forces. The volunteer at this station should be concerned with whether the participant's code contains a 1 or 2, a 3 or 4, or a Y or Z. If the teen's code contains a 1 or a Y, the volunteer should say, "I'm sorry, you cannot serve in the United States Armed Forces." If the teen's code contains a 3, the volunteer should say, "You will not be permitted to participate in combat." Topics of discussion that may arise from the teens' experiences at this station might include women's role in the military, as well as how the elderly and the disabled are viewed in our country.

Employment Agency

At this station, teens will attempt to obtain a job. The volunteer at this station should be concerned with several parts of the participant's code. If the teen's code contains a 3, the volunteer should say, "This job pays $10 an hour, but for you it pays $7.60." If the teen's code contains an X, the volunteer should say, "I'm sorry, you are not qualified for any job through this agency." If the teen's code contains a 1, 9, 0, or Y, the volunteer should say, "I'm sorry, that position has been filled." Topics of discussion that may arise from the teens' experiences at this station might include gender equality, as well as sexual discrimination and harassment in the workplace. It may also be interesting to note how external features such as skin color, age, or a physical disability can effect employers' snap judgments about job applicants. This could lead to a discussion about the merits of equal opportunity hiring practices.

Airport

At this station, teens will attempt to take a flight. The volunteer at this station should be concerned with whether the participant's code contains a 1 or 2, or a 9. If the teen's code contains a 1, the volunteer should say, "Please wait here while we find someone to assist you." Then, that teen should be made to wait a long time while other teens come and go. If the teen's code contains a 9, the volunteer should say, "Please step aside while we check to make sure your passport is in order." This teen should also be made to wait a long time. The volunteer might also glare suspiciously at the teen from time to time while he or she waits. Topics of discussion that may arise from the teens' experiences at this station might include the merits and disadvantages of racial profiling practices, as well as the inconveniences people with physical disabilities have to endure.

College Admissions Office

At this station, teens will attempt to enroll in college. The volunteer at this station should be concerned with whether the participant's code contains a 1 or 2, or a T or X. If the teen's code contains a 1, the volunteer should say, "There are 5 student dormitories, but you only have your choice of two of them." If the teen's code contains an X, the volunteer should say, "I'm sorry, you cannot attend this university." Topics of discussion that may arise from the teens' experiences at this station might include how physically disabled individuals are denied some opportunities because of institutions' failure to comply with ADA regulations, as well as how those without a high school degree have fewer opportunities available to them. It is important to point out here that, unlike one's race, age, or gender, it is within one's power to change one's level of education.

Real Estate Office

At this station, teens will attempt to buy a house. The volunteer at this station should be concerned with whether the participant's code contains a 2 in conjunction with a 7, or a 9 or 0. If the teen's code contains both a 2 and a 7, the volunteer should say, "Are you sure you want to buy a house? I have some nice rental properties I could show you," or "How about something a little smaller?" If the teen's code contains either a 9 or a 0, the volunteer should say, "The neighborhoods you're looking in don't seem appropriate for you. I'll try to find something a little more suitable for someone like you." A topic of discussion that may arise from the teens' experiences at this station might be how dangerous, and often inaccurate, assumptions are.

Traffic Stop

As the teens are wandering from station to station, the volunteer acting as a police officer will stop each individual as part of a routine "traffic stop." If a teen's code contains either a 9 or a 0, the volunteer will say, "Please step out of the car," or "It doesn't seem like you belong in this neighborhood. Where were you headed?" The volunteer might also issue a traffic ticket for something minor like a broken taillight or failure to wear a seat belt. If the teen's code contains a Q, however, the volunteer should politely chitchat with the teen and refrain from issuing a ticket. A topic of discussion that may arise from the teens' experience at the "traffic stop" might be how people—particularly men—of color are treated differently by law enforcement officials, in stores and in courtrooms.

After the teens have visited each station, gather everyone together in a large, welcoming circle conducive to having a discussion. Start the conversation by asking a sampling of teens what their experiences were and how they felt about the way they were treated. At this point (although some of the participants may already have guessed what portions of their code mean), reveal what each letter or number represents, for clarification. Make sure the teens understand that the reactions they received at each station are stereotypical, and not always played out in such blatant, straightforward manners. However, similar instances of discrimination take place every day. There is no need to structure the ensuing dialogue to a large degree, but if you prefer to feel more prepared, here are some questions you may consider posing in addition to the suggested topics for discussion already mentioned above:

- Which group seemed to receive the most discrimination? Which group seemed to receive the most opportunity?
- Which is the only factor that is truly within one's power to change?
- Were any of the reactions deserved? If so, which ones?
- Do you see yourself differently now?
- Do you think our attitudes and assumptions about people are learned? Similarly, do people learn how to treat others poorly, or is this inherent in human nature?
- What outside forces might affect the way we view people?

Three videos featuring Jane Elliott's experiment—*The Angry Eye* (2001), *Blue-Eyed* (1996), and *A Class Divided* (1984)—are likely available through your library. It may be a good idea to show excerpts from one of these films to drive home some of the points intended by this program.

Time, Cost, and Supplies

There are no major costs or supplies associated with this program, but it will pack a big punch nonetheless. Approach teachers to invite their participation at least three months before you hope to hold this program. Then, at least six weeks before, line up the volunteers needed for each station. If you plan to use one of the films mentioned above, make sure to track down a copy well in advance.

Promotion

As with any experiment, this program would not work if the participants were aware of all the factors involved. This makes it almost impossible to advertise the program to teen library customers or to the general public. The best way is to personally approach teachers in your area to invite their classes' participation. To make this more appealing to teachers, try to find tie-ins with their curriculum, and invite them to visit www.janeelliott.com to gain a better understanding of the need for a program like this. You may also consider inviting teens who regularly visit the library, but be sure to keep the details of the "experiment" a secret.

Collection Connection

Fiction

Aleutian Sparrow—Karen Hesse

Black and White—Paul Volponi

Deliver Us from Evie—M. E. Kerr

The Divine Wind: A Love Story—Garry Disher

Eight Seconds—Jean Ferris

Geography Club—Brent Hartinger

A Heart Divided—Cherie Bennett

Lizzie Bright and the Buckminster Boy—Gary D. Schmidt

Milkweed—Jerry Spinelli

Mississippi Trial, 1955—Chris Crowe

Necessary Roughness—Marie G. Lee

Spite Fences—Trudy Krisher

To Kill a Mockingbird—Harper Lee

Uncommon Faith—Trudy Krisher

Whale Talk—Chris Crutcher

Who Will Tell My Brother?—Marlene Carvell

Witness—Karen Hesse

Nonfiction

A Dream of Freedom: The Civil Rights Movement from 1954 to 1968—Diane McWhorter

Getting Away with Murder: The True Story of the Emmett Till Case—Chris Crowe

Let Me Play: The Story of Title IX: The Law That Changed the Future of Girls in America—Karen Blumenthal

To Establish Justice: Citizenship and the Constitution—Patricia McKissack

The Voice That Challenged a Nation: Marian Anderson and the Struggle for Equal Rights—Russell Freedman

With Courage and Cloth: Winning the Fight for a Woman's Right to Vote—Ann Bausum

---

When Time Is Short and Money Is Tight…

Ask area restaurants to donate pizzas for a Pizza Taste-Off.

Hold a limerick-writing contest in honor of St. Patrick's Day.

Host a Monopoly tournament.

REFERENCES

Januszewski, J. (1997). The art of the mix FAQ. Retrieved August 14, 2005, from the Art of the Mix, http://www.artofthemix.org/writings/faq.asp#1.

Kral, B. (2000, September). The eyes of Jane Elliott. *Horizon Magazine*. Retrieved August 31, 2005, from http://www.horizonmag.com/4/jane-elliott.asp.

Chapter 4

APRIL

April is National Financial Literacy Month, which is why the program with punch in this chapter focuses on money matters. "The Real World" aims to teach teens the importance of making wise financial choices as young adults. Then, since spring has officially arrived and warmer days are sure to be beckoning teen drivers, it's also the perfect time to celebrate National Car Care Month with a program that will teach teens the basics of purchasing, maintaining, and enjoying their cars. Finally, April 22 is the annual observation of Earth Day, the birth of the modern environmental movement. "Share the Love" rolls taking care of the environment—and each other—into one feel-good program.

THE REAL WORLD ($-$$$) (GRADES 9–12)

Remember that episode of *The Cosby Show* where Cliff and Claire Huxtable turn their house into "the real world" to teach their son, Theo, a lesson? Upon arriving home, Theo is startled to find his living room turned into a bank; the kitchen had become a restaurant where nothing was free; and the bedroom had become a one-room apartment for which he had to pay rent and buy furniture. According to *Young Money*, "Many young adults are ill prepared to take charge of their personal finances. Results from the 2002 Students in Free Enterprise report (SIFE) show that only 38 percent of college students prepare a monthly budget, 32 percent are currently in credit card debt and less than half understand how the stock market works" (Richards 2003). As evidenced by this statistic, clearly, Theo is representative of many young adults who are not learning the basics of money management. High school economics classes often teach abstract concepts pertaining to the economy, the stock market, and our country's national debt, but personal finance topics such as balancing a checkbook and building a solid credit history would be more helpful to teens about to enter the "real world." This program is designed to empower teens with the ability to make wise life decisions that affect their financial futures.

At the start of this program, teens will draw a profession out of a hat, be given an income with which to work, and then visit stations designed to challenge them with financial windfalls and pitfalls. Although this "real world" simulation is a game based on *chance*, it will be important to point out to the participants that life is based on *choices*. For the purposes of this program, the teens will not be able to change their professions or alter their family sizes, but make sure to emphasize that life's rules are more flexible, and often more forgiving. The choice to pursue higher education could lead to a better job; the choice to spend wisely could result in a large savings; and the choice to make wise investments can lead to owning a home. The reverse, of course, also holds true. Choices like dropping out of high school, for instance, will often result in limited opportunities and lower wages. The participants will be surprised by how much it costs to live in the real world, and they may even set higher goals for themselves based on this eye-opening experience.

How

Once a date has been set for this program, volunteers need to be recruited for each station representing the costs of the real world. A real estate office, a grocery store, a car dealership, a child care provider, a health insurance provider, a utility and a phone company, and a shopping center could be the stations representing life's expenses. In addition, volunteers will be needed for a Bank station, a Chance station, a Mad Money station, and an SOS station. This program provides a great opportunity to form partnerships with area businesses and organizations, so make sure to capitalize on this perk by involving representatives from a local realtor, a car dealer, or a bank. Once the volunteers have been secured, it is time to prepare the materials for each station. You may choose to use the materials provided for you in Appendix D.

The Bank

For convenience, the bank station is where several things happen to get the teens started. As they arrive, each teen draws a profession and a corresponding monthly salary from a hat. They also need to draw for a family size. These can be printed out on labels so each participant can attach it to the back of their checkbook ledger for quick reference. After learning their "lot in life," each teen receives his or her first paycheck but not before the correct taxes are deducted. The volunteer "bankers" are there to help teens calculate their net earnings, and give them a balance to write on a checkbook ledger. Reactions from the teens will probably vary at this point. While one teen may be elated because he "became" an airline pilot with a monthly salary of $10,000, another will grumble because she is a fast-food restaurant employee who has to support three children on minimum wage. Some of these students will ask if his or her spouse can contribute to the family's income, but for the purpose of this program, all households are single income. This is usually a good time to point out the varying levels of education required for each job in order to provoke thought about the relationship between higher education and earning potential.

Instruct the bank station's volunteers to help teens understand the following points:

- This is a game based on chance. In real life, you may have many choices to make which will affect your financial futures.

- Taxes are usually withdrawn from pay before we ever see our money.

- Taxes pay for most of the services in our communities.

- Taxes vary according to the amount of your salary and the size of your family.

- Pay yourself first. You should try to put a portion of your income in a savings account each month, even if it is only a couple of dollars.

Let volunteers at this station know that the first twenty minutes or so of the "Real World" will be very busy. After that, one of them may be asked to help control the crowd or even help at another table. The other volunteer should stay at the bank in case someone needs to make a deposit or a withdrawal from checking or savings. Or some of the students who finish first may want to ask questions about banking before they leave.

After stopping at the bank station, the teens must visit each of the other stations in any order they choose. Everyone must purchase something at every station and deduct the amount from their checking account ledger, but volunteers should be instructed to allow the teens to be creative with their choices. Examples of this are given for each station, and the option sheets for each station are provided in Appendix D.

The Real Estate Office

Several housing options are presented to the teens at this station. They may choose to buy one of three different homes, or they may decide to rent one of three different apartments. Volunteers at this station should be sure to note each teen's family size to help him or her make realistic housing choices. If time permits, they should also point out the following:

- A security deposit is required before renting an apartment; this often amounts to the first and last month's rent. Extra deposits are often required for pets.
- One should make a down payment before attempting to purchase a house; 10 percent of the purchase price is the customary amount.
- Everyone pays real estate taxes when they own a home.
- Everyone needs either renter's or homeowner's insurance to protect against losses.
- Most insurance companies offer a discount to customers who buy a home/rental policy along with an automobile policy.

The Grocery Store

At this station, teens need to choose a monthly food plan. The food plans provided are estimated costs for food at home for different-sized families, and include thrifty, low-cost, moderate, and liberal options. Teens should understand that these figures are for food eaten at home only. Meals eaten out in restaurants or fast-food places fall under the "entertainment" banner. Volunteers at this station should explain that food is usually the most flexible part of any family's budget. There are many ways to save money at the grocery store and still have a nutritious diet that can help keep one's family healthy. This would be a good time to point out the following:

- Healthy snacks such as fruits and vegetables are cheaper than chips and soda.
- Buying ingredients for a meal is almost always cheaper than frozen dinners or prepackaged meals.
- There is potential for saving by choosing generic rather than name-brand items.
- Many items other than food, such as paper products, cleaning supplies, cosmetics, and personal hygiene products, are also purchased at the grocery store.

The Car Dealership

If a teen's dream includes living in a big city, public transportation might be the first choice for getting around. Otherwise, most young adults have a dream car in mind. Choices for transportation include public transportation, a sports car, a midsize sedan, a small truck, and a compact car. Since it will be important for the teens to realize that the cost of a car includes more than the purchase price, all expenses for the different vehicles have been included (i.e., insurance, tax and license fees, gas and maintenance). Volunteers should start by briefly explaining the available options for transportation as well as the following expenses that go along with owning a car:

- Insurance is required and covers more than just replacement value. It's also helpful in the event of a possible lawsuit.
- Tax and license fees vary by the area where one lives. Those registration fees often increase and need to be paid every year.
- Gas and maintenance also vary according to the vehicle one chooses to own and the condition one chooses to keep it in. These costs, too, continue to rise each year. For instance, the students have probably either noticed themselves or heard their parents complain about the high price of gas.

The Child Care Provider

Every teen who draws a family with children will need to visit this station. For the purposes of this program, every family with children has only one employed parent and, therefore, one income. (It is assumed that there is some reason why one spouse cannot work, such as being between jobs and looking for work every day, or being disabled, or being in college.) It will be fun for you and the volunteers to see some surprised expressions on the teens' faces at this station because this is one of life's expenses that young adults usually have no idea is so costly.

The choices available for child-care are a day care facility (called Real World Day Care) and a babysitting service (called TLC Babysitters). After the participants realize that children are expensive to raise, they may make alternate suggestions for ways to care for them. Make sure volunteers are aware that they can freely discuss these possibilities as long as the suggestions are reasonable and safe. For instance, if a teen suggests that "Grandma" can babysit, volunteers may choose to tell him/her that Grandma still works full-time herself, or that she can babysit only two days a week. In this instance, costs for day care can be reduced, but not eliminated entirely.

The Health Insurance Provider

Volunteers at this station should start by presenting the individual health insurance plans to each teen. Costs for two medical options and two dental options are provided; however, some terms like "co-pay" and "deductible" may need to be explained to the teens. At this station, teens should learn the following:

- Insurance choices are getting more and more complicated every year. It is important to educate oneself on the constantly changing options.
- There is no health insurance that pays for all health costs. Only about half of Americans have dental insurance of any kind.
- Just as with auto insurance, the higher the deductible, the lower the insurance premium (or monthly expense).
- Living without any health insurance is like playing Russian Roulette. Without insurance, the costs of one illness could result in bankruptcy.

The Utility and Phone Companies

Every teen has to pay *something* for utilities and phone, but if the teens try to get creative with these expenses, volunteers may try to work with them. For instance, trash pickup could be one place to save money if a teen chooses to live in the country. Volunteers should also point out that the cost of water, gas, and electricity can vary according to family size, or size of home. For apartment dwellers it could be included in the rent amount. Also, even though teens may beg to differ, cell phones and cable are optional items because they are "wants," not "needs." Likewise, make sure the teens understand that long distance plans are not automatically a part of one's telephone bill; they must be added on if one plans on making long distance calls.

The Shopping Center

Many people would argue that items purchased at the shopping center station are wants, not needs. At one time or another, though, everyone must take care of at least some of these expenses. Therefore, each teen should be required to spend at least some of their money on store items. Volunteers should start by presenting each teen with the available options. The clothing amounts are based on about 5 percent of one's total income, although people with limited resources do not spend that much of their money on clothes. The participants should be allowed to negotiate this amount if they decide that they can get along with less. In addition, different amounts for furniture of high quality, moderate price, and low price are available. Volunteers should be instructed to be flexible with these options, but *only at the suggestion of the teen.* Finally, the costs of owning a washer and dryer versus doing laundry at a Laundromat are provided. Teens will need to decide which route is more economical for them based on their family size.

The Chance Station

The chance station represents just what the name says—all of those things in life that just happen by chance. Every teen at the Real World program will draw one situation from the chance bag. These situations run the gamut from TV repair to gift buying to receiving an inheritance! If a student happens to draw a chance card that involves having children and they have none, tell volunteers to allow them to throw that card back in and draw another one, but this is the only situation in which a second draw will be allowed.

Instruct the volunteers to explain to the teens that these situations happen all the time in life, and are hard to plan for. While some chances will be welcomed, others will create a real financial hardship. At this station, the participants should realize that having a savings account can be a real lifesaver when life's unexpected expenses come up!

The Mad Money Station

This station is called "mad money" because everything provided here is outside the realm of everyday needs. Teens who find themselves with very limited resources may choose not to visit this station. Volunteers should start by presenting the available options, but they may also remind the teens that there are many activities that are fun and free!

A giving guide for charitable donations to the many worthwhile organizations that provide service to our communities is provided for the teens' consideration. They may choose to give any amount, or nothing at all, but this would be a good opportunity to explain what a tax deduction is.

In addition, each participant should look at the "dream" options to think about the things they'd like to do someday. At this point, volunteers should remind the teens that if they do not start a savings plan for some of their dreams, they may never happen! While most dreams cost a lot of money, long-range planning and saving can make dreams come true. To help illustrate this point, and because many money advisors believe that "paying oneself first" is the best and surest way to build a savings account, a table portraying the wise practice of starting a savings plan early in life has been provided for you to hand out to all of the participants. They will be pleasantly surprised with the amount of savings that can accumulate over time with the benefit of compound interest working for them. Savings are very important for future college expenses and for retirement, although it is difficult for most teenagers to imagine their lives this far into the future.

The SOS Station

Teens should be encouraged to visit the SOS station if they find they do not have enough money to pay for all of their family's needs. The volunteers at this station will be responsible for helping teens see any options open to them for stretching their resources as far as they can; however, encourage the volunteers not to get bogged down. Some situations offer very little hope of actually "making it," and it is not possible to make sure everyone succeeds at this game. A brief discussion about wants versus needs may be helpful at this point. Other possible options include

- Downsizing their home, car, anything...send the teens back to other stations for this option.
- Giving something up, but only if it is not in the "need" category.
- If they are single, volunteers could suggest a roommate to share housing costs.
- An extra part-time job might be necessary. Be sure to mention that this might incur more babysitting or auto expenses. Part-time jobs should only be for up to twelve hours a week and minimum pay. For instance, twelve hours per week at the federal minimum wage rate of $5.15 per hour equals an extra $61.80 per week before taxes are deducted.
- Allow creative solutions from students, but use good sense. In other words, keep it realistic.
- A *very last* resort could be community resources such as WIC or federal programs such as welfare; however, volunteers should not encourage this option.
- If there is time, encourage teens to prepare for a better-paying job for their future in the *real* "real world."

Remind the teens that this is a game, and they drew their jobs and families by chance today. They have the power now, however, to make choices that would prevent an SOS situation from happening in their real lives.

Promotion

Finding an audience for a financial literacy program could be tough. Topics like saving, investing, and budgeting are often a hard sell to most teenagers. To ensure a good turnout, you should consider contacting local economics or life skills teachers to see if they are interested in bringing a class or two to the library for a field trip. This could result in meeting teens who might not normally visit the library, as well as future partnership opportunities with your school system. You could even offer to take this program on the road in cases where field trips are not possible. If you examine these opportunities and reach a dead end, however, try to use catchy phrases and gimmicks to convey that the program will be fun as well as educational. For instance, custom-made fortune cookies with messages reading "Find Your Fortune" could be handed out with school lunches. If you invite employees from a local bank to help with this project, you may even be able to entice teens with program promotions offering free money. Some banks are willing to offer $10–$20 for students who sign up for checking accounts. You could also play up the "Real World" angle due to the appeal of the popular MTV reality show by the same name.

Time, Cost, and Supplies

Since many of the materials are provided for you in Appendix D, this program should not take too long to plan. Make sure to contact volunteers at least a couple of months ahead of time, and then send them reminders about a week or so before the program. Allow a couple of hours to gather and photocopy materials for each station.

Costs for this program can be held to a minimum since the only supplies you really need are a few sheets of blank labels, paper, calculators, and pencils. You can spice things up, though, by giving teens fun, but useful, freebies at each station. Here is a list of suggestions:

Bank—gold foil–wrapped chocolate coins, a calculator

Real Estate Office—catalogs to inexpensive but hip furniture stores like IKEA

Grocery Store—granola bar, an apple, a gift certificate to a local grocer

Car Dealership—road map, key chain, information about AAA

Utility/Phone Companies—calling card, cell phone carrying case

Child Care Provider—candy pacifier, information from the local Red Cross about babysitting workshops

Health Insurance Provider—sample package of band-aids, dental floss, a toothbrush

Shopping Center—coupon to a favorite teen store

Mad Money Station—coupons to restaurants, bowling alleys, or video rental stores and, for their dreams, a piggy bank, coin purse, or a book about investing and/or saving

Chance Station—a lottery ticket

Should you decide to add these giveaways to your program, your costs will increase unless you ask the volunteers for each station to bring something from their company or organization. However, companies like U.S. Toy and Oriental Trading Company often have items for very inexpensive prices.

Collection Connection

Fiction

Begging for Change—Sharon Flake (Jump at the Sun, 2003)

Bucking the Sarge—Christopher Paul Curtis (Wendy Lamb Books, 2004)

Money Hungry—Sharon Flake (Jump at the Sun, 2001)

Nonfiction

Cha-ching! A Girl's Guide to Spending and Saving—Laura Weeldreyer (Rosen Publishing Group, 2000)

Complete Idiot's Guide to Money for Teens—Susan Shelly (Alpha, 2001)

Generation Y Money Book: 99 Smart Ways to Handle Money—Don Silver (Independent Publishers Group, 2000)

Get in the Game!! The Girls' Guide to Money and Investing—Vanessa Summers (Bloomberg Press, 2001)

How to Be a Teenage Millionaire—Art Beroff (Entrepreneur Press, 2000)

How to Survive in the Real World: Financial Independence for the Recent Graduate—James Lowell (Penguin, 1995)

I Want to Be Rich! A Teenager's Modem to Money; Financial Planning for Teenagers—Karin Humbolt (Reynolds Publishing Group, 1998)

Money: How to Make It, Spend It, and Keep Lots of It—Todd Temple (Broadman and Holman Publishers, 1998)

Money Matters for Teens—L. Allen and Lauree Burkett (Moody Publishers, 2001)

Money Matters for Teens Workbook—Larry Burkett and Todd Temple (Moody Publishers, 1998)

Neale S. Godfrey's Ultimate Kids' Money Book—Neale S. Godfrey (Simon and Schuster Children's Publishing, 1998)

Please Send Money: A Financial Survival Guide for Young Adults on Their Own—Dara Duguay (Sourcebooks, 2001)

Real World Math: Money and Other Numbers in Your Life—Donna Guthrie (Millbrook Press, 1998)

Teen Guide to Personal Financial Management—Marjolijn Bijlefeld and Sharon K. Zoumbaris (Greenwood Press, 2000)

ROAD TRIP ($$) (GRADES 10–12)

Do you remember what it felt like when the first of your friends got a driver's license? For most teens, this is an important rite of passage and for many of them, it's the first step toward independence. At first, there is nothing better than cruising along with the windows down, the music up, and friends in the back seat. The prospect of taking a road trip can seem like a huge adventure for newly licensed drivers. But then, the novelty wears off and minor frustrations like flat tires and the cost of gas threaten to spoil the fun.

A little knowledge can go a long way, however. In recognition of National Car Care Month, this program features local mechanics and car salespeople who can teach teens what to look for when buying a car, as well as basic car maintenance tips. Many adults go through life not knowing the first thing about how cars work, causing them to rely on the advice of car mechanics and salespeople. This program will give teens a leg up when it comes to owning and maintaining a car so that they can avoid common mistakes at the car dealership, prevent roadside breakdowns, and feel more comfortable behind the wheel. For libraries in urban areas where public transportation is the norm, you may want to focus more on types of cars and car customization.

How

It's entirely possible to run this program on your own, but you may make a better impression on the teens if you invite local experts to run the show. Call car dealerships or garages to ask them to consider bringing a car or two if you have the space for them in a nearby parking lot. Teens will probably retain more information if they can look under the hood while the mechanic demonstrates basic maintenance tips. Also, examples of used vehicles can help teens visualize what kind of car they can afford, and, as an added bonus, you can really make a splash with teen motorheads if the car dealership is willing to display some new, or classic, models. Next, come up with an agenda for the program so that you can provide the experts with an idea of what you want the teens to learn. Some suggestions for topics are provided here, but it's important to note that this is not a program intended to teach teens how to be better drivers. Presumably, they learn those skills through driver education courses, so it is not necessary to repeat the information at this program.

Buying a Car

Buying a car can be an intimidating experience. There are several things teens should consider when shopping for their first car. First, instruct them to note the mileage and the condition of the car. Encourage them to ask the salesperson if the vehicle has ever been in an accident. Second, remind them about the rising cost of gas, and provide examples of the varying fuel economies for different kinds of cars. For instance, a 2001 Jeep Cherokee gets sixteen miles to the gallon around town, resulting in an annual cost of $1,510 in gas, while a 2001 Ford Escort gets twenty-six miles to the gallon for an annual gas expense of $937 (U.S. Department of Energy 2005). This would be a good time to point out that manual transmissions offer better fuel economy than automatic transmissions. Finally, guide them to resources like *Consumer Reports*, *Kelley Blue Book*, or www.edmonds.com for information about repair costs and reliability, and for help with negotiating a fair purchase price.

Basic Car Maintenance

Even if you cannot find a car dealership willing to participate in this program, the section above is easy enough to conduct yourself. However, if you are not mechanically inclined, it would be best to have a local mechanic help out with this portion of the program. If you cannot locate a professional, consider contacting teachers of vocational education programs to see if they or their students would be willing to assist you. Basic car maintenance consists of changing flat tires and checking their air pressure; attaching new wiper blades; adding windshield wiper fluid; checking the oil, automatic transmission fluid, and coolant; and jumping a dead battery. If possible, it would be interesting to demonstrate how to change the oil and spark plugs as well. Search the Internet for a car maintenance checklist, print and photocopy it, then pass it out to the participants.

Tips for Road Trips

One of the best things about driving is road trips with friends, but they can turn into frustrating rather than exciting adventures if the proper precautions are not followed. Give teens a simple true/false quiz at the start of this portion of the program to help them gauge how much they know about traveling safely. This would be a good time to introduce teens to the advantages of having a AAA membership. The roadside assistance AAA offers in times of emergency brings peace of mind when traveling long distances, and the agency also provides free road maps. Ask AAA to provide some state highway maps for your teens to keep in their cars. Then, go over the correct answers to the quiz to jumpstart a quick discussion about things like roadside emergency kits, how to read a road map, safe places to stop, the dangers of driving while tired, or how to deal with road rage.

Tricking Out Your Ride

Just for fun, at the end of the program, invite the teens to look through various books featuring new and classic cars. If you know a local car enthusiast, you could even wrap things up with a slide show of restored or tricked out cars in the same spirit as MTV's *Pimp My Ride*. As they leave the program, send the teens on their way with parting gifts of things like key chains, car air fresheners, or fuzzy dice.

Promotion

An eye-catching bulletin board or display is a great way to promote this program. You could cover a flat surface with road maps and attach plastic or Matchbox® cars to the map in various positions to mark out a route. You could also make a display that resembles a driver's view through a windshield, with a road stretched out in the distance, dice hanging from a rearview mirror, and photocopies of different book jackets used as road signs. Another display idea is to use lots of different road signs like "Dangerous Curves Ahead" or "Yield," with the phrase "Are We There Yet? Tips for Your Road Trip" to advertise the content of the program. Consider distributing flyers about the program to driver education teachers, parents, AAA, the local department of motor vehicles, or even car dealerships. Doing this will help you target new teen drivers.

Time, Cost, and Supplies

You could get away with spending very little for this program, especially if you recruit local professionals to help you. Conceivably, the only expenses you will have would be for paper, snacks, road maps (if AAA will not donate them), and giveaways. It also should not take too long to prepare for this program, although you should contact car dealerships and/or mechanics several weeks ahead of time.

Collection Connection

Fiction

The Bean Trees—Barbara Kingsolver (Harper Perennial, 1989)

The Beetle and Me—Karen Romano Young (Greenwillow, 1999)

The Car—Gary Paulsen (Harcourt Children's Books, 1994)

Guitar Highway Rose—Brigid Lowry (Holiday House, 2003)

Hit the Road—Caroline B. Cooney (Delacorte Books for Young Readers, 2006)

My Road Trip to the Pretty Girl Capital of the World—Brian Yansky (Cricket Books, 2003)

On the Road—Jack Kerouac (Penguin Books, 1991)

Praying at the Sweetwater Motel—April Young Fritz (Hyperion, 2003)

Road Trip—Melody Carlson (Multnomah, 2003)

Rules of the Road—Joan Bauer (Puffin, 2000)

Sister Slam and the Poetic Motormouth Roadtrip—Linda Oatman High (Bloomsbury USA Children's Books, 2004)

Stetson—S. L. Rottman (Puffin, 2003)

Taking Chances—Stephanie Doyon (Simon Pulse, 1999)

Travels with Charley: In Search of America—John Steinbeck (Penguin, 1980)

Walk Two Moons—Sharon Creech (HarperCollins, 1994)

West with Hopeless—Carolyn Lieberg (Dutton Books, 2004)

ZigZag—Ellen Wittlinger (Simon and Schuster Children's Publishing, 2003)

Nonfiction

Auto Repair for Dummies—Deanne Sclar (John Wiley, 1999)

Behind the Wheel: Poems about Driving—Janet S. Wong (Margaret K. McElderry, 1999)

Car Smarts: Hot Tips for the Car Crazy—Phil Edmonston (Tundra Books, 2003)

Cars of the Fast and the Furious—Eddie Paul (Motorbooks International, 2003)

Clueless about Cars: An Easy Guide to Car Maintenance and Repair—Lisa Christensen (Firefly Books, 2004)

The Driving Book: Everything New Drivers Need to Know but Don't Know to Ask—Karen Gravelle (Turtleback Books, 2005)

The Everything Car Care Book: How to Maintain Your Car and Keep It Running Smoothly—Mike Florence (Adams Media Corporation, 2002)

Everything You Need to Know about Being a Teen Driver—Adam Winters (Rosen Publishing Group, 2000)

How to Buy a Car: A Former Car Salesman Tells All—James R. Ross (St. Martin's Publishing Group, 2001)

Inside Monster Garage—Dan Rosenberg, editor (Monster Garage, 2003)

Kelley Blue Book Used Car Guide—Kelley Blue Book

Real U Guide to Buying Your First Car—Johanna Bodnyk (Real U Guides, 2004)

Responsible Driving (student edition)—American Automobile Association (Glencoe/McGraw-Hill, 1999)

Road Trip USA: Cross-Country Adventures on America's Two-Lane Highways—Jamie Jensen (Avalon Travel Publishing, 2002)

Teenage Roadhogs—Michael Schein (MacMillan General Reference, 1997)

Used Car Buying Guide—Consumer Reports

SHARE THE LOVE ($) (GRADES 6–10)

Despite the cliché that teens are egocentric and self-involved, the fact is, many teens are still innocent enough in their youthfulness to embrace altruism. Perhaps the concept of "making a difference" is appealing, or maybe cynicism just hasn't found a toehold yet. In any case, I fondly remember sending a donation to the World Wildlife Federation to "adopt" a humpback whale when I was in high school. Later, in college, I helped paint a shelter for mentally ill homeless people in downtown Cincinnati, and I volunteered with an adult literacy program. As an adult, I never seem to have extra time to commit to service-oriented projects, but I still look for ways to have an impact—as many librarians do every day. Similarly compelled artist Sharon Vogt felt the "desire to 'do something positive' after September 11—or, at the very least, make someone some-where smile" (Puente 2003). The result of Vogt's inclination is the Found Art! Project wherein hundreds of artists—professional and amateur alike—create small works of art for the sole purpose of leaving them in public places for other people to find and take home. The mission statement of Found Art! reads, "Found Art! strives to make the world a better place right now by empowering people across the globe to share on a soul level. We believe in the power of art to communicate and heal. We believe all people are creative and that the expression of that creativity opens the heart of both the creator and the receiver. Open hearts com-municate at a deeper level, are naturally more compassionate, and are more aware and concerned about our global family" (Found Art!, www .found-art.com).

"Share the Love" is a program that will appeal to teens on a variety of levels. At its most basic level, it is a craft program. But, in celebration of Earth Day, which is itself a humane and philanthropic cause, the crafts are examples of recycled art, which environmentally conscious teens will appreciate. After making their recycled crafts, the teens will be encour-aged to participate in the Found Art! project in an effort to spread joy in their communities, heighten awareness of environmental concerns, and form connections to others through art. "Share the Love," through the distribution of ecologically friendly art, aims to make the world a better place to live.

How

The tenet of this program is very simple: to create something out of nothing, then leave it for someone else to enjoy. Before allowing the teens to make the crafts described below, introduce the concept of recycled art to them in relation to Earth Day. Briefly explain that the modern environ-mental movement began on April 22, 1970, when millions of Americans staged a protest against pollution, deforestation, and other practices harmful to the environment in an effort to bring such issues to the forefront of governmental agendas. The first Earth Day was a huge success in that it resulted in the formation of the United States Environmental Protection Agency, as well as the passage of the Clean Air, Clean Water, and Endangered Species acts. Since then, Earth Day has become a global observance, and continues to help make inroads for the protection and preservation of the environment (Earthday Network 2005).

Recycled art ties in very nicely with the principles of Earth Day in that it uses old or used items to create something new, attractive, and useful. In this way, it recycles objects that would normally clog up our landfills after being thrown away. Recycled art has gained in popularity, not only because of its inherent environmentally friendly message, but also because it is often whimsical in nature. After explaining these points to the teen participants, share examples of recycled art that you have located in art books or on the Internet. Then, encourage them to think about the things they would normally throw away as objects that have the potential to become something useful or beautiful, or both. Laura C. Martin, in her book about recycled crafts, does a good job of explaining the philosophy behind the recycled art movement, including its benefits for the environment as well as tips for reducing waste. Although the book is better suited for younger children—there is only one craft, making paper bead bracelets, that would be of interest to teens—it does include a useful checklist for determining an object's "trash to treasure" potential. Martin challenges her readers to think about an object as a potential art project by imagining what it would be like turned upside down; covered with cloth, paper, or paint; hung up on a wall; or separated into different parts (Martin 2004).

After describing recycled art to the teens, allow them to try their hands at making a couple of craft projects. Set up two stations with the supplies for each craft, and invite the teens to get started. While they are working, tell them about the Found Art! project. Explain the concept behind Found Art! and read the mission statement to them. If you have the technology handy, show the teens the Found Art! Web site so they can fully grasp the concept, and view some of the beautiful things people have created for others' enjoyment. It is important to point out that the only rule for participating in this project is that the art should have a positive message. Some of the pieces people have created actually have inspirational messages attached to them. Let the teens know that they don't have to donate their new creations to the Found Art! movement. If they choose to participate, however, the art they are creating at this program is a perfect way to get started with Found Art! Since it symbolizes ecological concerns, encourage the teens to craft environmentally friendly messages on paper luggage tags to attach to their creations. The Native American proverb "We do not inherit the earth from our ancestors; we borrow it from our children" or John Muir's statement "When one tugs at a single thing in nature, he finds it attached to the rest of the world" are examples of the types of things the teens might choose to write on their tags. Then, instruct the teens to adhere an "I Found One!" sticker to the back of their luggage tag so that the recipient of their creation can leave a comment on the Web site. (The stickers can be downloaded for free from www.found-art.com.) It may be a good idea to pass out multiple stickers to the participants in case they choose to create other works of art for the movement in the future. Finally, encourage them to leave their creations in places where people will serendipitously stumble across them, such as hospital waiting rooms, park benches, bus or subway seats, and even libraries. Advise the teens to ask for permission to leave their creations, except when leaving them in public places like parks. Other recycled craft ideas can be found at Kinder-Art (www.kinderart.com/recycle/) and the Imagination Factory's Trash Matcher (www.kid-at-art.com/htdoc/matchtmp.html).

CD Clocks

New clocks can be made using old, scratched CDs or the AOL discs that often arrive through the mail. Instruct the teens to decorate the shiny side of the CD with paint pens, and remind them to leave space for at least the twelve, three, six, and nine o'clock position indicators. They can use Roman or Arabic numbers to indicate these clock positions; alternatively, you could provide stickers or small colored stones for them to glue on in these spots. Then, show the teens how to attach the purchased gear box and clock hands.

Picture Holder

Using wire coat hangers and foraged stones, bark or driftwood, teens can make a simple picture holder. Instruct the teens to use wire cutters to cut about a twelve-inch piece of wire from the hanger. If this feels like a safety hazard to you, cut the pieces ahead of time. Then, have the teens bend one end of the wire into free-form shapes, making sure to create at least one loop that will hold a picture. Next, they should wrap the other end of the wire around a rock, stone, or piece of salvaged wood to form the holder's base.

Time, Cost, and Supplies

This is really a quick, easy, and cheap program to coordinate, but its impacts are far reaching. You will only need to set aside enough time for promoting the program, collecting the craft supplies, and printing out the Found Art! stickers from the Web site. A supply list consists of

old CDs

paint pens or markers

clock parts and hands

stickers or colored stones (optional)

glue (optional)

wire hangers

wire cutters

stones, rocks, driftwood, or salvaged wood

paper luggage tags

markers, crayons, or colored pencils

quotation books

Clearly, most of these supplies will be easy to obtain for free, keeping costs for this program to a bare minimum.

Promotion

Pique teens' curiosity for this program with a display containing a garbage bag filled with paper towels or balled-up newspaper to appear full. Affix a large question mark on the garbage bag, and surround the bag with crushed aluminum cans, balled-up newspaper, and candy wrappers. Create a logo for the program by lettering its title, "Share the Love," around a picture of the Earth. Then, entice teens with the hook "Celebrate Earth Day with a Trash to Treasure Creation" under the logo. Solidify the concept with bookmarks featuring the eco-fiction and nonfiction titles listed below.

Collection Connection

Fiction

The Beasties—William Sleater (Puffin, 1999)

California Blue—David Klass (Scholastic Paperbacks, 1996)

Downriver—Will Hobbs (Laurel Leaf, 1995)

Eva—Peter Dickinson (Laurel Leaf, 1990)

The Exchange Student—Kate Gilmore (Houghton Mifflin, 1999)

Flush—Carl Hiaasen (Knopf Books for Young Readers, 2005)

Free Fall—Joyce Sweeney (Laurel Leaf, 1999)

Green Thumb—Rob Thomas (Aladdin, 2000)

Home Free—Kathryn Lasky (Simon and Schuster Children's Publishing, 1985)

Hoot—Carl Hiaasen (Knopf Books for Young Readers, 2002)

Nausicaa of the Valley of Wind series—Hayao Miyazaki (Viz Media)

Night of the Whale—Jerry Spinelli (Laurel Leaf, 1988)

Rats—Paul Zindel (Hyperion, 2000)

Saving the Planet and Stuff—Gail Gauthier (Grosset and Dunlap, 2003)

Seedfolks—Paul Fleischman (HarperCollins, 1997)

The Spirit Window—Joyce Sweeney (Laurel Leaf, 1999)

The Talking Earth—Jean Craighead George (Harper Trophy, 1987)

Tangerine—Edward Bloor (Harcourt Children's Books, 1997)

Up a Creek—Laura E. Williams (Henry Holt and Company, 2001)

The Weirdo—Theodore Taylor (Harper Trophy, 1993)

Nonfiction

Dr. Art's Guide to Planet Earth: For Earthlings Ages 12 to 120—Art Sussman (Chelsea Green Publishing Company, 2000)

The Race to Save the Lord God Bird—Phillip M. Hoose (Farrar, Straus and Giroux, 2004)

Silent Spring—Rachel Carson (Mariner Books, 2002)

Teen Guides to Environmental Science—John and Peter Mongillo (Greenwood Press, 2004)

Walden—Henry David Thoreau (Dover Publications, 1995)

A Walk in the Woods—Bill Bryson (Broadway, 1999)

When Time Is Short and Money Is Tight...

Have the teens help run an Easter-egg hunt in cooperation with the Children's Department of your library.

Hold a "Stump the Librarian" contest for National Library Week.

Host an anime screening on a Saturday afternoon.

REFERENCES

Earthday Network (2005). History of Earth Day. Retrieved April 17, 2005, from Earthday Network Web site: http://www.earthday.net/resources/2005 materials/history.aspx.

Found Art! (n.d.). What is Found Art? Retrieved April 4, 2005, from Found Art! Web site: http://www.found-art.com/how.php.

Martin, L. (2004). *Recycled crafts box: Sock puppets, cardboard castles, bottle bugs and 37 more earth-friendly projects and activities you can make.* New York: Storey Publishing.

Puente, M. (2003). Found Art! project out to heal the world. *USA Today.* Retrieved April 4, 2005, from http://www.usatoday.com/life/2003-07-28-found-art_x. htm.

Richards, K. (2003). Build your credit and your future. *Young Money.* Retrieved January 10, 2005, from http://www.youngmoney.com/credit_debt/cred it_basics/030127_03?source=aha_pfi.

U.S. Department of Energy (2005). Find a car. Retrieved January 18, 2005, from Fuel Economy Web site: http://www.fueleconomy.gov/feg/findacar.htm.

Chapter 5

MAY

A couple of yearly observations this month are the driving force behind two of the three programs contained in this chapter. May is National Mental Health Month, making it an opportune time to shed some light on self-injury, a growing problem for many teenagers. On a lighter note, May is also National Book Month, making it the ideal time to promote reading to teens soon to have free time on their hands. Sandwiched in between these two programs is an entertaining program highlighting 1950s pop culture at a recreated drive-in movie theater featuring a cult favorite.

NATIONAL MENTAL HEALTH MONTH
($-$$) (GRADES 7–12)

Self-injury (SI), or the act of intentionally hurting oneself, is not a new concept to mental health professionals, but mainstream society is hearing more and more about it in recent years. The first time many people learned of self-injury was in 1995 when Princess Diana spoke about her use of cutting as an unhealthy coping mechanism. As unsettling as it may be, the reality is that nearly 1 percent of the population has engaged in some form of SI at least once (American Self-Harm Information Clearinghouse). This rate is much higher among teenaged girls, who are four times more prone to self-injurious behavior than boys (Warner 2002). Since so many self-injurers hide the marks of their behavior, it's conceivable that the rates could be even higher than what the research has shown.

Although cutting seems to be the most talked-about form of SI, there are many other manifestations such as branding or burning, pulling out hair, head banging, bruising, and even excessive body piercing. This program, though, will focus primarily on cutting. Teen cutters, according to KidsHealth.org, do not have the proper coping mechanisms in place to deal with stressful situations. As a result, cutting can be a way to release the built-up tension, anger, shame, and pain in an effort to gain control over the situation. Some teens who cut may have been abused or mistreated in some way so that "[s]elf-injury may feel like a way of 'waking up' from a sense of numbness after a traumatic experience" (Lyness 2005). Additionally, mental health problems such as depression, bipolar disorder, and obsessive-compulsive disorder can trigger cutting. In any case, psychologists say that cutting can itself become a compulsion, making it difficult to stop. Unfortunately, though, cutting has also claimed fad status in recent years, making it a way for overly dramatic teens to gain attention or appear rebellious.

Clearly, SI is an issue that warrants discussion. This program, using Patricia McCormick's book *Cut* as a medium, will create a safe environment for dialogue about SI among teens familiar and unfamiliar with SI, their parents, and mental health professionals in order to shed light on the disorder, and offer help to those who cut themselves.

How

Although other programs in this book may be enhanced, or simplified, by consulting with professionals such as teachers, counselors, art instructors, or photographers, it is absolutely imperative to seek the assistance of mental health professionals for this particular program. As librarians, we are not qualified to give advice about SI; however, it is entirely appropriate for you to lead the book discussion about *Cut* as long as there is at least one person nearby who is qualified to answer questions specific to SI that may arise. Therefore, before going further with planning this program, it is necessary to confirm the availability of someone from the mental health field to assist you. You may choose to invite just one expert, but it may be more interesting and beneficial to form a panel of people including psychologists or psychiatrists, school counselors, and even some reformed cutters.

After securing a panel, familiarize yourself with the topic by reading some professional literature and consulting organizations such as the American Academy of Child and Adolescent Psychiatry (www.aacap.org) and the American Psychological Association (www.apa.org). Of course, it will be necessary to read *Cut* in order to facilitate the book discussion, but you may also want to read a selection of other titles about SI, many of which are included in the Collection Connection section below. Finally, formulate a set of questions, such as those suggested below, to act as a discussion guide to the book.

- How is Callie's cutting connected to her silence at the beginning of the book?
- Callie is at Sea Pines with a group of young girls with a myriad of health issues: bulimia, anorexia, drug addiction, and so on. How are all of these "issues" related to one another?
- How does Callie's relationship with her father evolve throughout the book? Does this help her healing process? How?
- Tattooing, branding, and piercing have become "fashionable." What is the difference between these acts of body modification, and cutting?
- By the end, what did Callie discover as the root cause of her cutting? Could anything have been done to prevent this behavior?
- Guilt and feelings of powerlessness often contribute to cutting. What role did these emotions play in Callie's life?

After discussing the book, open the conversation up to a frank dialogue about self-injury—what it is, how to cope with it, and how to help others who may engage in this self-destructive behavior. To move the discussion along, invite each panelist to share five to ten minutes worth of advice, information, or testimonials. Then encourage the program participants to ask the panelists questions. In case participants are hesitant or too embarrassed to ask questions aloud, it may be a good idea to provide them with paper and pencils so that they can write down their questions instead. Then, you or one of the panelists can collect and read them for the group.

Some value-added ideas for this program include

- Showing an educational video such as *Self-Injury: From Suffering to Solutions*; *Hidden Scars, Silent Wounds: Understanding Self-Injury*; or *Skin Deep: Understanding Self-Injury*.
- Showing scenes from *Thirteen* (Twentieth Century Fox, 2003); see Chapter 6 for information about obtaining a public performance license.
- Reading aloud "A Hole New World," a short essay on piercing by Kelly Milner Halls featured in Michael Cart's literary anthology *Rush Hour: Face*. Run this idea by one of the professionals on your panel first, though, to make sure the essay won't have a triggering effect on teens dealing with SI.
- Providing recent news articles on the topic.
- Passing out copies of a biography of, or an interview with, Patricia McCormick.

Time, Cost, and Supplies

If your budget is small but your library is part of a large system or consortium, it will be possible to request copies of *Cut* via interlibrary loan for each of the participants. In order to obtain enough copies for everyone, request that all interested teens and parents sign up for the discussion about a month ahead of time. (This means you will have to promote the program at least six weeks before the panel discussion will actually occur.) Then, once the books have arrived, allow about two weeks for the participants to read the book before gathering to discuss it. *Cut* is a fairly short book, so this should be ample time. If, however, there is money in your budget, an easier way to handle this is to purchase multiple copies of the book so that they will be available to pass out to interested teens and their parents as they sign up for the program. So, other than promotional materials and, possibly, books, there are no other supplies or costs associated with this program.

Although you will have to plan ahead should you decide to loan the books, this program should still not take more than a few hours to organize since contacting the panel members and obtaining the books are the only two major tasks you'll need to complete.

Promotion

This may go without saying, but this program is for a specific audience (i.e., teens who engage in SI, or are concerned for a friend or family member who does, or teens who are curious and/or interested in psychology and mental health). Therefore, it would probably be a waste of energy—and perhaps even inappropriate—to develop a bulletin board promoting it. Alternatively, prepare a flyer that briefly describes SI, lists book titles about the topic, and, of course, advertises the book and panel discussion. Distribute these flyers to school counselors, doctors' offices, and child psychologists. You may also consider partnering with your local schools for this program, in which case it may be possible to send the flyer home to parents along with grade reports or other announcements. Make sure to promote this important program in your library's newsletter, and again, if you have a relationship with your local schools, in their newsletter as well. Press releases to newspapers might also be effective in this case since a large portion of your target audience is parents or other concerned adults.

Collection Connection

Fiction

America—E. R. Frank (Simon Pulse, 2003)

The Bell Jar—Sylvia Plath (Perennial, 1999)

Breathing Underwater—Alex Flinn (HarperCollins, 2001)

Checkers—John Marsden (Laurel Leaf, 2000)

Chinese Handcuffs—Chris Crutcher (Harper Trophy, 2004)

A Clockwork Orange—Anthony Burgess (W.W. Norton and Company, 1986)

Crosses—Shelley Stoehr (Writers Club Press, 2003)

Cut—Patricia McCormick (Push, 2002)

Damage—A. M. Jenkins (Harper Trophy, 2003)

Dancing on the Edge—Han Nolan (Harcourt Children's Books, 1997)

Dead Girls Don't Write Letters—Gail Giles (Roaring Brook, 2003)

The Facts Speak for Themselves—Brock Cole (Front Street, 1997)

---

*Indicates titles specific to cutting.

Freewill—Chris Lynch (HarperCollins, 2001)

Girl, Interrupted—Susanna Kaysen (Vintage, 1994)

I Am the Cheese—Robert Cormier (Knopf Books for Young Readers, 1977)

I Never Promised You a Rose Garden—Joanne Greenberg (Signet, 1989)

*Kat's Fall—Shelley Hrdlitschka (Orca Book Publishers, 2004)

Kissing Doorknobs—Terry Spencer Hesser (Delacorte Books for Young Readers, 1998)

Lisa, Bright and Dark—John Neufeld (Puffin, 1999)

*Luckiest Girl in the World—Steven Levenkron (Penguin, 1998)

Multiple Choice—Janet Tashjian (Henry Holt and Company, 1999)

Ordinary People—Judith Guest (Penguin, 1982)

*Saint Jude—Dawn Wilson (Tudor Publishers, 2001)

*Sleeveless—Joi Brozek (Phony Lid Publications, 2002)

Staying Fat for Sarah Byrnes—Chris Crutcher (Harper Trophy, 2003)

Stop Pretending: Or, What Happened When My Big Sister Went Crazy— Sonya Sones (Harper Trophy, 2001)

Touching Spirit Bear—Ben Mikaelson (HarperCollins, 2001)

*Tribes—Arthur Slade (Wendy Lamb Books, 2002)

Up on Cloud Nine—Anne Fine (Delacorte Books for Young Readers, 2002)

The Watcher—James Howe (Simon Pulse, 1999)

Whale Talk—Chris Crutcher (Greenwillow, 2001)

When Dad Killed Mom—Julius Lester (Silver Whistle, 2001)

When She Was Good—Norma Fox Mazer (Scholastic Paperbacks, 2000)

You Don't Know Me—David Klass (Harper Trophy, 2002)

Nonfiction

*The Body Project: An Intimate History of American Girls—Joan Jacobs Brumberg (Vintage, 1998)

*A Bright Red Scream: Self-Mutilation and the Language of Pain— Marilee Strong (Penguin, 1999)

The Burn Journals—Brent Runyon (Knopf Books for Young Readers, 2004)

Coping with Self-Mutilation: A Helping Book for Teens Who Hurt Themselves—Alicia Clarke (Rosen Publishing Group, 1999)

Skin Game: A Memoir—Caroline Kettlewell (St. Martin's Press, 1999)

GREASE AT THE DRIVE-IN ($$$$)
(GRADES 6–9)

Who doesn't love the movie *Grease*? Since its release in 1978, this cult-favorite musical starring Olivia Newton-John and John Travolta has inspired teens—and adults, I must admit—to belt out tunes from its appealing soundtrack. I have a sneaking suspicion, in fact, that even those who claim *Grease* is corny, surreptitiously sing along with its soundtrack in the shower. Its corniness, though, is part of its appeal. The movie—if you haven't seen it—revolves around the on-again-off-again romance between a squeaky-clean Australian foreign-exchange student named Sandy (played by Newton-John) and a tough-guy greaser with a big heart named Danny (played by Travolta). Set against the backdrop of all-American Rydell High School during the 1950s, this film has all the ingredients of a classic teen movie: a dance, a couple of love triangles, a crazy group of friends, a false-alarm pregnancy scare, impending graduation, and a beauty makeover. The 1950s time frame also lends *Grease* some kitschy charm through songs like "Beauty School Dropout" and "Grease Lightning." The songs themselves have lasting appeal, too. In fact, clubs and radio stations often still play a dance remix made from a few of the more popular tunes.

This program is purely for fun. Capitalizing on the teen appeal of *Grease*, a recreated 1950s drive-in movie theater will set the stage for a film screening followed by a karaoke session, giving teens license to sing their favorites from the movie's soundtrack.

How

Before proceeding with the planning for this program, consult Chapter 6 of this book for a discussion of public performance licenses. Then, after making sure you have the resources available to offer a public screening of *Grease*, obtain a copy of the movie and the soundtrack. To enhance the atmosphere, put some thought into re-creating the feel of a 1950s drive-in movie theater. If you have an outdoor space, it would be fun to show the film outdoors. A white wall or sheet and a power source would be all the extra equipment you would need for this. Set up a snack shack in one corner, offering typical theater treats such as popcorn, soda, retro candy (available at www.nostalgiccandy.com), and ice cream bars. If you can get your hands on some classic intermission advertisements, show one or two of these to entice the teens to visit the snack shack before the film begins.

Also, just before the movie begins, pass out a list of film blunders so the teens can have fun watching for them. Lists of these errors as well as trivia about the movie can be found on the Internet Movie Database (www.imdb.com) and Movie Mistakes (www.moviemistakes.com).

For added fun, stop the movie about halfway through for an inter-mission, during which the teens can participate in a couple of activities inspired by 1950s pop culture. For instance, challenge the teens to a simple hula-hoop contest in which whoever can keep their hoop up the longest wins a prize. Or unwrap several kinds of frozen TV dinners and ask the teens to write down what each item is. Those who correctly identify the most items would win. Inexpensive items like Silly Putty® and 3-D glasses could serve as the prizes for these quick activities. Then, it's on with the show!

After the movie, kick off a karaoke contest by asking groups of teens to come up and sing their favorites from the *Grease* soundtrack. If you have access to a karaoke machine, this will be easy to accomplish. If not, though, you could hire a DJ who specializes in karaoke. This is perhaps not the least expensive way to go, but the DJ may be willing to donate his or her services. In any case, make sure to have all of the *Grease* selections, as well as other favorites from the 1950s that teens would recognize. After each group or individual has performed, have the audience vote for their fa-vorite by applause. Award prizes like movie tickets or CDs of the *Grease* soundtrack to whoever receives the loudest ovation.

Time, Cost, and Supplies

There are some costs associated with this program, specifically for snacks and prizes, assuming you already have the public performance license needed to show the movie. A list of items you'll most likely need to purchase includes

popcorn

cans of soda

ice cream bars

candy

ice

napkins

hula hoops

several frozen dinners

Silly Putty

3-D glasses

copies of the *Grease* soundtrack, or movie tickets (to give as prizes)

Check dollar stores for some of the above items since they often carry toys such as hula hoops for a lot less. Also, when confronted with the wide range of frozen dinners available, keep in mind that for the purpose of this contest, cheaper is better. Fairly unsavory-looking selections like creamed spinach and Salisbury steak will probably be harder to identify than some of the newer, fancier meals on the market today. Other items you'll need to acquire include

a VHS or DVD copy of *Grease*

the *Grease* soundtrack

a cooler (for the ice cream and the soda)

a karaoke machine, or a DJ

a projector

a white sheet or a screen (if showing the movie outdoors)

extension cords (if showing the movie outdoors)

Promotion

Promoting this program should be a cinch if you tie the approaching end of the school year to that of Rydell High's with phrases like "Get the Gang Together One Last Time" or "Celebrate 'Summer Nights.'" Invite the teens to dress like Pink Ladies and T-Birds for an evening of retro fun. Decorate a bulletin board to look like a jukebox with the song choice buttons labeled with the program's specifics—such as the date and time—instead. Surround the jukebox with old 45s and other 1950s para-phernalia. Of course, make sure to link the program to your collection with a display of some of the titles listed below.

Collection Connection

Fiction (set in the 1950s)

Catch a Tiger by the Toe—Ellen Levine (Viking Juvenile, 2005)

The Education of Robert Nifkin—Daniel Pinkwater (Graphia, 2005)

Gidget—Frederick Kohner (Berkley Publishing Group, 2001)

Grease—Ron De Christoforo (Pocket, 1998)

How Far Would You Have Gotten if I Hadn't Called You Back?—Valerie Hobbs (Scholastic, 2003)

Jericho Walls—Kristi Collier (Henry Holt and Company, 2002)

Kira-Kira—Cynthia Kadohata (Atheneum, 2004)

Memories of Summer—Ruth White (Farrar, Straus and Giroux, 2000)

Mississippi Trial, 1955—Chris Crowe (Puffin, 2003)

Sonny's House of Spies—George Ella Lyon (Atheneum, 2004)

Waiting to Disappear—April Young Fritz (Hyperion, 2004)

Nonfiction

The American Drive-In Movie Theater—Don Sanders (Motorbooks International, 2003)

American Pop Icons—Susan Davidson (Guggenheim Museum Publications, 2003)

As Seen on TV: The Visual Culture of Everyday Life in the 1950s—Karal Ann Marling (Harvard University Press, 1996)

The Beatles: 10 Years That Shook the World—Paul Trynka, editor (DK Adult, 2004)

Frenchy's Grease *Scrapbook: "We'll Always Be Together!"*—Didi Conn (Hyperion, 1998)

Rock & Roll Generation: Teen Life in the '50s—Editors of Time Life Books (Time Life Books, 1998)

Rocket Boys—Homer Hickam (Delta, 2000)

CATCH A TITLE WAVE ($$$$) (GRADES 7–10)

If your teen summer reading statistics could use a boost, "Catch a Title Wave" is the perfect program to try, and May is a great time to try it.

National Book Month is celebrated in May, and it is also near the end of the school year. So, by using this time to promote the materials and services your library has to offer, it is more likely that the information will stay fresh in teens' minds until school lets out for the summer.

All of the programs contained in this book have a strong tie to young adult fiction and nonfiction titles; however, this program specifically showcases books and promotes reading as a worthwhile, and even cool, activity. Through coordinated class visits to your library, "Catch a Title Wave" celebrates reading luau-style in a festive, tropical atmosphere in an effort to make the library a preferred destination for teens over the course of the long, hot summer.

How

Rather than being held one afternoon for what could turn out to be a dismally small audience, "Catch a Title Wave" is designed to be enjoyed by classrooms full of teens during the school day. Therefore, a lot of coordination with your local schools will be necessary to make this happen. Think of it as an open house of sorts, with classes visiting the library in shifts throughout each day. The number of days this program will run will depend on how many schools there are in your area. Typically, students have to take some form of English or reading for every year they are in school. So, to reach as many teens as possible—and because this program ties in nicely with English and reading—make a list of these teachers and plan on contacting them individually to schedule a time for their class visit. A sample spreadsheet (Appendix E) has been included to help simplify this scheduling process. As you gauge the size of the schools, you may need to narrow down your audience considerably. In a very small, rural area, it is quite possible to entertain every teenaged student from seventh through twelfth grade. Obviously, though, this will not be possible everywhere. For larger school systems, consider targeting only middle-schoolers or even just one grade.

To simplify the process, you could view this program as a wonderful partnership opportunity that could be advantageous. Contact the school library and media specialists for the schools you would like to target in order to invite them into the planning process. With their help, it may be possible to "take this show on the road," making it more enticing for teachers to participate in that it would be simpler to visit their own school's library rather than the public library that may or may not be conveniently located.

Either way, after scheduling the class visits, determine whether or not there will be enough staff to handle this program all day, or, in the case of larger populations, all week. It may be necessary to recruit coworkers, volunteers, or the Friends of the Library to help out. In this case, use the last column on the scheduling spreadsheet to indicate who will staff each time slot.

Now comes the fun part: creating a luau-style celebration of reading. First, set the tone with some Hawaiian music or a CD of ocean sounds playing in the background. As the class arrives, invite each teen to guess how many jelly beans are in a jar, and then write the number on a small entry form and drop it in a box. (Choose tropical-flavored jelly beans such as coconut, pineapple, passion fruit, orange, and so on.) Use the information from the entry forms to create a mailing list that you could use to send reminders about upcoming summer reading activities, then notify the teen with the best guess at the end of "Catch a Title Wave."

As with any teen program, plan to serve food. These two recipes were inspired by tropical climes and would go nicely with some sort of fruit punch.

Aloha Kabobs

2 cans of chunk pineapple

bunch of red grapes

quart of strawberries, sliced in half

bag of mini marshmallows

wooden skewers

Cut the wooden skewers in half, then thread two pieces of each kind of fruit onto them along with a couple of marshmallows. Makes about 20–30 kabobs.

Pineapple Spread

12-oz. package of cream cheese, softened

1 c. crushed pineapple, drained well

1 c. coconut flakes

1 tsp. lemon juice

½ tsp. ground ginger

½ c. chopped pecans (optional)

Beat cream cheese until fluffy; fold in other ingredients and mix well. Serve with crackers or pita bread. Serves about fifty.

As the teens snack on their tropical treats, entertain them with a few booktalks that have been prepared ahead of time. Chances are, you already have several to choose from, but if you need inspiration, consult any of the fine resources written by Joni Bodart, or these Web sites:

ALA Booktalking
www.ala.org/ala/yalsa/profdev/booktalking.htm

The Booktalker
www.thebooktalker.com

Booktalks Quick and Simple
nancykeane.com/booktalks/

You may choose titles that share the tropical theme already established, or books that correlate with the theme your library has chosen for upcoming summer reading activities. Alternatively, you could highlight some of the newest, hottest titles with high teen appeal along with some of the titles on their required summer reading lists.

After booktalking a few titles, give the teens a chance to browse some genre book displays set up around the program space, and to voice their own opinions about books. The Mastics-Moriches-Shirley Community Library and the William Floyd High School in New York held a similar program they called a "book blitz," during which teens could pose with their favorite books and a few fun, beachy props for group photos taken with Polaroid® film. Browse through catalogs like Oriental Trading or U.S. Toy to find props like straw hats, plastic coconut tumblers, and flower leis. You could even bring some tropical-printed shirts, lawn chairs, and a beach umbrella from home to add to the fun. The Mastics-Moriches Library also used this time to record teens' testimonials about their favorite books. It is possible to replicate this idea by setting a video camera on a tripod in front of which teens can sit to record themselves describing books they've enjoyed. Cover the background with black fabric or paper so the quality is consistent for each testimonial. With the teens' permission, it would be useful to splice these testimonials together with footage taken during summer reading programs to use as a promotional piece in the future.

Finally, with time permitting, hold a quick limbo contest using a broomstick and the game's anthem, "Limbo Rock" by Chubby Checker.

The winners could receive advanced reading copies you may have lying around, T-shirts promoting that year's summer reading program, or bookmarks. Then, send the teens on their way back to school with information about your summer reading activities, lists of their required summer reading, and, if needed, library card applications.

Time, Cost, and Supplies

This program could get expensive if you live in an area with a large school system. If costs pose a problem, serve just one of the treats, and use a digital camera to take the pictures of teens posing with their favorite books. (Note: To ensure each group of teens receives their photo, it will be necessary to collect their e-mail addresses. This can be accomplished by numbering a sheet of paper and asking at least one member from each group to list his or her e-mail address.) Also, since this program could be considered a kickoff for your library's teen summer reading program, you may be able to use some of the funds dedicated to that purpose to help ease the financial burden. The supplies and equipment you will need include

CDs of Hawaiian music, ocean sounds, and/or limbo music

CD player

large jar (exact size depends on how many bags of jelly beans you purchase for the contest)

jelly beans

container for raffle slips

pencils

video camera with tripod

black fabric or paper

tropical props for photographs

Polaroid camera and film, or digital camera

broomstick

small prizes for limbo contest

chunk pineapple

red grapes

strawberries

mini marshmallows

wooden skewers

cream cheese

crushed pineapple

coconut flakes

lemon juice

ground ginger

pecans (optional)

This could also be a fairly time-intensive program to implement in that several hours will probably be necessary to schedule the class visits. In addition, the program itself may run for as long as a full week in order to reach a large student population, but the impact on summer reading statistics may well be worth the extra effort.

Promotion

It is not necessary to promote "Catch a Title Wave" in-house, as the audience for this program is a ready-made one. Therefore, design a colorful flyer to mail to your targeted teachers along with a letter describing the benefits of the program. In the letter, state that you will be following up with each of them individually to schedule their class visit. Then, set aside a fair amount of time to contact each of the teachers via e-mail or telephone to start filling in the schedule for the day(s) or week. Keep in mind that teachers may be more responsive if you ensure them that your library offers several copies of each title on their students' required (or suggested) summer reading lists, and that you may even booktalk one or two of them at the program. To link the program with some familiar faces, you could—as the Mastics-Moriches-Shirley Community Library did—take pictures of teachers, coaches, and administrators with their favorite books and make them into READ posters. And, again, by partnering with school library media specialists and holding the program on their turf, it may make it easier for teachers to bring their classes.

Collection Connection

Fiction

Dr. Franklin's Island—Ann Halam (Laurel Leaf, 2003)

The Goats—Brock Cole (Farrar, Straus and Giroux, 1990)

Island Boyz—Graham Salisbury (Wendy Lamb Books, 2002)

Island of the Blue Dolphins—Scott O'Dell (Yearling, 1987)

Lord of the Flies—William Golding (Berkley Publishing Group, 1959)

Red Palms—Cara Haycak (Wendy Lamb Books, 2004)

Robinson Crusoe—Daniel Defoe (Modern Library, 2001)

Wild Man Island—Will Hobbs (HarperCollins, 2002)

When Time Is Short and Money Is Tight...

National Salsa Month—host a salsa dancing class!

In celebration of Cinco de Mayo, host a taco-building party.

Invite a balloon artist or clown to teach teens how to sculpt balloons; recruit your newly talented teens to volunteer their services during the children's summer reading program.

REFERENCES

American Self-Harm Information Clearinghouse (n.d.). Retrieved June 3, 2005, from American Self-Harm Information Clearinghouse Web site: www.selfinjury.org.

Lyness, D. (2005). Cutting. Retrieved June 3, 2005, from KidsHealth Web site: http://www.kidshealth.org/teen/your_mind/feeling_sad/cutting.html.

Warner, J. (2002). Self-injury no longer rare among teens. Retrieved June 3, 2005, from WebMD Health Web site: http://my.webmd.com/content/article/53/61375.htm.

Chapter 6

JUNE

Because the summer months are often packed with teen summer reading programs and activities, the chapters for June, July, and August each contain only two programs, supplemented by a film series that kicks off in June. Since school is not in session, the programs in this chapter take advantage of teens' free time. Many schools these days expect students to perform some kind of volunteer service before graduation. "Green Teens" is a community beautification project that can help teens fulfill this requirement. Summer is also the perfect time to launch a visual poetry contest since the weather is nice enough for teens to grab a camera and hit the great outdoors after months of feeling cooped up in classrooms. Finally, "From Print to Silver Screen," detailed in this chapter, is a three-month-long film series featuring movies that have been adapted from books, perfect for the avid reader who now has time to read for pleasure.

GREEN TEENS ($$$$) (GRADES 7–12)

"Green Teens" is a two-part program that will teach teens the basics of gardening and landscape design. Teens with a knack for nature, however, will probably not be the only ones interested in this program since, as mentioned above, many schools require their students to complete community service hours before graduation. While "Green Teens" will help teens fulfill that requirement, it also meets several of their developmental needs. Teens will find an outlet for constructive use of their free time, as well as an opportunity to learn new skills through this service project. In addition, the hands-on experience enforces positive values such as responsibility and teamwork while providing a channel for creative expression. By participating in "Green Teens," teens will gain a sense of empowerment through the decisions they will need to make, and the program will help build their self-esteem by giving them the chance to contribute something meaningful to their community.

How

This program consists of two parts. First, participants will attend a two-hour workshop at which they will learn the basics of gardening and landscape design, and sketch a rough layout of the garden space to be planted. The second part of the program will consist of implementing the design scheme on "planting day."

Before planning the details of this program, space for a garden needs to be obtained. In order to complete the planting in one day, make sure to select a fairly small space; one measuring 20 feet by 20 feet is likely to be plenty large enough. There are several options for you to consider and explore when trying to find a space to plant. The first, most obvious, choice is to claim a spot in your library's landscaping for teens to plant. Your library may even have a courtyard that needs some sprucing up. If this seems like a feasible idea, be sure to obtain permission from your building's administration or board of directors. Also, make sure that the garden can be properly watered and cared for by someone other than you or your teen participants. In other words, it's not reasonable to assume that the teens participating in this project, many of whom will be graduating, will water and weed the garden. Nor is it realistic for you to take on this added responsibility yourself. Rather, consult your library's building and maintenance staff (if you have one) to see if they are willing to care for the garden. Chances are, the library where you work already has some landscaping that needs to be maintained, so this will probably not be a problem. If your library contracts with an outside landscaping company, make sure that its employees are willing to care for the teens' plantings on their regular visits to your building.

The second option is to partner with your community's park department. Park staff may be quite willing to allow the "Green Teens" to plant a garden in a space they normally plant themselves. This way, you and your library will not be responsible for maintaining the garden. If you choose this route, invite park staff to attend—or even lead—the workshop. This will ensure that the garden fits within their specifications and that the correct plants are chosen. The most obvious benefits of this option are that the park staff will shoulder much of the responsibility, and that a mutually beneficial partnership can be established.

Finally, the third option for finding a garden space is to explore "Adopt-a-Spot" opportunities within your community. Many cities allow civic organizations to plant gardens in designated locations in parks, on boulevards, or in residential neighborhoods. If this is the route you choose, you may want to partner with organizations—like your local garden club, for example—so that responsibility for the garden can be shared with a group that has knowledge and expertise. This is especially important if you don't have a green thumb.

Next, you will need to determine how this project will be funded. If you've ever planted a garden yourself, you know how expensive plants—particularly, perennials—can be. If you are fortunate enough to have a healthy budget for teen programming, purchasing plants is the easiest route to follow, but make sure to set a budget for the project first so costs don't get out of hand. If your garden will be on library property, however, your library's building budget is a logical source of funding. Most of us, though, will need to consider outside funding or soliciting donations. If partnering with a garden club is an option (in the case of utilizing an Adopt-a-Spot program, for instance), members of the club may be willing to purchase the plants in exchange for the teens' labor. If your local park department is willing to donate a spot they would normally plant anyway, ask them to purchase the supplies. The final option is to contact a local greenhouse or home improvement store to ask them to donate plants. If this looks like the route you'll have to follow, be sure to inquire far in advance of your program. Oftentimes, chain stores ask that donation requests be made to their corporate headquarters, which can slow the process, and it will be necessary to know their answer before going ahead with this program.

Once the garden space has been obtained and a funding source for the plants has been secured, it's time to start planning the workshop. While it's entirely possible for you to teach this yourself—especially if you're an avid gardener—you may want to consider asking someone from a greenhouse, a landscaping company, or a gardening club to provide their expertise. Don't forget to ask your coworkers if any of them have the know-how; your best resource could be right under your nose! Regardless of who leads the workshop, however, the participants will need to learn some basic concepts before the proper plants can be selected.

Where you live will be the largest deciding factor for choosing the type of garden to plant. Florida gardens, for instance, are much different than those in New England. This would be a good time to explain the difference between annuals and perennials. Beyond regional geography, the garden's exact location also steers plant choices. Explain to the teens the different factors to consider in landscape design, such as amount of sunlight, soil composition, and moisture. After this introductory tutorial, provide them with an illustrated list of suggested plants and flowers so they can use it as a guide in choosing how they want their garden to look. Next, pass out blank garden plans that have only the perimeter and major objects like trees sketched out. Allow each teen the chance to design the garden using the plants from the suggestion list. It may also be fun to split the teens into teams for better idea generation. Be sure to have plenty of gardening books available for the teens to browse through for inspiration.

At this point, allow the teens to break for a snack. Pizza is always an easy and popular choice, but if you really want to get into the spirit of things, you could serve salads. While they are eating, teens can continue to look through the books you've provided or take virtual tours of famous gardens such as the Biltmore Estate Gardens in North Carolina (www. biltmore.com/explore/gardens/virtualtour.shtml) or the Royal Botanical Gardens in England (www.rbgkew.org.uk/plants/index.html). This is also a good opportunity for a "commercial break" during which you can congratulate the teens for participating in such a worthy project and draw their attention to the books about other types of community service, listed in the Collection Connection section of this program.

After the break, the teens will share their individual ideas of how the garden should look and vote on the best idea. Again, if you are not a gardening guru, it would be wise to have an expert there to help teens determine which of their ideas is most feasible. Next, explain the basic steps for planting a garden. This will help teens determine the division of labor for planting day. Pass around sign-up sheets for three different jobs: Dirt Diggers, Seed Sowers, and Plant Managers. The Dirt Diggers will be responsible for clearing the land of debris and weeds, breaking up the soil with hoes, applying topsoil, and digging holes for plants and flowers. The Seed Sowers will place seeds and plants in the holes, cover them up with soil, water the fresh plantings, and fertilize them if necessary. Finally, the Plant Managers will oversee the project, making sure that the garden plan is followed by marking off sections with stakes, helping their peers properly place the plants, and identifying the plants with markers after spreading mulch around them. Before the teens leave, have them self-address postcards to be used as reminders for planting day.

The second part of this program should take place a week or so after the workshop so the teens don't forget what they've learned. Shortly after the workshop, send the participants their self-addressed postcards reminding them of the date, time, and location of planting day. Offer another date as a backup in case the weather doesn't cooperate. In addition, the postcards should contain a checklist of items to bring such as gardening tools and gloves, a brown-bag lunch, and extra clothes in case of chilly weather. It might be a good idea to list the tools needed for each job to ensure that your group has what they need to complete the job. It would be a disaster to end up with fifteen rakes and no hand trowels! Next, arrange for delivery of the plants and other materials such as topsoil and mulch.

On planting day, make sure to have a very clear idea of what the finished project should look like. Set a timetable for the project and work to make sure the project is finished that day. For this to happen, you may consider recruiting parent volunteers to help out, but if you were careful to select a fairly small space for the garden, or if the teens will be working alongside members of a garden club, this may not be necessary. When the work is completed, take a group picture of the teens beside the garden they worked so hard to create. Then, present them with award certificates stating the number of community service hours they completed, along with small gifts like potted African violets, spring bulbs, or seed packets.

Time, Cost, and Supplies

"Green Teens" is a fairly ambitious program. Quite a bit of preparation time will need to be devoted to the project, particularly as you decide where the garden should be, and how the plants will be supplied. Also, while most programs last a few hours from start to finish, this one will cover the better part of two days. If you already have a fair amount of gardening wisdom to impart to the teens, you will also need to devote time to studying the garden space and determining what plants would work best. Recruiting community partners, however, will keep both time and costs to a minimum. Not only will they be the ones to prepare most of the materials for the workshop, but they may also be your funding source for purchasing the plants, topsoil, mulch, and fertilizer. Costs can also be kept lower by asking the teens and other library coworkers to loan their garden tools for the project. If an outside donor is secured, you may only need to budget for the following supplies:

salad ingredients or pizza for lunch during the workshop

paper supplies, including postcards, postage, and award certificates

film

potted African violets or seed packets

garden gloves

Promotion

The easiest way to promote this program is to capitalize on the community-service angle. Many teens will jump at the chance to earn service hours while working alongside their friends on a sunny afternoon. Before school lets out for the summer, contact guidance counselors, building principals, and teachers to let them know about the program opportunity that you have to offer. A display within the library can help advertise this further. Catch teens' attention with posters and flyers urging them to "Get Involved," "Have a Voice," and "Make a Difference." Illustrate your point by displaying the books found in the Collection Connection section below, about teens making their mark on the world. Photographs, not drawings or cartoons, portraying teens working on important projects will drive the point home and inspire them to pick up a flyer advertising "Green Teens." Another option is to turn "Green Teens" into an intergenerational program by promoting it to garden clubs. Invite club members to spend quality time with their children or grandchildren through a two-day volunteer program to benefit and beautify the community. Finally, though the contingent may be small, don't miss the opportunity to promote "Green Teens" in-house to nature-loving teens. Mount a large poster of a garden or flowers on green cloth or paper to serve as the backdrop for a collection of gardening books. Use tools such as a watering can, a hand trowel, and gardening gloves to add interest to the display, but to prevent the display from attracting little old ladies instead of teenagers, try to find photographs of teens working on a garden to portray the idea behind the program.

Collection Connection

Fiction

The Adventures of Blue Avenger—Norma Howe (Henry Holt and Company, 1999)

The Ancient One—T. A. Barron (Philomel, 1992)

Blue Jean: What Young Women Are Thinking, Saying, and Doing—Sherry Handel (Blue Jean Press, 2001)

Flush—Carl Hiaasen (Knopf Books for Young Readers, 2005)

God of Beer—Garrett Keizer (HarperCollins, 2002)

Going, Going—Naomi Shihab Nye (Greenwillow, 2005)

The Gospel according to Larry—Janet Tashjian (Henry Holt and Company, 2001)

A Heart Divided—Cherie Bennett and Jeff Gottensfeld (Delacorte Books for Young Readers, 2004)

Hoot—Carl Hiaasen (Knopf Books for Young Readers, 2002)

Hope Was Here—Joan Bauer (Putnam Publishing Group, 2000)

Nothing but the Truth—Avi (Scholastic, 1991)

The Outcasts of 19 Schuyler Place—E. L. Konigsburg (Atheneum, 2004)

Seedfolks—Paul Fleischman (HarperCollins, 1997)

Sledding Hill—Chris Crutcher (Greenwillow, 2005)

Up a Creek—Laura Williams (Henry Holt and Company, 2001)

Vote for Larry—Janet Tashjian (Henry Holt and Company, 2004)

Who Will Tell My Brother?—Marlene Carvell (Hyperion, 2002)

The Year They Burned the Books—Nancy Garden (Farrar, Straus and Giroux, 1999)

Nonfiction

Catch the Spirit: Teen Volunteers Tell How They Made a Difference—Susan K. Perry (Franklin Watts, 2000)

It's Our World, Too!—Phillip Hoose (Farrar, Straus and Giroux, 2002)

It's Your World—If You Don't Like It, Change It: Activism for Teenagers—Mikki Halpin (Simon Pulse, 2004)

The Kid's Guide to Social Action: How to Solve the Social Problems You Choose—And Turn Creative Thinking into Positive Action—Barbara A. Lewis (Free Spirit Publishing, 1998)

Kids with Courage: True Stories about Young People Making a Difference—Barbara A. Lewis (Free Spirit Publishing, 1992)

The Race to Save the Lord God Bird—Phillip Hoose (Farrar, Straus and Giroux, 2004)

Rosa Parks: My Story—Rosa Parks (Dial Books, 1992)

Take Action! A Guide to Active Citizenship—Marc Kielburger (Wiley, 2002)

Teen Power Politics: Make Yourself Heard—Sara Jane Boyers (21st Century, 2000)

Teens with the Courage to Give: Young People Who Triumphed over Tragedy and Volunteered to Make a Difference—Jackie Waldman (Conari Press, 2000)

Volunteering: The Ultimate Teen Guide—Kathlyn Gay (Scarecrow Press, 2004)

Youth! The 26% Solution—Wendy Lesko (Information USA, 1998)

IN FOCUS: A VISUAL POETRY CONTEST ($-$$$$) (GRADES 7–12)

Who doesn't love looking at pictures? Most of us, though, would rather be behind the camera than in its focus. Teens brim with creativity, but not all of them are great at writing poems or painting masterpieces. Photography, however, is a teachable art form that many teens have embraced. While taking pictures is a great creative outlet, it's also a skill many people wish they had while traveling or celebrating important milestones. A workshop, therefore, will teach teens the basics of taking great pictures so that, later in life, they'll rarely be disappointed with the quality of their keepsakes. As a bonus, the ensuing visual poetry contest will encourage teens to be creative with their new knowledge, allowing them to explore different photography methods and techniques. June is the perfect month for this contest because the weather is nice, school is out for the summer, and outdoor activities like festivals, sporting events, and barbecues make great subjects. This two-part program starts with a workshop that will teach teens photography basics and end with a contest culminating in an awards ceremony show-casing the participants' creativity and skill as budding shutterbugs.

How

Before launching the visual poetry contest, plan to host a workshop that will give teens who are new to this art form a basic understanding of the skills, equipment, and techniques needed to take good pictures. The en-suing contest may be open to all teens—even those who are more ex-perienced photographers—but you may consider making the workshop mandatory, thereby limiting contest participation to the amateurs who attend the workshop. In any case, you'll need to decide who will lead the workshop. You may decide that you have enough basic knowledge to be helpful to the teens, but if you have a tendency to forget to take the lens cap off before snapping a picture (as I do), it may be better to ask a professional to impart his or her expertise. In this case, ask the owner of a photography studio, a professional portrait photographer, or just an amateur with a great eye to help out.

Learning any new skill has to start with a fundamental understanding of the terminology. Start the workshop with an explanation of basic words like backlighting, overexposure, and panoramic. An extensive glossary can be found at www.nikonians.org/html/resources/photography-glossary. html. Some of the terms contained in this glossary are for very advanced photographers, but many are commonly used and should help dispel teens' confusion. To make this overview a bit more fun or interactive, try playing a matching game with the words and definitions, and tossing rolls of film to the participants who answer the questions correctly. Next, point out the parts of a camera and explain what their functions are. Choose to either have a camera handy for this quick overview, or pass out a printed diagram of a camera. One can be found at http://library. thinkquest.org/11355/html/partsofcamera.htm.

Finally, for something as visual as photography, the best way to demonstrate solid picture-taking skills is to show examples of good and bad pictures. At the workshop, show teens sample pictures that were taken using simple techniques, to improve their quality. Taking pictures at eye level, choosing a plain rather than distracting background, taking vertical pictures, and moving the camera closer to the subject are all ways to improve pictures. Next, show examples of common problems to avoid like red eye, reflections or light streaks, and fuzzy or blurry images. Kodak has a wonderfully helpful Web site (www.kodak.com) that explains how to troubleshoot these common problems. It also has an interactive demo that will allow your teen participants to practice choosing angles, backgrounds, and lighting for perfect pictures. Consider using this site, particularly if you plan on leading the workshop yourself, to illustrate your points. Other useful Web sites include

PhotoSecrets
www.photosecrets.com

Fodor's Focus on Photography
www.fodors.com/focus/

FotoFinish Tutorials
www.fotofinish.com/resources/centers/photo/index.htm

Depending on how long you want the workshop to be, you may also choose to include information specific to digital photography, but keep in mind that many teens may not have access to a digital camera. This information could include the best way to print digital images, as well as an overview of the software (e.g., Adobe Photoshop, FotoFinish, and Picasa) used to enhance or alter photographs. Whether or not you choose to include this information may also depend on what kinds of pictures you want to allow as contest entries. If you decide to allow digitally enhanced, edited or designed pictures, it would be best to create a separate category for these entries. Doing so would make judging fairer, and it may also attract teens who have an interest in gadgets or computer graphics.

To enhance the workshop, allow teens the chance to browse through photography books to discover the style they enjoy most. Black-and-white, still-life, action, nature, or animal photography are examples of the kinds of photography books to have available. It would also help the participants if they could take turns with a digital camera while being "coached" by the volunteer expert. Another idea is to provide each teen with a cardboard rectangle with a hole in the middle. Allot some time outdoors for them to practice finding subjects and framing them within the square so they can fine-tune their abilities before using real film. Finally, give each teen a disposable camera and coupons for film developing before they leave.

The second part of "In Focus" consists of the visual poetry contest. At the workshop, announce the theme for the contest and pass out rules and entry forms. Keeping the contest wide open could overwhelm some teens who have no idea what style they like, or what subjects they're most attracted to. So, while it's not necessary to create a theme, it could give teens a starting point, or a focus (so to speak), for their lens. General, indiscrete themes could result in creative and surprising interpretations. Examples of these are Beauty, Life, and Emotion. To make it less ambiguous, try Nature, Babies, or a specific emotion like Pride, Grief, or Joy. Other themes could embody your community's spirit, like a particular festival or celebration indigenous to your area, or themes like Patriotism, Civic Pride, Our Heroes, or Architecture. Still other themes that could result in some really interesting images include

Odd Jobs

Unusual Pets

Body Art

Unique Hobbies

Music or Poetry

Gotcha!

Opposites Attract

Who I Am

As the deadline for the contest nears, make sure to have qualified people available to judge the work and award prizes. It would be best to award first, second, third, and honorable-mention prizes to teens in two or three separate age or grade categories to ensure that 12-year-olds are not competing against more experienced 18-year-olds. The winners should be announced at an awards and recognition ceremony, at which all of the participants' work is displayed. Prizes could consist of a gift certificate to a camera supply store, free rolls of film, or a book on photography. After the ceremony, it would be nice to make the entries into a traveling display for your community. Your library system may have branches, making it easy to showcase the entries at each library location for a couple of weeks. This works particularly well if the contest is citywide and not specific to your building. However, if your library is independent or just on the small side, contact other venues such as hospitals, schools, or civic centers to see if they are willing to display the work for a short period of time.

Time, Cost, and Supplies

If a volunteer expert is employed to lead the workshop, the time it takes to prepare for this program can be kept to a minimum. If, however, you choose to lead the workshop yourself, allow several hours to prepare the materials, browse and bookmark helpful Web sites, and plan an agenda for the program. Regardless of who leads the workshop, you will be responsible for arranging other matters. For example, if your budget is tight, allow time to solicit donations such as disposable cameras and film from a local vendor. Also, plan on giving at least one month's notice to the contest judges, and line up locations for the traveling display at least three months ahead of time. Use the few weeks between the workshop and the contest deadline to make final arrangements for the awards ceremony, like printing certificates, planning the refreshments, and purchasing or collecting the prizes.

Again, the most economical way to run this program is to solicit prizes, ensuring that costs would be kept to promotional materials and printing for handouts and award certificates. If, however, your budget is healthy enough to purchase some things, plan on spending about $10 for each workshop participant. This would cover the cost of one disposable camera or one roll of film for each teen. Alternatively, you could approach stores that offer film developing to ask if they are willing to donate coupons good for one free roll to be developed. Prizes for the visual poetry contest can be as small or extravagant as your budget allows since gift certificates can be purchased in any denomination and photography books vary widely in price. Don't forget to budget for snacks and refreshments for both the workshop and the awards ceremony.

Supplies for this program, other than workshop giveaways and contest prizes, simply consist of paper and printing for promotional materials and cardboard for the subject-framing exercise.

Promotion

A key piece to promoting this program should be a flyer with an at-tached registration form. To get as many entries as possible, it will be necessary to blanket your community with these flyers, which should communicate all of the information needed to enter the visual poetry contest. Clearly state the contest rules and include things like size regulations, whether the photographs should be matted or framed, as well as whether or not digitally altered or enhanced photographs will be accepted. List pertinent dates such as the day of the workshop, the deadline for contest entries, the day by which winners will be notified, and the day of the awards ceremony. The entry form, in addition to asking for names, ages, and contact information, should ask teens to indicate what kind of camera they used and supply the title of their photograph. Also, require the teens to certify their work by having them sign a statement such as "I certify that the work submitted is mine and is completely original. I grant XYZ Library the right to use my name and my work in their publications without recourse." Strategically place these flyers at camera shops, photo processing locations, bookstores, and, if possible, copy shops since they often have self-serve photo processing machines.

Within the library, promote the program with a display of "photographs" that your teen volunteers or advisory board members help you string onto fishing line using binder clips. These will actually be just black paper rectangles glued onto slightly larger white paper rectangles to resemble developing pictures dripping dry in a darkroom. For the middle "photograph," cut out one large, white question mark and glue it on top of the black rectangle. Under the string of "pictures," letter the phrase "Watch What Develops..." followed by the details of your visual poetry workshop and contest. Alternatively, if your contest has a specific theme, fill your display with realia and pictures that represent the theme. For instance, our visual poetry contest centered around an annual community festival, so I filled a display case with balloons, artificial cotton candy, popcorn, as well as pictures of Ferris wheels and parades. In any case, make sure plenty of registration forms are stacked near the display along with photography books and fiction titles featuring teens who take pictures. If you decide that attendance at the workshop is not mandatory for entering the contest, provide handouts illustrating basic photography techniques as well.

Collection Connection

Fiction

Born Confused—Tanuja Desai Hidier (Scholastic Press, 2002)

Carolina Autumn—Carol Lynch Williams (Delacorte Books for Young Readers, 2000)

Making the Run—Heather Henson (Harper Trophy, 2003)

One Shot—Susan Glick (Henry Holt and Company, 2003)

Picture Perfect—Elaine Marie Alphin (Carolhoda Books, 2003)

Pictures, 1918—Jeanette Ingold (Puffin, 2000)

Rain Is Not My Indian Name—Cynthia Leitich Smith (HarperCollins, 2001)

Razzle—Ellen Wittlinger (Simon and Schuster Children's Publishing, 2001)

Shooting Monarchs—John Halliday (Margaret K. McElderry, 2003)

The Spirit Catchers: An Encounter with Georgia O'Keeffe—Kathleen Kudlinski (Watson-Guptill Publications, 2004)

Spite Fences—Trudy Krisher (Laurel Leaf, 1996)

Spitting Image—Shutta Crum (Clarion Books, 2003)

Stop Pretending: What Happened When My Big Sister Went Crazy—Sonya Sones (Harper Trophy, 2001)

Nonfiction

America 24/7—Rick Smolan (DK Adult, 2003)

The Complete Idiot's Guide to Digital Photography—Steven Greenberg (Alpha, 2002)

Girl Culture—Lauren Greenfield (Chronicle Books, 2002)

In Focus: National Geographic's Greatest Portaits—National Geographic (National Geographic, 2004)

Odd Jobs: Portraits of Unusual Occupations—Nancy Rica Schiff (Ten Speed Press, 2002)

One Nation: America Remembers September 11, 2001—Life Magazine (Little Brown, 2001)

Photography: An Illustrated History—Martin W. Sandler (Oxford University Press, 2002)

Photography Guide for Kids—Neil L. Johnson (National Geographic Children's Books, 2001)

Restless Spirit: The Life and Work of Dorothea Lange—Elizabeth Partridge (Viking, 1998)

Teach Yourself Photography—Lee Frost (McGraw-Hill, 2004)

Teen Ink: Written in the Dirt: A Collection of Short Stories, Poetry, Art and Photography—Stephanie H. Meyer, editor (HCI Teens, 2004)

Through the Lens: National Geographic's Greatest Photographs—Leah Bendavid-Val, editor (National Geographic, 2003)

FROM PRINT TO SILVER SCREEN ($$)
(GRADES 9–12)

It seems that Hollywood has been producing a lot of movies adapted from books these days, and an increasing amount of these are titles for children or teenagers. Perhaps the success of J. K. Rowling's *Harry Potter* series accounts for this trend; it certainly seems to have inspired several adult authors, like Carl Hiaasen, James Patterson, and Joyce Carol Oates, to begin writing fiction for teens. It stands to reason, therefore, that the motion picture industry also sees great potential (i.e., money) in making movies based on novels intended for the younger set. While the industry's aim is probably not entirely altruistic, movies based on books get kids reading! Just as reading a great book makes one want to watch it come to life on-screen, seeing the film version of a really great story could entice teens to seek out the book on which it was based. In addition, "films provide excellent opportunities for . . . discussion—and not just at the end of the film" (Teasley & Wilder 1997).

In the air-conditioned comfort of your library, this program, lasting for the duration of the summer, will help teens explore topics based on books, movies, and the relationship between the two. You may choose to show movies as often as you like—from once a week, to once a month—because this section simply offers a basic outline that can be customized for each discussion.

How

Before you plan your series, you must first determine if your library has a public performance license to show movies. Due to copyright restrictions, it is against the law to publicly show entertainment movies—even if a fee is not charged—that have been produced solely for use in one's home. A Movie Copyright Compliant Public Performance Site License, however, makes it legal for you to show movies within the library, as long as the studio that produced the movie is covered under the license. Licenses can be purchased from either of these two companies: The

Motion Picture Licensing Corporation (www.mplc.com), or Movie Licensing USA (www.movlic.com).

If, however, your library cannot afford to purchase a public performance license, you could opt to rent titles from Swank Motion Pictures (www.swank.com). Swank distributes films to entities that wish to exhibit them publicly, such as cruise ships, charter buses, churches, schools—and libraries. Although they hope you'll buy a twelve-month umbrella license from them, this company does offer the latest titles in VHS, DVD, 16mm, and 35mm for one-time showings. The cost for these varies based on the number of cardholders your library has, so you will need to contact them to determine the cost-effectiveness of this program. Be aware that an umbrella license *could be* cheaper than renting three or four individual titles for the course of the summer, especially if you work in a small library. Swank also offers edited versions of R-rated titles.

A final option for showing movies publicly in your library is to restrict yourself to movies in the public domain. Public domain films are those whose copyright licenses expired and were never renewed, or those that were never registered for copyright protection to begin with. Lists of public domain films can be obtained on the Internet from the following sources:

Buy Out Footage
www.buyoutfootage.com

Desert Island Films
www.desertislandfilms.com

RetroFilm Media International
www.retrofilm.com

These sites do sell copies of the films, but you may find that you have some of them in your collection. Some of the more interesting offerings of these companies include classic cartoons, old Three Stooges shorts, famous speeches such as Martin Luther King, Jr.'s "I Have a Dream" speech of 1963, classic commercials, movie trailers, and intermission ads such as the famous "Let's All Go to the Lobby" ad from the 1950s. For the purposes of this program, films in the public domain will probably not work as well as current films because of their age, limited relevancy to teens, and lack of connection to books. However, this is the cheapest route to go, and worth mentioning in case you decide to alter this program to revolve around a theme like classic horror movies.

After working out the legalities of showing movies publicly, it's time to choose which book-based films you want to use. The books listed in the Collection Connection section of this program could serve as a jumping-off point for brainstorming. Online resources such as the Mid-Continent Public Library's comprehensive "Based on the Book" Web site (www.mcpl.lib.mo.us/readers/movies/) should also prove to be quite helpful.

When choosing the films, there are several factors to consider. First, it should probably have some teen appeal. For example, teens would likely find *Clueless* (Paramount, 1995) starring Alicia Silverstone a more fun and interesting adaptation of Jane Austen's *Emma* than Gwyneth Paltrow's film adaptation of the same name. Likewise, *10 Things I Hate About You* (Touchstone, 1999) starring Heath Ledger and Julia Stiles probably has more teen appeal than the BBC production of Shakespeare's *Taming of the Shrew*. Because these movies modernize classic stories, this opens the door for discussions about timeless themes as well as comparisons of how things have changed since the story was first told.

It may seem obvious to some, but another factor to consider is the films' ratings. After thinking of a great movie, check with the Motion Picture Association of America (www.mpaa.org) just to be sure its rating is what you thought it was, and to see what elements of the movie might give concerned parents pause.

Next, consider offering a variety of genres for your film series. It might be more interesting to choose one movie based on a fictional title, one based on a true story or biography, and one based on a graphic novel series like *X-Men* or *Hellboy*. On the other hand, you could base your book-based film series on a theme, like superheroes, classic fiction, medieval fiction, fairy tales, or science fiction. Doing it this way may allow you to tie "From Print to Silver Screen" into the theme you've chosen for your teen summer reading program as well.

After choosing the films, make sure multiple copies of the novels on which they're based are available in your library system. If you have an umbrella license and only need to obtain your library's copy of each film, don't forget to place reserves on them as well so you're sure to have them in hand in plenty of time! In fact, it might be a good idea to reserve two copies of each film in case one arrives damaged or scratched. Next, decide what your discussion questions will be. While it's possible to customize questions for each discussion, a set has been provided for you here that can easily be used for any book-based film that you choose.

- Did the film stay "true" to the novel? In other words, did it capture the book's essence?
- Most films alter some aspects of a novel's story—mostly to cut down its length. What did this film change or leave out? Why do you think these aspects were altered or deleted?
- Consider the film's depiction of the book's characters. Would you have cast the same actors? Why or why not?
- In your opinion, was the movie or the book better? Why?
- Did the film's soundtrack enhance certain scenes? Which ones?
- How did the movie set and/or special effects match up to what you pictured in your mind's eye as you read the book? Did the movie visually represent anything differently than how you interpreted it?
- Do you think this movie would entice others to read the book if they haven't already? Why or why not?

With any book discussion, film based or not, it's a good idea to incorporate some tricks to keep things lively and more interactive. For instance, instead of passing out the questions and assuming the role of "teacher" with your teen participants as the "students," tape large pieces of paper to the walls of the meeting area and write the questions on them. Invite the teens to write their opinions on the poster paper with colored markers. Another idea involves picking a buzzword associated with the story line and passing out confetti for the teens to throw—or M & Ms for them to eat—each time the word is said. For instance, throughout a discussion about the book and movie *Holes*, the word "fingernails" might be mentioned a couple of times. It's fun to watch the teens' reaction when their peers unwittingly say the buzzword. Finally, if the discussion drags, or if you run out of time, consider a "lightning round" during which teens must give a one-word response to certain questions. This will quicken the pace and raise the energy level of your discussions.

In addition, incorporating some value-added ideas into the discussion will make things more interesting. For instance, sharing interviews with the author and/or the director and stars of the film would lend an insider's perspective. If the story is a period piece, you could invite a local historian to share what life was like in your community during that time period. Chances are, your library has a collection of old newspapers and photographs—even realia—representing life in your community throughout its history; these items could be used to enhance the historian's presentation. Finally, if the story is based on actual events, try to dig up some pictures or news articles about the events to encourage teens to delve deeper into the topic.

Time, Cost, and Supplies

If you choose to use the questions I've provided for you above, you will not need to invest a lot of preparation time in this program. Although you will need to read the books ahead of time, it might be nice to watch their film adaptations right along with your teen participants, provided you are certain the movies' contents are appropriate. If you choose to use a value-added idea such as those suggested above, you should also devote a little time to lining up a guest speaker, or tracking down news articles, photographs, and the like. If your library already has a public performance license, this program will also be very cost-effective. Snacks during the movie could consist of microwave popcorn, soft drinks, and candy traditionally sold in movie theaters, such as Raisinets®, Goobers®, or Junior Mints®. The only other supply you will need is paper for promotional materials. Optionally, you could buy multiple paperback copies of the books to ensure every participant is able to read it before coming to the library to watch the movie. Or you could just buy a couple of copies of each book to use as door prizes. Consider contacting your local theater or video rental store to see if they would be willing to donate movie tickets, gift certificates, or movie posters to use as giveaways or trivia contest prizes.

Promotion

There are some important things to keep in mind when promoting movies to be shown in your library. Even with a public performance license, advertising the movies' titles to the general public is disallowed. While this may seem limiting, keep in mind that there is a fine line between the general public and your library's customers. Because public performance licenses are site specific, you should feel free to promote the program in-house using titles and even movie posters. You may also advertise the titles of the movies in your library's newsletter, assuming it is mailed only to your library's cardholders. You may not, however, use movie titles in any promotional materials aimed at the public at large. This includes press releases to newspapers or television stations, billboards, and flyers posted in local businesses. To promote the program using these avenues, you may only name the title of the film series itself instead of listing individual movies. Another loophole exists in vague wording. For instance, you could state, "We will be discussing the movie adaptations of J.R.R. Tolkien's body of work." If you have additional questions about promoting a film series at your library, contact the company from whom you purchased the license or rented the film, or contact the American Library Association's Office of Information Technology Policy at 1-800-941-8478.

Since school is out for the summer, promoting this program to area teachers is not a viable option. Therefore, while keeping the rules for properly promoting your film series in mind, consider targeting bookstores and small movie theaters that show indie films, as well as cultural or civic centers and local theater groups. An attention-grabbing display for in-house promotion could consist of a black or red curtain drawn back to reveal a large white paper square representing a movie screen. The phrase "Coming to a library near you..." along with large reproductions of the movie posters should be placed on the "screen." Try to obtain old 35mm movie reels to stack in the display; you could even wind some of the film around stacks of books about movies. Heap a bowl with popcorn and place this in the display if you're working with a secure space. Finally, be sure to place flyers that explain the who, what, when, and where of the program near the display.

Collection Connection

Fiction

About a Boy—Nick Hornby (Riverhead Books, 1998)

Around the World in 80 Days—Jules Verne (Puffin, 2004)

Because of Winn Dixie—Kate DiCamillo (Candlewick, 2000)

Charlie and the Chocolate Factory—Roald Dahl (Puffin, 1998) (*Willy Wonka and the Chocolate Factory*)

Confessions of a Teenage Drama Queen—Dyan Sheldon (Candlewick, 2002)

Drive Me Crazy—Todd Strasser (Simon Pulse, 1999)

Ella Enchanted—Gail Carson Levine (HarperCollins, 1997)

Emma—Jane Austen (Bantam Classics, 1984) (*Clueless*)

Freak the Mighty—Rodman Philbrick (Scholastic Paperbacks, 2001) (*The Mighty*)

Harry Potter series—J. K. Rowling (Arthur A. Levine)

Holes—Louis Sachar (Farrar, Straus and Giroux, 1998)

I Know What You Did Last Summer—Lois Duncan (Laurel Leaf, 1999)

I, Robot—Isaac Asimov (Spectra, 1991)

Jurassic Park—Michael Crichton (Knopf, 1990)

Little Women—Louisa May Alcott (Signet Classics, 2004)

Lord of the Rings trilogy—J.R.R. Tolkien (Del Rey)

The Notebook—Nicholas Sparks (Warner Books, 1999)

The Outsiders—S. E. Hinton (Puffin, 1997)

Pay It Forward—Catherine Ryan Hyde (Pocket, 2000)

The Princess Bride—William Goldman (Del Rey, 1987)

The Princess Diaries—Meg Cabot (HarperCollins, 2000)

A Series of Unfortunate Events—Lemony Snicket (HarperCollins)

Someone Like You / That Summer—Sarah Dessen (Speak, 2004) (*How to Deal*)

Speak—Laurie Halse Anderson (Farrar, Straus and Giroux, 1999)

Taming of the Shrew—William Shakespeare (Washington Square Press, 2004) (*10 Things I Hate About You*)

To Kill a Mockingbird—Harper Lee (Warner Books, 1988)

Tuck Everlasting—Natalie Babbitt (Farrar, Straus and Giroux, 1985)

A Walk to Remember—Nicholas Sparks (Warner Books, 2000)

Where the Heart Is—Billie Letts (Warner Books, 1995)

Nonfiction

Friday Night Lights: A Town, a Team, and a Dream—Buzz Bissinger (De Capo Press, 2003)

Perfect Storm: A True Story of Men against the Sea—Sebastian Junger (W.W. Norton, 1997)

Rocket Boys—Homer Hickman (Delta, 2000) (*October Sky*)

When Time Is Short and Money Is Tight...

Host a Welcome Summer party complete with hot dogs and an ice cream sundae social.

Have a science fiction movie marathon one day, showing films like *X-Men*, *E.T.*, and *Star Wars*.

Hold a passive contest challenging teens to create their own new su-perhero complete with costume and super power; award a gift cer-tificate to a comic bookstore.

REFERENCE

Teasley, A., and Wilder, A. (1997). *Reel conversations: Reading films with young adults*. Portsmouth, NH: Boyton/Cook Publishers.

Chapter 7

JULY

Summer is in full swing, and so, too, is your teen summer reading programming. Since "From Print to Silver Screen," detailed in Chapter 6, continues this month, the two very different programs contained in this chapter will entertain your teen patrons who aren't avid readers. "Summer under the Stars" offers science-minded teens a chance to learn how to read the night sky, while a unique take on the currently popular *Fear Factor* television program will ask teens questions like "Are you afraid of the dark?"

SUMMER UNDER THE STARS ($$$)
(GRADES 7–10)

One hot summer night between ninth and tenth grades, a group of my friends and I ventured out to our community's reservoir to watch a meteor shower. I grew up in the distinctly flat area of northwest Ohio, so our reservoir was the highest point in the area. The water's expanse was also fairly large, which afforded a view of the night sky unobstructed by trees or buildings. As we all lay on blankets and looked up at the sky, we laughed and told ghost stories, poked fun at one another, and talked without inhibitions about entering high school in the fall. While all of this had little to do with astronomy, there was something about the night sky above us that led us to question our futures and feel a great sense of freedom at the same time. Occasionally, however, our conversation would be injected with exclamations of "There's one!" or "Oh, did you see *that?*" as meteors flashed across the darkness. I recall wishing I knew more about what I was looking at, particularly the constellations, but, regardless, there was something magical about that night. Looking back, I can't help but think the moon and the stars had something to do with it.

Most of us are magnetized by the romantic notions associated with stars and other heavenly bodies. Teens are no different. If promoted carefully, this program will attract a broader audience than just those with an interest in astronomy or science. While designed with the ultimate goal of teaching teens a little about astronomy, "Summer under the Stars" will also afford them a chance to simply hang out with each other on a warm summer evening. Sometimes there's nothing better than that.

How

The first thing you should decide when considering this program is whether or not your library is located in an area suitable for stargazing. Downtown Manhattan, for example, may not be the best place for viewing stars because of the city's light pollution, but it can be minimized by the use of telescopes, in which case it will almost certainly be necessary to enlist the help of a local expert. If your library is situated in a suburban or rural area, there shouldn't be a problem viewing stars with the naked eye, but you may want to find a local expert anyway. He or she would have the knowledge to answer all of the teens' questions, and an enthusiasm for the subject you may not be able to impart yourself. A science teacher, a physics professor, or an amateur astronomer may be willing to assist you. Or consult the International Planetarium Society's (www.ips-planetarium.org) Planetarium Finder to locate the nearest local expert.

Before heading outdoors to stargaze, gather your teen participants together for no more than twenty to thirty minutes to explain a few things about astronomy. Since astronomy is such a wide topic, and the teens will no doubt be anxious to get outdoors, limit the informational content to constellations. First, describe how the night sky has been a navigational tool for centuries, and how stars have inspired poets and artists since the beginning of time. Provide a few examples of songs or paintings that portray this fact, like Van Gogh's *Starry Night*. Invite teens to shout out other works of art or poems about stars if they can think of any. Then, briefly explain what stars are, what they are made of, and how they are formed. Finally, show the teens a chart of the night sky and point out major constellations that should be visible that evening. Edmund Scientific (scientificsonline.com) manufactures several products that can enhance this aspect of your program. Although most telescopes are too expensive for library budgets, a home planetarium kit can be purchased from this company for about $30. This tool projects constellations onto the ceiling while a CD narrates the star show, giving teens an idea of what to look for when they're outside. To make this more interesting, provide the myths behind the constellation names, and explain how their seasonal appearances in the night sky were often associated with important activities like harvests. The Hawaiian Astronomical Society (www.hawastsoc.org/deepsky/) is an excellent resource for locating the myths associated with each constellation.

While some of your participants may want to just casually observe the stars while snacking and chatting, some may be eager to locate the constellations that have been described to them. A star hunt is one activity that will keep these teens engaged. There are a few basic tools necessary for your serious teen stargazers. Cardboard paper towel holders can be used as sighting tubes, which will help block out ambient light from nearby buildings or street lamps. Flashlights are necessary for reading star guides and making notes in the dark, but they should be covered with either red cellophane or a brown paper bag to lessen their beams' impact on night vision. Finally, star and planet locators (also available from Edmund Scientific for $2.50), can be adjusted to any day and time and will assist the teens with locating constellations relative to the horizon. After arming them with these three tools, challenge the teens to find certain constellations in the night sky.

Another activity you could utilize in addition to, or in lieu of, the star hunt is encouraging the teens to find and name their own constellations. Star frames are useful tools for this exercise, and can be made from wire coat hangers. Instruct the teens who want to discover their own constellations to stretch the coat hangers from a triangle shape into a diamond shape. Holding these up to the sky helps frame clusters of stars, making it easier to find patterns and shapes. They can then draw and name the constellations on black construction paper using a white crayon or colored pencil, then turn their discoveries in for a chance to win a prize. If you feel your participants may be more sophisticated stargazers, more activities like these can be found in Richard Moeschl's wonderful book about astronomy (Moeschl 1993).

After arriving at the outdoor location, teens can lie on blankets, sleeping bags, or lawn chairs to observe the stars and chat with their friends. If your teens aren't appreciative of night sounds like chirping crickets, consider playing background music to enhance the atmosphere. Mazzy Star's *So Tonight That I Might See* (Capitol 1993) and REM's *Automatic for the People* (Warner Brothers 1992) are perfect for stargazing. Provide bowls full of Little Debbie Star Crunch® Cosmic Snacks and Moon Pies®. As teens search for constellations old and new, collect their findings and award prizes later. If you choose to give a small prize to every participant, packages of glow-in-the-dark stars or celestially themed picture frames or stationary would be economical. Or if you choose to give one large prize to the teen with the most original constellation, a copy of *National Audubon Society Field Guide to the Night Sky*, or the more elaborate gift of naming one's own star through the International Star Registry (www.starregistry.com) are good ideas.

Time, Cost, and Supplies

If you decide not to use a local expert for this program, you will need to allot a couple of hours for collecting information about stars, constellations, and the mythology behind them. Because this portion of the program is meant to be brief, however, don't go overboard in compiling information—basic facts should suffice. For instance, it would be easy to spend a couple of hours discussing the mythological roots of the constellations, but for the purpose of this program, simply introduce the concept and provide one or two examples. Then, pass out bookmarks listing a few resources for the teens to look into in their leisure time. Plan on spending another hour ordering tools such as the home planetarium kit and the star and planet locators, in addition to buying snacks and prizes.

Depending on what prizes you decide to buy, this program can be fairly cost-effective. Many of the supplies listed here can be gathered from the library or your home. You could also ask the teens to bring their own flashlights and lawn chairs or blankets.

star and planet locators (optional)

home planetarium kit (optional)

flashlights

red cellophane or brown lunch bags

cardboard paper towel tubes

wire hangers

black construction paper

white crayons or colored pencils

sleeping bags, blankets, or lawn chairs

snacks

music

Promotion

Cover a space on an open wall with black paper. Then, with a white crayon or colored pencil, place "stars" on the paper, drawing lines between them to show the shapes of the constellations. A large heading reading "Summer under the Stars" should attract the attention of your teen patrons. The nonfiction books listed in the section below can highlight your collection while helping to promote the program. With the exception of *Light Years* by Tammar Stein, the fiction books listed below do not share an astronomy theme, but their titles all contain words pertaining to the idea. If you choose to display these books, or list them on a bookmark, you could link them to the program by stating, "These books are out of this world." Distribute flyers promoting the program to your local planetarium as well as stores for hobbyists and amateur astronomers. Be sure to list a rain date on the flyer in case the forecast calls for rain or clouds which would block out the stars.

Collection Connection

Fiction

Counting Stars—David Almond (Delacorte Books for Young Readers, 2002)

Daughters of the Moon series—Lynne Ewing (Volo)

The Earth, My Butt, and Other Big Round Things—Carolyn Mackler (Candlewick, 2003)

Heaven—Angela Johnson (Simon and Schuster Children's Press, 1998)

Heaven Eyes—David Almond (Delacorte, 2001)

The Heaven Shop—Deborah Ellis (Fitzhenry and Whiteside, 2004)

The Hitchhiker's Guide to the Galaxy—Douglas Adams (Del Rey, 2002)

Keeping the Moon—Sarah Dessen (Viking, 1999)

Light Years—Tammar Stein (Knopf Books for Young Readers, 2005)

Number the Stars—Lois Lowry (Houghton Mifflin, 1989)

Planet Janet—Dyan Sheldon (Candlewick, 2003)

Rock Star Superstar—Blake Nelson (Viking, 2004)

Saving the Planet and Stuff—Gail Gauthier (Grosset and Dunlap, 2003)

Second Star to the Right—Deborah Hautzig (Puffin, 1999)

Stargirl—Jerry Spinelli (Knopf Books for Young Readers, 2000)

The Star of Kazan—Eva Ibbotson (Dutton Juvenile, 2004)

A Step from Heaven—An Na (Front Street, 2001)

Walk Two Moons—Sharon Creech (HarperCollins, 1994)

When Kambia Elaine Flew In from Neptune—Lori Aurelia Williams (Simon Pulse, 2001)

Wolf Star—Tanith Lee (Puffin, 2002)

Nonfiction

Astronomy: A Visual Guide—Mark A. Garlick (Firefly Books, 2004)

The Book of Constellations: Discover the Secrets in the Stars—Robin Kerrod (Barrons Educational Series, 2002)

Brief History of Time—Stephen Hawking (Bantam, 1998)

Hubble: The Mirror on the Universe—Robin Kerrod (Firefly Books, 2003)

National Audubon Society Field Guide to the Night Sky—Mark R. Chartrand (Turtleback, 1991)

Smithsonian Handbooks: Stars and Planets—Ian Ridpath (DK Adult, 2002)

Star Maps for Beginners—I. M. Levitt (Fireside, 1992)

The Ultimate Guide to the Sky: How to Find the Constellations and Read the Night Sky Like a Pro—John Mosley (McGraw-Hill, 1997)

LIBRARY FEAR FACTOR ($-$$) (GRADES 6–9)

In some strange way, teens love to be scared, grossed out, and repulsed. Haunted houses, roller coasters, ghost stories, horror movies, and the television show *Fear Factor* are all popular with teenagers—probably because they each involve a level of risk. By engaging in any of these activities, teens can enjoy pushing boundaries and testing their limits, but not without sacrificing their safety in any real or threatening way. A roller coaster, for example, is relatively safe, but its high speeds, terrifying heights, and gravity-defying loops offer a temporary thrill. Likewise, haunted houses can test one's fear of confined, dark places, for instance, but we all know that the monsters within them aren't real.

Some of these fears, though, are very real and difficult to conquer even if they seem irrational. Someone who is deathly afraid of heights is probably never going to get on a roller coaster, and you won't find someone with claustrophobia in a haunted house. Although this program primarily aims to entertain and does include a few gross-out activities, similar to programs you may already have tried, other fears and common phobias will also be explored. A wrap-up discussion afterward will help teens identify what they're afraid of and may even help them identify other, more serious, risk-taking behaviors.

How

Shortly after the teens arrive, pass out a list of funny phobias. A fairly comprehensive one can be found at www.ojohaven.com/fun/phobias.html. Since the list is pretty long, you can pick and choose some of the more bizarre phobias, such as those given below:

Abluthophobia—fear of bathing

Arachibutyrophobia—fear of peanut butter sticking to the roof of the mouth

Aulophobia—fear of flutes

Dextrophobia—fear of objects on the right side of the body

Domatophobia—fear of being in a house

Papaphobia—fear of the Pope

Phobophobia—fear of phobias

Pogonophobia—fear of beards

Russophobia—fear of Russians

Technophobia—fear of technology or arts and crafts

This quick activity will serve as an icebreaker, because it's pretty likely that the teens won't actually have any of these phobias, but they'll certainly find them amusing. After introducing the concept of phobias, the real fun begins! You can use any number of common phobias to put the teens to the test. This chapter, however, details four: glossophobia (fear of speaking in public); entomophobia (fear of insects) or arachnophobia (fear of spiders); phasmophobia (fear of ghosts); and emetophobia (fear of vomiting). Challenges designed to test each of these fears will take place in four rounds. The teens must complete each challenge successfully before advancing to the next round.

Many teens, and adults for that matter, are nervous—if not terrified—of public speaking. It's a rare person who can perform in front of an audience without any jitters. For the first challenge, every teen will be asked to stand in front of the group and recite something. Many of the participants will shrug this off nonchalantly until you explain what it is they must recite in order to qualify for the next round. Prior to the program, find several poems, songs, or book excerpts that would be especially embarrassing to read aloud, and print them off on slips of paper. Place the readings in a hat or bucket and have the teens select one at random. Examples include the *Barney* theme song, a sappy love poem, or a PG excerpt from a romance novel. Anything that involves singing, or phrases like "They gazed lovingly into each other's eyes" is sure to make even the bravest teen balk a little. The participants who read an entire excerpt or poem, or sing an entire song, are allowed to advance to the second round.

Spiders, mice, snakes, and insects are all frequently feared things, so teens who wish to advance to the next round must touch or handle one of these creepy-crawly creatures. This challenge can be altered based on the availability of local experts or animal handlers. A local pet store owner may be willing to bring mice or snakes to your program. Or you could ask an entomologist or herpetologist from a zoo or university to bring a sampling of insects, spiders, or snakes to frighten your teens. There are even companies that specialize in school and library visits. Bugman Educational Enterprises (www.bugs.org) and Bugworks (home.comcast.net/~ajkozol/website5/) are two such companies. Other avenues to try include local cooperative extension offices or 4-H programs, extermination companies like Orkin® (www.orkin.com), and amateur entomology or herpetology clubs or societies.

The third round will dare the teens to confront their fear of ghosts. First, find a sampling of ghost stories. (Some good collections to try are included in the Collection Connection section below.) If possible, create a spooky atmosphere by holding the program after the library closes so that the entire building will be darkened. Move the group of teens into a dark, quiet corner of the library away from the program space. Then, using a flashlight, read a couple of short, creepy ghost stories to them with eerie music playing in the background. After you have finished reading the stories, send each teen back to the program space one by one, alone. Walking through the darkened library at night after hearing a ghost story is sure to get the participants' hearts pumping. To creep them out even more, you could stage a few "bumps in the night" while you are reading. Since this program works best after-hours, you will likely need an assistant or a volunteer to help out, if only for liability issues. Ask this person to stay behind to prepare the next challenge, with the intent that he or she will also be able to slam a door—or open a creaky one—at a planned moment during the ghost story session.

Those who have braved their fears and made their way back to the main program space can advance to the next round. The fourth round will challenge their fear of vomiting with a buffet of unappetizing foods. Many libraries have conducted programs involving eating contests such as this one, so many recipes with high "gross-out" factors are available on the Internet. Pickled pigs' feet, cow's tongue, blood pudding, sweetbreads, and brains are some of the more extreme foods you could purchase. Or if you don't really want the teens to vomit, consider baby food, or more common things disguised as something else—peeled grapes as eyeballs, for instance. Again, many examples can be found on the Internet. If you choose to enlist the help of an entomologist for the second challenge, you could ask him or her to bring chocolate-covered crickets or mealworms for this challenge. Alternatively, you could bake something featuring edible insects. To prepare the insects, rinse them in a fine-mesh colander and pat them dry, then cook in a 200 degree oven until they are crispy (Iowa State University Entomology Department 2000). Cut them into pieces before using them in these two recipes:

Banana Worm Bread

½ c. shortening

¾ c. sugar

2 bananas, mashed

2 c. flour

1 tsp. soda

1 tsp. salt

½ c. chopped nuts

2 eggs

¼ c. dry-roasted army worms (available from pet store supply companies or www.grubco.com, but you must roast them first, using the directions above)

Mix together all ingredients. Bake in greased loaf pan at 350° for about one hour.

Chocolate Chirpie Chip Cookies

2¼ c. flour

1 tsp. baking soda

1 tsp. salt

1 c. butter, softened

¾ c. sugar

¾ c. brown sugar

1 tsp. vanilla

2 eggs

12 oz. chocolate chips

1 c. chopped nuts

½ c. dry-roasted crickets (available from pet store supply companies or www.grubco.com, but you must roast them first, using the instructions above)

Preheat oven to 375°. In a small bowl, combine flour, baking soda, and salt, and set aside. In a large bowl, combine butter, sugar, brown sugar, and vanilla; beat until creamy. Beat in eggs. Gradually add flour mixture and insects, mix well. Stir in chocolate chips. Drop by rounded measuring teaspoonfuls onto ungreased cookie sheet. Bake for eight to ten minutes (Iowa State University Entomology Department 2000).

Remember to cover the tables with plastic tablecloths or butcher paper to aid with cleanup, and be sure to have wastebaskets nearby for those who are inclined to spit out food.

At the end of the program, the teens who finish all four challenges successfully can receive a prize. At this point, you may also choose to discuss these and other phobias in order to help teens understand what scares them and why. Ask them to share which challenge was hardest, or what other phobias they may have. Finally, you could engage them in a discussion about the teen tendency to engage in thrill-seeking behaviors—including some that are risky, like drug use.

Time, Cost, and Supplies

Besides tracking down someone to bring snakes, mice, spiders, or insects, this program should not take long at all to prepare. Allot time for finding readings for the first challenge, ghost stories for the third challenge, and foods or recipes for the final challenge. A few hours is all you should need to track down these things, in addition to the following supplies:

hat or bucket

flashlight

eerie music and a CD player

plastic tablecloths or butcher paper

wastebaskets (lined with plastic bags)

prizes (copy of a book of ghost stories, gift certificates for pizza, or packages of gummy worms)

Conceivably, the only things you may need to purchase are the food items and prizes, which will help keep the cost of this program low. Hopefully, the help you enlist for the second challenge will agree to donate their time, which will also save your budget.

Promotion

You can really have fun promoting this program with a display entitled "What Are You So Afraid Of?" Fill the display space with things like a jar full of mealworms or rubber snakes, insects, and spiders. The more disgusting the items are, the more attention the display will attract. You could even hold a passive contest asking teens to guess how many mealworms are in the jar. The prize could be a jar of the same size filled with something more savory, like gummy worms. The flyers should entice teens to face their fears by asking "Do You Have What It Takes?" It would be wise, however, to make the flyer serve double duty as a registration form since it is important to get parental permission and ask about food allergies for this program.

Collection Connection

Fiction

Complete Stories and Poems of Edgar Allan Poe—Edgar Allan Poe (Doubleday, 1966)

The Fear Place—Phyllis Reynolds Naylor (Aladdin, 1996)

Fearless series—Francine Pascal (Simon Pulse)

Great Ghost Stories—R. Chetwynd-Hayes, editor (Carroll and Graf Publishers, 2004)

The New Young Oxford Book of Ghost Stories—Dennis Pepper, editor (Oxford University Press, 1999)

Night Terrors: Stories of Shadow and Substance—Lois Duncan (Simon Pulse, 1997)

Nonfiction

Eat-a-Bug Cookbook—David George Gordon (Ten Speed Press, 1998)

Everything You Need to Know about Phobias—Erin M. Hovanec (Rosen Publishing Group, 2000)

Extreme Cuisine: The Weird and Wonderful Foods That People Eat—Anthony Bourdain (Periplus Editions, 2004)

Guts: The True Stories behind Hatchet and the Brian Books—Gary Paulsen (Delacorte Books for Young Readers, 2001)

Man Eating Bugs: The Art and Science of Eating Insects—Peter Menzel (Ten Speed Press, 1998)

Phobias: Revealed and Explained—Richard Waters (Barron's Educational Series, 2004)

Pop-Up Book of Nightmares—Gary Greenberg (St. Martin's Press, 2001)

Pop-Up Book of Phobias—Gary Greenberg (Harper Entertainment, 1999)

When Time Is Short and Money Is Tight . . .

Beat the heat of summer with a reading marathon—teens who read the longest (e.g., at least four out of the six hours) will be invited to attend a pizza party afterward.

Invite teens to a book swap where they will trade their own old books with each other.

Hold a *CSI*-like program for budding forensic scientists. Demonstrate handwriting analysis, fingerprint dusting, and other crime scene techniques.

REFERENCES

Iowa State University Entomology Department (2000). Iowa State University lectures: Insect horror film festival. Retrieved February 24, 2006, from the Iowa State University Lectures Web site: http://lectures.iastate.edu/lecture/849.

Iowa State University Entomology Department (2000). Iowa State University's tasty insect recipes. Retrieved February 11, 2005, from Insects: Iowa State University Entomology Web site: http://www.ent.iastate.edu/misc/insects asfood.html.

Moeschl, R. (1993). *Exploring the sky: Projects for beginning astronomers*. Rev. Ed. Chicago: Chicago Review Press.

Chapter 8

AUGUST

By now, summer reading activities are winding down, but you're probably gearing up for back-to-school programming and planning your fall agenda. That's why this chapter—just like the two before it—contains only two new program ideas to supplement the film series that will be wrapping up at the end of this month.

TEENS TEACHING TEENS ($) (GRADES 6–10)

In ninth grade, my communications teacher gave her freshman students an assignment that has stuck with me all these years. My classmates and I each had to give a three-minute instructional speech about something we were good at. Although I am certain the purpose of this project was to improve our speaking skills and ability to give clear instructions to a group, that's not why I remember the assignment so well. First of all, I recall having quite a bit of difficulty coming up with a skill or talent of mine. Wasn't I good at *anything*? As the deadline neared, the only things I could think of didn't seem remarkable to me in any way—being a good reader, for instance, just came naturally to me. The phrase "jack of all trades, master of none" kept repeating itself in my head, until I finally settled on a speech about how to wrap a present. Sitting there waiting for my turn, I watched as one by one my peers stood up to share their talents. I was amazed at everything my classmates could do: cooking, communicating in sign language, and French-braiding hair are some of the things I remember wishing I could do, too.

This episode from my own teenage years served as inspiration for "Teens Teaching Teens," a program that showcases the talents of local teens so they can learn from each other and take pride in the unique skills they possess. This program will get teens thinking about what things come naturally to them, which, in turn, could help them pinpoint a future college major or career choice. For instance, a teen who has grown up in a bilingual home may not think of his second language as a unique skill. This program, however, may help him realize his gift and discover ways to cultivate it into a career as a translator. Similarly, someone who has always been complimented on her neat handwriting probably takes her penmanship for granted. But if she attends the showcase and meets someone with a talent for calligraphy, she would realize how her skill could grow into something bigger. "Teens Teaching Teens" will offer participants the chance to learn a little about themselves and their peers, but it may even expand their horizons to include new hobbies or interests.

How

Since your local teens are the stars of this program, all you really need to do is secure a location and invite them to participate by signing up. First, canvas your teen advisory council to see what talents each of them have and encourage them to participate. You may also consider asking them, or other teens with whom you have established relationships, if there are any other students at their schools who could contribute something unique to the showcase. After personally inviting them, cultivate more talented teens by making a flyer and distributing it to teachers. The promotional display described below will also help unearth more participants. Each teen with a talent will be offered a table to display their craft or skill, so the number of teens who can participate is limited only by how large your space is.

Some teens may have trouble identifying what their skills are, like I did back when I was a freshman. Help them out with these suggestions:

- Knitting
- Cooking or baking

- Drawing manga
- Photography
- Playing a musical instrument
- Dancing
- Sewing or designing clothes
- Making crafts
- Being a good friend or listener
- Staying organized
- Martial arts
- Playing a sport
- Singing
- Writing poetry or short stories
- Telling jokes
- Identifying constellations
- Fixing computers
- Designing Web pages
- Gardening
- Wrapping presents
- Hair braiding
- Woodworking
- Speaking another language
- Babysitting
- Fixing cars
- Shopping for bargains
- Acting
- Party planning

While this list can help teens start thinking about what skills they may be able to share with their peers, it certainly is only a guideline. Encourage them to customize their display or demonstration to reflect their own personalities and unique gifts. Another thing to keep in mind is that specialized displays may be more interesting than ones showcasing general skills. For instance, if a teen is a great baker, advise her to demonstrate something specific, like how to bake homemade bread or frost a cake. This will serve as one example of what she can create in the kitchen and would be less overwhelming to those who are visiting that station in an effort to learn. If she desires, suggest that she create handouts listing her other culinary talents, or tried-and-true recipes.

The day of the program, arrange the stations around the program space in a way that encourages a steady flow of traffic. At each station, place a sign stating the teen's name along with his or her talent. In addition, supply each station with a stack of books pertaining to the skill that will be showcased there. As the visitors stream in, hand them each a flyer listing the different stations and where they are located. You may also want to have some background music playing to lend some festivity to the atmosphere. After the "open house" portion of the program, divide the group of demonstrators in half and ask one half to demonstrate their skills while the other half watches. Then have the groups switch. This would enable all of the participating teens to see what their peers' talents are.

Time, Cost, and Supplies

Again, since the teens are the presenters for this program, they will each be responsible for bringing the supplies necessary to showcase their talents. Therefore, costs for this program can be held to a bare minimum. Paper, printing or photocopying services, and refreshments are the only supplies needed. Similarly, this program shouldn't take a lot of time to plan. Most of the work will be completed a month or so ahead of time when recruitment of the talent and promotion of the program will take place.

Promotion

Books are at the center of this promotional display. Use the book list below to showcase the nonfiction books written by teens under the heading "Talented Teens." Then, utilize realia to highlight the specific talent about which each book was written. For example, stack a few rolls of duct tape next to Ellie Schiedermayer's book, or put some stacks of play money next to Jay Liebowitz's book. You may also want to make small placards for each book stating, for example, "Jay made money in the stock market at the age of 16!" or "Michelle Kwan won an Olympic medal in figure skating at the age of 18!" Near your display, make sure to stack registration forms for would-be participants, and prominently display the date, time, and location of the program, enticing others to see what local teens can do. You may also consider making the list of fiction titles written by teens into a bookmark to further highlight your library's collection.

Collection Connection

Fiction (written by teen authors)

Black Stallion—Walter Farley, 15 (Random House Books for Young Readers, 1991)

Crazy—Benjamin Lebert, 16 (Vintage, 2001)

The Distant Summer—Sarah Patterson, 16 (Pocket Books, 1983)

Doormat—Kelly McWilliams, 15 (Delacorte Books for Young Readers, 2004)

Eragon—Christopher Paolini, 18 (Knopf Books for Young Readers, 2003)

Frankenstein—Mary Shelley, 19 (Pocket Books, 2004)

In the Forests of the Night—Amelia Atwater Rhodes, 14 (Laurel Leaf, 2000)

The Outsiders—S. E. Hinton, 16 (Puffin, 1997)

The Prophecy of the Stones—Flavia Bujar, 13 (Miramax, 2004)

Seventeenth Summer—Maureen Daly, 17 (Simon Pulse, 1985)

Twelve—Nick McDonell, 18 (Grove Press, 2002)

Nonfiction (written by teen authors)

Anne Frank: The Diary of a Young Girl—Anne Frank, 14 (Bantam, 1993)

Dave's Quick and Easy Web Pages—Dave Lindsay, 15 (Erin Publications, 2001)

The Diary of Latoya Hunter—Latoya Hunter, 14 (Vintage, 1993)

Got Tape? Roll Out the Fun with Duct Tape!—Ellie Schiedermayer, 17 (KP Books, 2002)

Heart of a Champion—Michelle Kwan, 17 (Scholastic, 1997)

Katie.com: My Story—Katie Tarbox, 15 (Plume Books, 2001)

Organizing from the Inside Out for Teens—Julie Morgenstern and her daughter Jessi Morgenstern-Colon, 19 (Owl Books, 2002)

Please Don't Kill the Freshman—Zoe Trope, 17 (Harper Tempest, 2003)

Rick and Lanie's Excellent Kitchen Adventures: Chef-Dad, Teenage Daughter, Recipes and Stories—Rick Bayless and his daughter Lanie, 13 (Stewart, Tabori and Chang, 2004)

A Rose Grew from Concrete—Tupac Shakur, 19 (MTV, 1999)

Teen Angst? Naaah ... A Quasi-Autobiography—Ned Vizzini, 19 (Laurel Leaf, 2002)

Teens Cook: How to Make What You Want to Eat—Megan and Jill Carle, 19 and 16 (Ten Speed Press, 2004)

Things I Have to Tell You: Poems and Writing by Teenage Girls—Edited by Betsy Franco (Candlewick, 2001)

Wall Street Wizard—Jay Liebowitz, 18 (Simon and Schuster Children's Publishing, 2000)

Within Reach: My Everest Story—Mark Pfetzer, 17 (Puffin, 2000)

You Hear Me? Poems and Writing by Teenage Boys—Edited by Betsy Franco (Candlewick, 2001)

Zlata's Diary: A Child's Life in Sarajevo—Zlata Filipovic, 13 (Penguin, 1995)

AROUND THE WORLD IN EIGHTY MINUTES ($$$-$$$$) (GRADES 6–9)

In general, teens are egocentric. It's not their fault—it's just a normal part of growing up and finding one's place in the world. This multicultural program familiarizes teens with cultures from around the globe, allowing them to step out of their current reality, if only for a little while. Hopefully, their eyes will be opened to the adventures of traveling, which could be of particular interest to suburban or rural-dwelling teens who are aching to get a glimpse of the outside world. In any setting, though, teens will gain an understanding of the different values, beliefs, and customs found in other countries, which will help to dispel myths and foster tolerance.

"Around the World in Eighty Minutes" is a virtual tour of eight different countries, designed to give teens a snapshot of life in other nations. Each of the eight countries is represented by a station featuring a map of the country, its national flag, regional cuisine, a small craft representing one aspect of the nation's culture, and other visual aids like books, pictures, or Web sites.

Teens are issued "passports" as they enter the program space; as they travel to each station, they receive stamps in their passports verifying their visit to that country and helping them become eligible for a prize drawing. Time at the various countries will be spent sampling different foods, practicing saying "hello," "goodbye," and "thank you" in new languages, looking at pictures or Web sites, making quick crafts, and even listening to the countries' national anthems.

How

This program takes a lot of preplanning, so it would be wise to start early, perhaps even three months ahead of time. The very first thing you must do is select the countries you want to highlight. I have chosen Egypt, France, India, Iran, Japan, Thailand, Spain, and Poland. You may, of course, choose different countries depending on the demographics of your community. For example, if many of your teens are Hispanic-American it would be a good idea to exclude countries such as Mexico, Puerto Rico or even Spain since your participants would already be familiar with the cultures of countries like these. On the other hand, if your community's makeup is shifting from a largely homogeneous population to a more diverse one, and there has been an increase in the Asian American contingent, for instance, it may be beneficial to highlight Korea, Laos, or Vietnam to increase teens' cultural awareness of their new classmates and neighbors. Current events should also steer your choices. September 11, for example, has highlighted a need for greater understanding of Arabic nations. In any case, attempt to select countries that represent each continent or major geographical region.

After the countries have been chosen, it's time to start researching their customs, eating habits, holidays, and religious practices. General encyclopedias, *Culture Grams*, and the *CIA World Factbook* (www.ciafactbook.com) are all great places to start gathering information to display at each station. If you have the technology available, search the Web for virtual tours of the countries you choose and invite the teen travelers to view them. You could also have each country's national anthem or traditional music playing, provided you have the technological capability. Photography books and phrase books should be displayed at each station, along with craft books and realia. For instance, materials at the Japanese station might include a photography book about Mount Fuji, a craft book on the art of origami, a set of chopsticks that the teens could try using, a kimono they could try on, some sushi spring rolls for them to taste, and supplies for them to make an ikebana picture.

Finally, photocopy the cover of a passport onto half a sheet of blue card stock and then fold it in half. Color copy the national flags of the countries you choose onto labels so the teens can get a "stamp" for each country they visit. As the participants enter the program space, you can hand them their passport and a plastic compass, and invite them to get started traveling the world.

The day of the program, stock each station with the craft supplies and instructions, food, and books you've chosen. If possible, put each country's name on enlarged maps showing the geography of the area behind each station to help guide teens "around the world." This might seem like a lot, but if you choose to use any or all of the eight countries I listed, you can use the crafts and recipes suggested in the sections that follow.

Egypt

A cartouche is like a nametag written in hieroglyphs that ancient Egyptian kings and queens used to wear around their necks. Cartouches were originally made of precious metals, so it's unlikely that teens would wear a paper cartouche necklace; therefore, have them make key chains instead. Find and photocopy a hieroglyph alphabet on golden or yellow paper. Instruct the teens to cut out the characters that spell their names, and then glue them in a vertical row on a piece of card stock. Next, cut the cartouche into an oval or rectangular shape, laminate it, and use a hole punch to make a hole on one end to attach a key ring.

Pita bread is an easy snack for this station and can be purchased at any grocery store. If you prefer to make your own, however, the recipe is as follows:

Pita Bread

2 tsp. dry yeast

1 c. warm water

3 c. flour

1 tsp. salt

Preheat oven to 350°. Dissolve the yeast in one cup warm water. Sift together the flour and salt, then mix with yeast and water. Work the mixture into dough and knead for several minutes. Cover the dough with a damp cloth and let rise in a warm place for three hours. Divide the dough into six equal portions and roll into balls. With either your hand or a rolling pin, pat and press each ball of dough into a five-inch circle about half-inch thick. Place on an ungreased baking sheet and bake for ten minutes, or until the pita are light golden brown.

France

Since France is so famous for its art museums, this quick craft highlights works from the Louvre and the Musee d'Orsay. Digitally cut and paste images of works found in these museums, such as the *Mona Lisa*, *Winged Victory*, and Cezanne's *Oranges and Apples* in one horizontal row on a standard-sized sheet of paper in the landscape position. Print these "cuffs" out in color. Instruct the teens to simply cut out the cuff and place in a Design-a-Mug® for a custom-made coffee mug. An alternative to this idea is to cut out the artwork and decoupage a wooden frame or box with the images.

Most teens probably haven't tried Brie cheese before; purchase some of this along with some crackers for a no-fuss snack at this station.

India

Mehndi is the ancient art of body adornment using henna extracts. Since it would be too time consuming to allow the teens to receive these temporary tattoos, this activity simply gives them an opportunity to practice the basic elements found in intricate mehndi designs. Photocopy traced outlines of your hand on legal-sized paper and give examples of some of the techniques used to create the designs. Then, instruct the teens to practice making mehndi designs on the paper using fine-tip black ink pens. Examples of patterns and mehndi design elements can be found by searching the Web, or in any of these books:

- *The Magic of Mehndi Pack*—Zaynab Mirza
- *Mehndi: The Art of Henna Body Painting*—Carine Fabius
- *Mehndi: The Timeless Art of Henna Painting*—Loretta Roome

Curry powder is one of the traditional spices used most often in India. For an example of ethnic cuisine at this station, make some instant rice and add a healthy quantity of curry powder along with salt to taste.

Iran

Arabic calligraphy is a beautiful form of writing that was initially used to adorn the Koran, but came to beautify functional objects as well as architecture, particularly mosques and palaces. For this craft, find an inspirational saying written in Arabic calligraphy and reproduce it in gray scale on a half-sheet of card stock. Instruct the teens to cut this into an oval and encourage them to color in the calligraphy and decorate the edges with designs. Then, punch holes in the card stock, laminate it, and attach colored yarn to make a door hanger or locker decoration. Make sure to tell the teens what the saying means in English!

Yogurt is a main part of the Iranian diet. Iranians also eat cucumbers and tomatoes with almost every meal. Therefore, a cucumber mint yogurt dip is the perfect snack for this station, and is likely to be something the participants haven't tried before.

Cucumber Mint Yogurt Dip

1 large cucumber, diced

salt to taste

2–3 cloves garlic, crushed

2 c. plain yogurt

white pepper to taste

1 T. dried crushed mint or 3 T. fresh mint, chopped

Dice cucumber, then place in colander with a little salt to drain excess water. Mix the yogurt and the garlic, then season to taste with salt and pepper. Mix in cucumber and mint. Serve with pita bread (which you've already made or purchased for the Egyptian station).

Japan

Ikebana is the ancient Japanese art of flower arranging that emphasizes the importance of living in harmony with nature. This craft will allow teens to mimic the beautiful twisting of branches and the careful placement of flowers with paint instead of real plants. Gather black, turquoise, orange, and red tempera paint, small art sponges, straws, and legal-sized paper. Make sure to cover this station with newspaper or butcher paper as this craft can get messy. In small paper cups, mix the black tempera paint with enough water so that it becomes very runny, and place spoons in these cups. Next, put some undiluted, colored tempera paint on small paper plates. Instruct the teens to use the spoons to dribble some black paint on a sheet of paper, and then use a straw to blow the paint across the paper to make interesting, treelike patterns. Next, have them dip the sponges in a paint color and dab it on the "branches" to represent flowers. Allow these pictures to dry until the end of the program.

What better snack is there for this station than sushi? If you think your teens would be willing to try it, buy some sushi with raw fish, but California rolls or vegetable spring rolls are a great alternative for a less-adventurous crowd. For a cheaper alternative, try rice crackers.

Thailand

Fire is one of the most common religious symbols because it represents primal energy and has purification abilities. As such, fire is used in many Buddhist rituals throughout Thailand, where Buddhism is the predominant faith. Luckily, candles are always popular with teenagers. For this craft, collect clean baby food jars, colored tissue paper, glue, small brushes, and tea lights. Teens simply paint a thin layer of glue on a glass jar and place torn tissue paper on top. When the jar is completely covered, they should brush another thin layer of glue over the entire jar to seal loose edges. Place a tea light inside for a colorful addition to any bedroom and as a tribute to the Buddhist faith.

Two easy options for a snack at this station are satay and pad thai. Both are sauces that can be found in the international food aisle of a grocery store or at an ethnic food store. Simply mix the sauce of your choice with cooked rice noodles, or you could just order takeout from a local Thai restaurant. Just be sure to have forks, plates, and napkins available at this station.

Spain

Many mosaics can be found throughout Spain because the Islamic art was brought to the Iberian peninsula by the Moors in the eighth century. Unlike many mosaics that have irregular gaps between jagged pieces of tile, the mosaics of Spain are mostly geometric in nature and fit together perfectly, or tessellate, to adorn a whole surface. To illustrate the art of tessellation, photocopy grids on transparency film and gather colorful permanent markers. Encourage your participants to create their own "mosaics" (inspired by examples you provide) by coloring in the squares of the grid in a pattern or design of their own. Have them cut the transparency into a shape, punch a hole in the top and attach a suction cup hook to make a sun catcher for their bedroom window.

An easy snack for this station could be some Spanish olives that you can purchase at a deli. However, if you want to give your teen travelers a sweet treat this time, you could offer flan, traditional Spanish custard.

Traditional Flan

¾ c. sugar

4 eggs

1¾ c. water

14 oz. of sweetened condensed milk

½ tsp. vanilla

⅛ tsp. salt

Preheat oven to 350°. Cook the sugar in a skillet over medium heat, stirring constantly until it is caramel colored. Pour the sugar into an ungreased nine-inch baking pan, making sure it covers the bottom completely. In a bowl, beat the eggs, then stir in the remaining ingredients. Pour over caramelized sugar. Set the pan in a broiler pan and fill the broiler with one inch of hot water. Bake fifty-five to sixty minutes in oven or until a knife inserted near center comes out clean. Chill. Loosen side of flan with knife and invert onto a serving plate.

Poland

In Poland, Christmas is called Gwiazdka, which means "star." With much anticipation, Polish children look for the appearance of the first star in the eastern sky on Christmas Eve. For this craft, teens will make Polish *gwiazdy* (little stars), which are a variation of what we call paper snowflakes, but are eight-sided and much more intricate. Starting with a nine-inch square of paper, instruct the teens to fold the paper in half to make a rectangle, and again to make another square. Next, fold the square corner to corner to make a triangle. Have the teens draw a curved line on the triangle as a guide to cut off the top, then draw symmetrical designs on both edges of the triangle. After the designs are cut out and the stars unfolded, they can be decorated with glitter.

Pierogies, which are dumplings traditionally stuffed with cheese, potatoes, and onions, are a staple of the Polish diet. Pierogies can easily be purchased in the frozen food section of any grocery store. Simply boil them in water ahead of time, then reheat and serve them with a side of sour cream for the program.

Promotion

For an eye-catching display, use colorful maps or a hodgepodge of national flags as a backdrop. Attach a plastic airplane to a globe and surround this with stacks of books that have a multicultural theme. If you don't have a globe, you could reproduce flags on a color printer and attach them to toothpicks that you can insert between the pages of books. For instance, a copy of *Born Confused* could have India's national flag sticking out of it. You may also consider filling a display case, if you have one, with realia from different countries. Entice teens with phrases like "Take a virtual tour" or "Sample ethnic cuisine." You will likely find an audience for this program with in-house promotion and displays, but you could also send flyers to foreign language or ESL teachers, community cultural centers, or ethnic food stores.

Time, Cost, and Supplies

It's likely pretty clear by now that this program will cost a bit and take some time to plan. If you choose to use the countries detailed here, allow about thirty minutes to one hour each to prepare the materials and instructions for the crafts and activities. Obviously, if you decide to research and plan activities for some other countries, it will take longer, but don't let this dissuade you from customizing the program. The virtual tour you plan should reflect your community as well as current events of the time. The day of the program, allow at least two hours to set up the stations in your program space.

A shopping list for craft supplies follows. However, your library may already have several items on the list.

key chain rings

laminating sheets

hole punch

yellow or gold card stock

picture-insert mugs

black fine-tip markers (like Sharpies®)

colored pencils

yarn

black, orange, and red tempera paint

straws

small craft sponges

butcher paper or newspaper

white unlined paper

small candles

baby food jars

colored tissue paper

glue

permanent markers in a variety of colors

transparency sheets

suction cup hooks

scissors

Plan to shop for the recipe ingredients only a day or two in advance of the program to prevent spoiling. A shopping list for these items follows:

yeast

flour

Brie cheese

crackers

rice

curry powder

plain yogurt

cucumber

mint

onion

garlic

white pepper

sushi or spring rolls

pad thai sauce or satay sauce

rice noodles

Spanish olives

sugar

eggs

condensed milk

vanilla extract

frozen pierogies

sour cream

Some of the food will not require assembling or cooking, such as the olives, brie, and sushi. You can follow the recipes provided for things like the curry rice and cucumber mint dip, but you may decide to save time by substituting with pre-made items from ethnic food stores or restaurants. Regardless, don't worry about having large quantities of each food available; the idea is for the teens to *sample* each thing—and chances are, not everyone will like everything enough to want seconds. Bon Voyage!

Collection Connection

Fiction

America Street: A Multicultural Anthology of Stories—Anne Mazer, editor (Persea Books, 1993)

American Eyes: New Asian-American Short Stories for Young Adults— Lori Carlson (Fawcett, 1995)

Angel on the Square—Gloria Whelan (Russia) (HarperCollins, 2001)

Before We Were Free—Julia Alvarez (Dominican Republic) (Knopf Books for Young Readers, 2002)

Behind the Mountains—Edwidge Danticat (Haiti) (Scholastic Paperbacks, 2002)

Born Confused—Tanuja Desai Hidier (India) (Scholastic Press, 2002)

Breadwinner—Deborah Ellis (Afghanistan) (Groundwood Books, 2001)

Broken Bridge—Lynne Reid Banks (Israel) (Harper Trophy, 1996)

Chandra's Secrets—Allan Straton (Sub-Saharan Africa) (Annick Press, 2004)

Crazy Loco: Stories—David Rice (Mexico) (Puffin, 2003)

Cuba 15—Nancy Osa (Cuba) (Delacorte Books for Young Readers, 2003)

The Divine Wind—Gary Disher (Japan) (Arthur A. Levine Books, 2002)

Dragonwings—Lawrence Yep (China) (HarperCollins, 1975)

The Education of Little Tree—Forrest Carter (Native American) (University of New Mexico Press, 2001)

The Fattening Hut—Pat Lowery Collins (Oceania) (Houghton Mifflin, 2003)

Finding Miracles—Julia Alvarez (Central America) (Knopf Books for Young Readers, 2004)

Fresh Girl—Jaira Placide (Haiti) (Wendy Lamb Books, 2002)

Future Perfect—Kat Corbett (Russia) (Writers Club Press, 2000)

Girls for Breakfast—David Yoo (China) (Delacorte Books for Young Readers, 2005)

Go and Come Back—Joan Abelove (Peru) (Puffin, 2000)

Habibi—Naomi Shihab Nye (Israel) (Simon Pulse, 1999)

Homeless Bird—Gloria Whelan (India) (HarperCollins, 2000)

The House on Mango Street—Sandra Cisneros (Hispanic American culture) (Knopf, 1994)

How the Garcia Girls Lost Their Accents—Julia Alvarez (Dominican Republic) (Algonquin Books, 1991)

Iqbal—Francesca D'Adamo (Pakistan) (Atheneum, 2003)

The Joy Luck Club—Amy Tan (China) (Putnam, 1989)

Kira-Kira—Cynthia Kadohata (Japan) (Atheneum, 2004)

Light Years—Tammar Stein (Israel) (Knopf Books for Young Readers, 2005)

Looking for Alibrandi—Melina Marchetta (Australia) (Knopf Books for Young Readers, 2006)

Many Stones—Carolyn Coman (South Africa) (Front Street, 2000)

Milkweed—Jerry Spinelli (Nazi-occupied Poland) (Knopf Books for Young Readers, 2003)

The Other Side of Truth—Beverley Naidoo (South Africa) (HarperCollins, 2001)

Out of Bounds—Beverley Naidoo (South Africa) (HarperCollins, 2003)

Parvana's Journey—Deborah Ellis (Afghanistan) (Groundwood Books, 2002)

Persepolis—Marjane Satrapi (Iran) (Pantheon, 2003)

Persepolis 2—Marjane Satrapi (Iran) (Pantheon, 2004)

Quincenera Means Sweet 15—Veronica Chambers (Mexico) (Hyperion, 2001)

Rain Is Not My Indian Name—Cynthia Leitich Smith (Native American) (HarperCollins, 2001)

Red Palms—Cara Haycak (Oceania) (Wendy Lamb Books, 2004)

Samir and Yonatan—Daniella Carmi (Palestine) (Arthur A. Levine Books, 2000)

Shabanu: Daughter of the Wind—Suzanne Fisher Staples (Pakistan) (Laurel Leaf, 2003)

Shiva's Fire—Suzanne Fisher Staples (India) (Farrar, Straus and Giroux, 2000)

Shizuko's Daughter—Kyoko Mori (Japan) (Fawcett, 1994)

A Single Shard—Linda Sue Park (Korea) (Clarion Books, 2001)

A Step from Heaven—An Na (Korea) (Front Street, 2001)

Ties that Bind, Ties That Break—Lensey Namioka (China) (Laurel Leaf, 2000)

Under the Feet of Jesus—Helena Maria Viramontes (Mexico) (Plume, 1996)

The Whale Rider—Witi Ihimaera (New Zealand) (Harcourt Children's Books, 2003)

When My Name Was Keoko—Linda Sue Park (Korea) (Clarion Books, 2002)

Who Will Tell My Brother?—Marlene Carvell (Native American) (Hyperion, 2002)

Zazoo—Richard Mosher (Vietnam/France) (Clarion Books, 2001)

Nonfiction

19 Varieties of Gazelle: Poems of the Middle East—Naomi Shihab Nye (Greenwillow, 2002)

Anne Frank: The Diary of a Young Girl—Anne Frank (Bantam, 1993)

Coming of Age in America: A Multi-Cultural Anthology—Mary Frosch, editor (New Press, 1995)

Cool Salsa: Bilingual Poems on Growing Up Hispanic in the United States—Lori Carlson (Henry Holt and Company, 1994)

Facing the Lion: Growing Up Maasai on the African Savanna—Herman Viola (National Geographic Children's Books, 2003)

When Time Is Short and Money Is Tight...

Have a passive contest commemorating August as National Inventor's Month; invite the teens to match an invention with its inventor for a prize drawing at the end of the month.

Hold a chess tournament.

Have a teen cooking contest where participants bring in their best concoction to be judged.

Chapter 9

SEPTEMBER

Forget January; for many of us September is the time of year that feels more like the start of a new year. As the heat of summer wanes, cooler air and the start of a new academic year somehow manages—along with freshly sharpened pencils and crisp, blank sheets of notebook paper—to jump-start many teens heading back to school. Teen librarians, too, are often moving full speed ahead, planning for classroom visits and after-school programming. This chapter contains two programs that will help teens prepare for a successful future. "Find Your Future" is a career-planning program with a unique spin, and the "Battle of the Sexes" is a scavenger hunt designed to orientate students to the library resources that will help them succeed in school and in life. Finally, "LOL @ Your Library" provides some comic relief at the end of the month.

FIND YOUR FUTURE ($) (GRADES 9–12)

Today's choices for new high school graduates are endless. Although a large percentage of teens go on to college, statistics show that the percentage of them who earn a degree is surprisingly low. According to a 2005 press release, "In October 2004, 66.7 percent of high school graduates from the class of 2004 were enrolled in colleges or universities" (U.S. Department of Labor 2005). However, the Center for the Study of College Student Retention (2005) states that "[i]n spite of all of the programs and services to help retain students…only 50 percent of those who enter higher education actually earn a degree." It's clear from these figures that some high school graduates are choosing college because they don't know what other options are available, or because they think four years of higher education will give them time to think about which career to choose. Some, unfortunately, may not even be academically prepared enough to pursue a four-year degree. To put it in real numbers, "about 2,800,000 students will graduate from high school this year [2005], 1,850,000 will attend college and only 925,000 of these students will earn a bachelor degree" (Center for the Study of College Student Retention 2005). These numbers belie the commonly held belief that pursuing higher education is the only way to make a decent living since, obviously, a large percentage of high school graduates enter the workforce right away, or after dropping out of college.

Giving teens enough time to think about their goals and lessening the pressure on them to attend college may help them make healthier decisions. In fact, *Time* magazine reports that a new demographic has emerged called "twixters," defined as those young adults between the ages of 18 and 25 who have put off the responsibilities of adulthood for several years, changing jobs and relationships frequently. At first glance, it may seem like too many young adults are indulging their Peter Pan complexes by delaying marriage and financial independence. But the article states that there may be some benefit to stalling. "It's not that [twixters] don't take adulthood seriously; they take it so seriously, they're spending years carefully choosing the right path into it … [but if] twixters are ever going to grow up, they need the means to do it" (Grossman et al. 2005).

Although college is the right choice for some, technical jobs, enlisting in the military, and even entrepreneurial ventures are three other valid career paths of which teens should be made aware through more systematic and deliberate career counseling. In this program, fun character trait quizzes and aptitude tests will help teens match their unique personalities and skill sets with today's hottest careers. Information on technical training programs and college majors will also be made available in an effort to present the whole picture to teens faced with the daunting question, "What do you want to do with your life?"

How

First off, it is important to mention that this program will probably run for two to three hours for about fifteen teens, and longer for a larger audience. Therefore, it may be wise to schedule "Find Your Future" for a Saturday morning or afternoon to avoid running into the dinner hour or competing with other evening activities during the school week. This program's runtime is a bit lengthy because there are several steps to the career selection process that should not be rushed. Also, although the main focus of this program is educational, there are some activities built in just for fun. It's possible to skip them, making the program run faster, but these activities make the program less boring and more interactive than an average career fair.

As the teens arrive and get settled, set the tone for the program with a fun icebreaker. Ask for three volunteers, then call the first teen over to you to pin a career title to the back of the shirt so it is not visible to him or her. The career titles should be preselected and can be anything from airline pilot, to pastry chef, to accountant. Turn the volunteer around so the rest of the audience can see the word, then instruct the volunteer to ask the audience a series of twenty yes-or-no questions in an effort to figure out the career title. If they have trouble getting started, give a few prompting starter questions such as "Do I need a college degree for this job?" or "Is this job dangerous?" If the volunteers guess what their "jobs" are within the twenty-question limit, toss them each a PayDay® or $100 Grand® candy bar.

Now that the audience is warmed up and more relaxed, welcome them and state the goals of the program. Next, pass out a (Career Inventory Worksheet) for the teens to use for the duration of the program. Before asking them to begin researching possible career options, instruct the teens to write down their top three job choices in the first column of the

Find Your Future
Career Inventory Worksheet

Top 3 Career Choices	Top 2 Choices from Each Code Group	Observations and Discoveries	#1 Choice to Pursue

Name_____Grade_____

E-mail Address_____

worksheet. If a teen has absolutely no idea what he wants to do, it's fine to leave this column blank.

At this point, ask the teens to assess their personalities using the Holland Code. According to Dr. John Holland, six different groups can be used to classify people and work environments. While the teens may identify with certain aspects of several of the groups, they are likely to feel stronger affiliations to only two or three of the groups. The letters that stand for these groups make up one's Holland Code (University of Missouri Career Center 2002). The University of Missouri Career Center has devised a Career Interest Game based on Holland's findings that the teens should use to find their Holland Code. Before setting them loose, however, let the teens know that career assessment tests are not perfectly accurate, and that the results of any such test do not definitively indicate which career path one should follow. Tests such as the Holland test are meant to act as a guide, not a crystal ball. These and the others listed below are all available electronically, so if at all possible, have the teens take them this way rather than on paper. Since it's very likely that there will not be enough computer stations for every participant, ask the teens to take turns, and offer a passive activity like a word search (Appendix F) as well as several reference sources to entertain those waiting for their turn. After the teens are finished determining their Holland Code, instruct them to pick their top two career choices from each code group and write them in the second column of their Career Inventory worksheet. For example, if a teen's Holland Code is ARS, she should select two career possibilities from the Artistic grouping, two from the Realistic grouping, and two from the Social grouping.

Next, allow the teens to explore these fun (i.e., less scientific) personality quizzes to see if the results lead to any insights about the careers they've considered so far:

The Animal in You Personality Test
http://www.animalinyou.com/survey.asp

Cheese Test . . . What Type of Cheese Are You?
http://cupped-expressions.net/cheese/quiz/

The Oreo Personality Test
http://www.aboutteens.org/jokes/oreo.htm

This activity is thrown in for fun, capitalizing on teens' affinity for these types of quizzes often found in magazines geared toward their age-group. If, however, you would rather keep this program on the serious side,

consider these personality tests instead of, or in addition to, the ones
above:

CareerLink Inventory
www.mpc.edu/cl/cl.htm

Enneagram Test
similarminds.com/cgi-bin/similarminds.pl

Temperament Sorter
www.advisorteam.com/temperament_sorter/register.asp?partid=1

In any case, the participants should enjoy delving into their personalities,
and the results will hopefully help them think about how their natural
inclinations fit with the careers they are considering. For instance, if a teen
has narrowed her career picks down to actress, comedian, or professional
clown, and the results from a personality quiz reveal that she is a reserved, shy person who enjoys quiet activities, perhaps she should give
some more thought to her future.

At this point in the program, have the teens use the third column of the
Career Inventory worksheet to write down any interesting observations,
contradictions, or ideas that have surfaced after taking the career tests and
personality tests, and looking through the reference sources available.
Then, encourage them to pick one career they think they'd like to learn
more about, and have them write that in the fourth column of the
worksheet. Have them note whether or not this choice differs drastically
from the three career choices they wrote down at the very beginning of
the program. Hopefully, by now the teens have a good idea of which
career path best suits them, but if they still need guidance, it may be a
good idea to have guidance counselors from the local school system or
career counselors from a local university on hand to answer students'
questions. A simple question and answer period may be sufficient, or, if
time permits, individual consultations might be in order.

At the very end of the program, collect the worksheets from the participants so you can send each of them a personalized e-mail with a profile
of their top career choice obtained from the online version of the *Occupational Outlook Handbook* (www.bls.gov/oco/). Along with this profile,
provide them with resources listed in a "site-seeing" tour to help them
learn more about the type of career path that correlates to that job. For
instance, if a teen chooses a career path that requires a college education,
direct him to these sites:

Collegeboard
www.collegeboard.com

College Depot
http://www.collegedepot.com/hs/hsarticles.htm

College Planning Resources for Teens
http://www.quintcareers.com/teen_college.html

Free Application for Federal Student Aid
www.fafsa.ed.gov

Mapping Your Future
www.mapping-your-future.org

The Princeton Review
www.princetonreview.com

If a teen chooses a career path that requires a vocational or technical education, direct her to these sites:

JobProfiles
jobprofiles.org/index.htm

Guide to Vocational and Technical Schools
www.vocational-technical-schools.com/

If a teen is attracted to the idea of starting her own business, direct her to these sites:

Entrepreneur Quiz
www.allthetests.com/quiz07/dasquiztd.php3?testid=1076428333

SBA: The Young Entrepreneur Online Guide to Business
www.sba.gov/teens/

Y & E: The Magazine for Teen Entrepreneurs
ye.entreworld.org/

If a teen chooses a career path that involves military service, direct him to these sites:

Military Careers
www.todaysmilitary.com/mc/t13_mc_milcar.php

My Future
www.myfuture.com

United States Air Force
www.airforce.com

United States Army
www.goarmy.com

United States Marines
www.marines.com

United States Navy
www.navy.com

If a teen wants, or needs, to enter the workforce directly after graduating from high school, direct him to these sites:

CareerBuilder
www.careerbuilder.com

HotJobs
www.hotjobs.com

Job Hunter's Bible
www.jobhuntersbible.com/

Monster
www.monster.com

Finally, if a teen is still confused about his choices, encourage him to explore these sites:

Gap Year
www.gapyear.com

The Peace Corps
www.peacecorps.gov

Time, Cost, and Supplies

Regardless of the large impact this program could have on teens, it is inexpensive to implement. The only supplies and equipment necessary are paper and pencils, computer stations, candy bars for the icebreaker, and resources from your library's collection such as those listed below. Preparation for "Find Your Future" should not take more than a couple of hours. You will need to prepare the icebreaker, the word search, and the

Career Inventory worksheet; bookmark the career and personality tests online (or print them out if it is possible to do so); and invite career and guidance counselors to attend.

Promotion

This program can be promoted in one of two ways. You may be able to attract a number of teens simply by playing up the angle of fun self-exploration through personality quizzes. To target a more specific audience (i.e., high school juniors and seniors), however, consider placing promotional pieces in guidance counselors' offices, at SAT or ACT testing locations, or at any career fairs your local schools may host. It may also be beneficial to mail a piece home to parents of graduating students to bring their attention to the service you hope to offer.

In-house, plan to cover a bulletin board or display case with street signs such as "Stop," "Yield," "Merge," and "One Way." You could even purchase a battery-operated replica of a stoplight to spice things up a bit. With the phrase "Find Your Future" prominently lettered in the display, along with stacks of books on topics like college and choosing a career, it should be clear to teens that this program will help them navigate the choices life has to offer as they embark on the journey from high school into the real world.

Collection Connection

Fiction (featuring teens with jobs)

The $66 Summer—John Armistead (Milkweed Editions, 2000)

Acceleration—Graham McNamee (Wendy Lamb Books, 2003)

Ashes of Roses—Mary Jane Auch (Henry Holt and Company, 2002)

The Beet Fields—Gary Paulsen (Laurel Leaf, 2002)

Before Wings—Beth Goobie (Orca Book Publishers, 2001)

Breaking Through—Francisco Jimenez (Houghton Mifflin, 2001)

Burger Wuss—M. T. Anderson (Candlewick, 2001)

Chill Wind—Janet McDonald (Farrar, Straus and Giroux, 2002)

Dunk—David Lubar (Clarion Books, 2002)

Frozen Rodeo—Catherine Clark (Harper Tempest, 2003)

Heart on My Sleeve—Ellen Wittlinger (Simon and Schuster Children's Publishing, 2004)

Help Wanted: Short Stories about Young People Working—Anita Silvey, editor (Little Brown, 1997)

Hope Was Here—Joan Bauer (Putnam Publishing Group, 2000)

Jesse—Gary Soto (Harcourt Children's Books, 1994)

Keeping the Moon—Sarah Dessen (Viking, 1999)

Lord of the Fries & Other Stories—Tim Wynne Jones (DK Publishing, 1999)

A Northern Light—Jennifer Donnelly (Harcourt Children's Books, 2003)

One Fat Summer—David Lipsyte (Harper Trophy, 1991)

Paul Has a Summer Job—Michel Rabagliati (Drawn and Quarterly, 2002)

Pool Boy—Michael Simmons (Roaring Brook, 2003)

Rain Is Not My Indian Name—Cynthia Leitich Smith (HarperCollins, 2001)

Razzle—Ellen Wittlinger (Simon and Schuster Children's Publishing, 2001)

Rules of the Road—Joan Bauer (Putnam Publishing Group, 1998)

Saving the Planet & Stuff—Gail Gauthier (Grosset and Dunlap, 2003)

That Summer—Sarah Dessen (Speak, 2004)

Truth about Forever—Sarah Dessen (Viking Juvenile, 2004)

Truth or Dairy—Catherine Clark (Harper Tempest, 2000)

Twists & Turns—Janet McDonald (Farrar, Straus and Giroux, 2003)

Wizards of the Game—David Lubar (Philomel Books, 2003)

Working Days: Short Stories about Teenagers at Work—Anne Mazer, editor (Persea Books, 1997)

Zipped—Laura McNeal (Knopf Books for Young Readers, 2003)

Nonfiction

145 Things to Be When You Grow Up—Russell Kahn and Jodi Weiss (Princeton Review, 2004)

Career Ideas for Kids Who Like Money—Diane Lindsay Reeves (Facts on File, 2001)

Careers in Focus series—Facts on File, editor (Facts on File)

The College Board College Handbook—College Board (College Board, 2005)

College Majors Handbook with Real Career Paths and Payoffs—Paul Harrington and Thomas Harrington (Jist Publishing, 2004)

Colleges That Change Lives: 40 Schools You Should Know about Even if You're Not a Straight-A Student—Loren Pope (Penguin, 2000)

Complete Idiot's Guide to Cool Jobs for Teens—Susan Ireland (Alpha, 2001)

Cool Careers without College series—Rosen Publishing (Rosen Publishing)

Creating Your High School Resume: A Step-by-Step Guide to Preparing an Effective Resume for Jobs, College and Training Programs—Kathryn Kraemer Troutman (JIST Works, 2003)

Entrepreneurship for Dummies—Kathleen Allen (John Wiley, 2000)

Girl Boss: Running the Show Like the Big Chicks—Stacey Kravetz (Girl Press, 1999)

A Girl's Guide to College: Making the Most of the Best Four Years of Your Life—Traci Maynigo (Blue Mountain Arts, 2003)

Harvard Schmarvard: Getting Beyond the Ivy League to the College That Is Best for You—Jay Mathews (Three Rivers Press, 2003)

The Insider's Guide to the Colleges—Yale Daily News, editor (St. Martin's, 2005)

Peterson's College Money Handbook—Peterson's Guides (Peterson's Guides, 2005)

Teen Dream Jobs: How to Find the Job You Really Want Now!—Nora Coon (Beyond Words Publishing, 2003)

The Teenage Entrepreneur's Guide: 50 Money-Making Business Ideas—Sarah Riehm (Surrey Books, 1990)

The Totally Awesome Business Book for Kids: With Twenty Super Businesses You Can Start Right Now!—Adriane G. Berg and Arthur Berg Bochner (Newmarket Press, 2002)

Whiz Teens in Business: Enjoy Yourself while Making Money: A Simple and Complete Guide for Teenagers to Starting and Managing Their Small Business—Danielle Vallee (Truman Publishing Company, 1999)

The Young Entrepreneur's Guide to Starting and Running a Business—
Steve Mariotti (Three Rivers Press, 2000)

Young Person's Occupational Outlook Handbook—U.S. Department of
Labor, editor (JIST Works, 2004)

A BATTLE OF THE SEXES ($) (GRADES 7–10)

The start of a new school year brings many teens into the library to
conduct research and find help with homework. Most students these days
are computer savvy, but that doesn't mean they have the requisite skills to
navigate a library. Knowing that teens' first inclination is often to "Google"
a topic to find information, teachers often restrict the number of Web sites
students can use for their reports and research papers. This forces teens to
come to the library in search of print sources or even subscription databases, which in turn requires librarians to happily brush up on their bib-
liographic instruction skills in order to guide students through the various
print and electronic resources available. Many teen services librarians have
used scavenger hunts in one form or another as a tool with which to do just
that. So, while scavenger hunts in libraries aren't exactly new, this one has
a unique spin that is sure to disguise the built-in educational element.

"A Battle of the Sexes" pits guys against girls to see which gender is
more adept at finding accurate information faster. Granted, whichever
side wins the contest should not presume to make any sweeping statements of superiority based on the outcome of this simple game. But,
hopefully, a healthy competitive spirit will encourage the participants to
try their hardest to win. Also, the questions will teach both guys and girls
a little bit more about one another.

How

The basic idea behind this program is that through specific questions,
each team will go in search of various library resources in order to find
letters that will ultimately need to be unscrambled to form a secret phrase.
Since time is of the essence in this contest, the participants may be inclined
to talk loudly and move around quickly from source to source. It may be
wise, therefore, to conduct this program after-hours. Before passing out
the clue sheets, though, take a few moments to orientate the teens to the
various sections of the library. Briefly go over the layout of the library,
pointing out the fiction, nonfiction, periodical, audiovisual, and reference
sections. Also, make sure that a few computers have your library's catalog

pulled up, and that a few more have your library's databases readily accessible. Next, divide the participants into teams of four, making sure that the teams consist of either all guys or all girls. Have them choose team names for themselves, then pass the clue sheets out to each team, staggering their starting points so they aren't stumbling over one another in search of answers. Explain that the questions are designed to see how much girls know about guys, and vice versa, but that they are based almost entirely on stereotypical interests of each gender. In other words, the questions are just for fun and should not be taken to mean that all guys like kung fu movies and all girls are interested in makeup. After passing out the clue sheets, make the participants aware of the time, and set a time by which they should finish.

Sample clue sheets have been provided in Appendix G. Obviously, these were created with a specific library's collection in mind, so it will probably be necessary to customize it a bit to reflect the holdings in your own building. You will notice that there are letters in parentheses after each clue; these are the letters each team should collect as they find the source and the answer to each question. The letters the guys' teams will collect make the phrase "Guys Are #1!" and the letters for the girls' teams spell out "Girls Rule!" For this aspect of the scavenger hunt to work smoothly, estimate how many teens you expect at the program, then divide by two. Divide this number by four to determine the number of teams for each side. For instance, if you expect twenty teens to participate, you may be able to safely bet that ten will be girls and ten will be guys. Therefore, you will have at least three teams of girls and three teams of guys. Using an Ellison machine—or just a computer—cut out as many sets of letters as there are teams for each side. Of course, if you opt to require that teens register for this program ahead of time, or if you ar-range for a teacher to bring his or her class to the library for the scavenger hunt, you will be able to more closely estimate the number of teams. In any case, after preparing the phrases, put the letters for each clue in an envelope and hide it in or near its respective item. For example, for the first question on the guys' clue sheet, you should put an envelope full of U's in the "V" volume of the encyclopedia. For questions requiring the use of an electronic database, there is obviously no place to hide the letters. Have the teens answer these questions, and collect the letters from you when they are finished with the hunt.

As the teens locate the resources for the questions on their team's clue sheet, they should write in the answers and collect the respective letters. When they are finished with the scavenger hunt, each team should hand in their clue sheets, at which time they can collect any of the letters won by answering the questions requiring the use of an electronic resource. As soon as their clue sheets have been checked over for accuracy, the teams can start to unscramble the letters they've collected. The first team to figure out the phrase wins the hunt!

To spice up the hunt even further, interrupt the scavenging for a reward challenge and an immunity challenge (similar to the popular television show *Survivor*). The reward challenge consists of a lightning round of gender-related trivia questions. Challenge the guys' teams with the following questions:

- What happens when lipstick "feathers"? (Answer: It bleeds beyond the lip line)
- What product can stop a run in panty hose? (Answer: Clear fingernail polish or hairspray)
- What is a cross between a one-piece bathing suit and a bikini called? (Answer: A tankini)
- What boy band did Nick Lachey (Jessica Simpson's ex-husband) once belong to? (Answer: 98 Degrees)
- Who wrote *The Notebook* and *A Walk to Remember*? (Answer: Nicholas Sparks)

Pose these questions to the girls' teams:

- What would you use to tie a Windsor knot? (Answer: A necktie)
- Who wears number 23 for the Cleveland Cavaliers? (Answer: LeBron James)
- What is a styptic pencil? (Answer: A product men use to decrease blood flow when they cut themselves shaving)
- What is a half-pipe? (Answer: A type of ramp used for skateboarding)
- What was the name of the crude and obnoxious male character in the *American Pie* movies? (Answer: Steven Stifler)

The gender that gets the most questions correct will win the reward challenge and receive the letter for one of the questions on their clue sheet.

A little later, have the teams reconvene once more for the immunity challenge. Ask each side to pick two members to represent their gender for this challenge. For round one, instruct one of the male contestants to raise one knee to a 90 degree angle, then hand him a razor (with its protective cover on), asking him to "shave" his entire leg—from ankle to hip—without putting his leg down. While he is attempting this challenge, one of the female contestants will have a go at tying a tie around her neck by using a set of instructions or a diagram. For round two, the other male contestant will need to walk in a pair of stiletto high heels from one location to another. Meanwhile, the female contestant will make an attempt at identifying several objects in a toolbox. Whichever side completes both rounds most successfully will receive immunity from having to unscramble the letters they collect at the end of the hunt.

By the end of the scavenger hunt, award a trophy to the "superior sex." If this program is highly successful, it may be possible to reuse this trophy from year to year in an annual "battle of the sexes." If you conduct this program in partnership with a school or classroom, suggest that the award be displayed in the school's trophy case until the next year. This could create healthy competition and heighten the anticipation for the next "battle." Also, time permitting, you may choose to serve pizza or some other snack at the end of the hunt.

With a lot of fun and silliness built into this scavenger hunt, it might be easy to lose sight of the ultimate goal: to familiarize teens with the library and the materials it has to offer. Before the program ends, therefore, gather the teens together to review a few things such as how to use the library's catalog, access the electronic databases, and find journal articles. If your library offers online reference in the form of e-mail or chat, take a moment to point this out as well. Finally, send the teens on their way with a library card application, a bookmark listing some of the key things to remember when conducting research at the library, and maybe even a small trinket promoting your library or reading. The American Library Association's (ALA) online store (www.alastore.ala.org) carries merchandise such as T-shirts, key chains, and water bottles.

Time, Cost, and Supplies

The clue sheets have been provided in Appendix G, so you will only have to spend time customizing the clues to reflect your library's collection, rather than creating them from scratch. Photocopying the clue sheets, cutting out the letters, and preparing the bookmarks are the other major tasks on the to-do list for this program. Make sure there will be a few computers available during the scavenger hunt so the participants can access the library's catalog and databases. You will also need to gather the following supplies for the immunity challenge:

disposable razor

pair of high heels

necktie

book or diagram demonstrating how to tie a tie

toolbox filled with tools (e.g., Phillips screwdriver, socket wrench, Allen wrench, etc.)

trophy (plastic, or the real deal)

Giveaways and snacks are optional, making this an inexpensive program requiring a minimal amount of preparation on your part. At the same time, however, the preparation the teens will receive should serve them well throughout the remainder of the school year.

Promotion

If you decide to conduct this program in conjunction with a school or teacher, in-house promotion will not be necessary. In this case, make a flyer advertising the availability of the program to the local schools, encouraging teachers to contact you to set up a day and time for the scavenger hunt. Take this opportunity to publicize other services you may offer to teen students and teachers, such as booktalks, for instance.

If, however, you decide to hold this program for the general teen public, an in-house display featuring large gender symbols (i.e., ♀ vs. ♂) under the heading "Join the Battle of the Sexes!" will catch their attention. Then, make two stacks of books—one containing titles great for boys and one containing titles great for girls—with a sign that asks, "How will your gender stack up?" Put flyers and a sign-up sheet in or near the display so that the teens can read about the scavenger hunt and sign up immediately.

Collection Connection

Fiction (for Guys)

The Afterlife—Gary Soto (Harcourt Children's Books, 2003)

Artemis Fowl series—Eoin Colfer (Miramax)

Black and White—Paul Volponi (Viking Books, 2005)

Cirque du Freak series—Darren Shan (Little Brown)

Damage—A. M. Jenkins (HarperCollins, 2001)

Doing It—Melvin Burgess (Henry Holt and Company, 2001)

Downriver—Will Hobbs (Laurel Leaf, 1995)

Downsiders—Neal Shusterman (Simon Pulse, 2001)

Ender's Game—Orson Scott Card (Tor Books, 1985)

Fat Kid Rules the World—K. L. Going (Grosset and Dunlap, 2003)

Fighting Ruben Wolfe—Markus Zusak (Push, 2002)

Freak the Mighty—Rodman Philbrick (Scholastic Paperbacks, 2001)

Girls for Breakfast—David Yoo (Delacorte Books for Young Readers, 2005)

The Goats—Brock Cole (Farrar, Straus and Giroux, 1990)

Heart of a Champion—Carl Deuker (Harper Trophy, 1994)

Hitchhiker's Guide to the Galaxy—Douglas Adams (Del Rey, 1995)

I Was a Teenage Professional Wrestler—Ted Lewin (Scholastic, 1993)

Jake, Reinvented—Gordon Korman (Hyperion, 2003)

Looking for Alaska—John Green (Dutton Juvenile, 2005)

Maniac Magee—Jerry Spinelli (Little Brown, 1990)

Monster—Walter Dean Myers (Amistad, 1999)

Net force series—Tom Clancy (Berkley Publishing Group)

No More Dead Dogs—Gordon Korman (Hyperion, 2000)

Oddballs—William Sleator (Puffin, 1995)

Out of Order—A. M. Jenkins (Harper Tempest, 2003)

Painting the Black—Carl Deuker (Houghton Mifflin, 1997)

The Perks of Being a Wallflower—Stephen Chobsky (MTV, 1999)

Rats Saw God—Rob Thomas (Simon and Schuster Children's Publishing, 1996)

Red Midnight—Ben Mikaelsen (Rayo, 2002)

Silent to the Bone—E. L. Konigsburg (Atheneum, 2000)

Slot Machine—Chris Lynch (Harper Trophy, 1996)

Soldier's Heart—Gary Paulsen (Delacorte Books for Young Readers, 1998)

Stormbreaker (and sequels)—Anthony Horowitz (Philomel Books, 2001)

Tangerine—Edward Bloor (Harcourt Children's Books, 1997)

Touching Spirit Bear—Ben Mikaelsen (HarperCollins, 2001)

Whale Talk—Chris Crutcher (Greenwillow, 2001)

Wild Man Island—Will Hobbs (HarperCollins, 2002)

Fiction (for Girls)

Angus, Thongs, and Full-Frontal Snogging (and sequels)—Louise Rennison (HarperCollins, 2000)

Battle Dress—Amy Efaw (Harper Trophy, 2003)

Beauty: A Retelling of the Story of Beauty and the Beast—Robin McKinley (HarperCollins, 1978)

Beetle and Me—Karen Romano Young (Greenwillow, 1999)

Boy Proof—Cecil Castellucci (Candlewick, 2005)

The Earth, My Butt, and Other Big Round Things—Carolyn Mackler (Candlewick, 2003)

Feeling Sorry for Celia—Jaclyn Moriarty (St. Martin's Griffin, 2002)

Forever—Judy Blume (Atheneum, 2002)

Gingerbread—Rachel Cohn (Simon and Schuster Children's Publishing, 2002)

Girl 15, Charming but Insane—Sue Limb (Delacorte Books for Young Readers, 2004)

Gossip Girl series—Cecily von Ziegesar (Little Brown)

A Great and Terrible Beauty (and sequel)—Libba Bray (Delacorte Books for Young Readers, 2003)

Grecian Holiday (and sequels)—Kate Cann (Avon)

Heart on My Sleeve—Ellen Wittlinger (Simon and Schuster Children's Publishing, 2004)

Keeping the Moon—Sarah Dessen (Viking, 1999)

Mates, Dates series—Cathy Hopkins (Simon Pulse)

My Cup Runneth Over: The Life of Angelica Cookson Potts—Cherry Whytock (Simon and Schuster Children's Publishing, 2003)

A Northern Light—Jennifer Donnelly (Harcourt Children's Books, 2003)

The Notebook—Nicholas Sparks (Warner Books, 1996)

The Princess Diaries series—Meg Cabot (HarperCollins)

Prom—Laurie Halse Anderson (Viking Juvenile, 2005)

Romiette and Julio—Sharon Draper (Atheneum, 1999)

Sisterhood of the Traveling Pants (and sequels)—Ann Brashares (Delacorte Books for Young Readers)

Sloppy Firsts (and sequel)—Megan McCafferty (Three Rivers Press, 2001)

Someone Like You—Sarah Dessen (Viking, 1998)

Speak—Laurie Halse Anderson (Farrar, Straus and Giroux, 1999)

Stargirl—Jerry Spinelli (Knopf Books for Young Readers, 2000)

That Summer—Sarah Dessen (Speak, 2004)

True Confessions of Charlotte Doyle—Avi (Scholastic, 1990)

A Walk to Remember—Nicholas Sparks (Warner Books, 1999)

What My Mother Doesn't Know—Sonya Sones (Simon and Schuster Children's Publishing, 2001)

Who Am I without Him?—Sharon Flake (Jump at the Sun, 2004)

Nonfiction (for Guys)

Concrete Wave: The History of Skateboarding—Michael Brooke (Warwick House Publishing, 1999)

Guts—Gary Paulsen (Delacorte Books for Young Readers, 2001)

How Angel Peterson Got His Name—Gary Paulsen (Wendy Lamb Books, 2003)

King of the Mild Frontier—Chris Crutcher (Greenwillow, 2003)

Phineas Gage: A Gruesome but True Story of Brain Science—John Fleischman (Houghton Mifflin, 2002)

The Radioactive Boy Scout—Ken Silverstein (Villard, 2005)

Rocket Boys—Homer Hickam (Delta, 2000)

The Teenage Guy's Survival Guide: The Real Deal on Girls, Growing Up, and Other Guy Stuff—Jeremy Daldry (Megan Tingley, 1999)

Nonfiction (for Girls)

33 Things Every Girl Should Know about Women's History: From Suffragettes to Skirt Lengths to the ERA—Tonya Bolden, editor (Crown Books for Young Readers, 2002)

33 Things Every Girl Should Know: Stories, Songs, Poems, and Smart Talk by 33 Extraordinary Women—Tonya Bolden (Crown Books for Young Readers, 1998)

Counting Coup: A True Story of Basketball and Honor on the Little Big Horn—Larry Colton (Warner Books, 2001)

Every Girl Tells a Story: A Celebration of Girls Speaking Their Minds—Carolyn Jones (Simon and Schuster Children's Publishing, 2002)

Girl Coming In for a Landing—April Halprin Wayland (Knopf Books for Young Readers, 2002)

Girls Got Game: Sports Stories and Poems—Sue Macy, editor (Henry Holt and Company, 2001)

GirlWise: How to Be Confident, Capable, Cool, and in Control—Julia Devillers (Three Rivers Press, 2002)

Let Me Play: The Story of Title IX: The Law That Changed the Future of Girls in America—Karen Blumenthal (Atheneum, 2005)

Shout, Sister, Shout!: Ten Girl Singers Who Shaped a Century—Roxane Orgill (Margaret K. McElderry, 2001)

Um, Like . . . OM: A Girl Goddess' Guide to Yoga—Evan Cooper (Little Brown, 2005)

LOL @ YOUR LIBRARY ($-$$$$)
(GRADES 7–10)

Everyone enjoys a good laugh from time to time, but anyone who's ever attempted to tell a joke to a crowd can attest that getting people to laugh isn't always easy. In fact, it's an art form. I clam up if I try to relate any funny story more sophisticated than a simple knock-knock joke, and I absolutely marvel at the moxie of stand-up and improv comedians who brave the ever-dreaded silences and polite chuckles of a live audience when a joke bombs. But one good joke can break the ice with an eruption of laughter that often spurs on the performer, carrying him or her through the rest of the set on a wave of hilarity. Achieving this success, however, takes training and practice.

Whether one is on the receiving or giving end of humor, the cliché stating that laughter is the best medicine has quite a bit of merit. In fact, humor can actually help children and their parents cope with serious illness as discovered through a study by Alicja Jarzab. Jarzab writes that the families she studied "perceived humor as a 'stress deodorant' and repeated its application all day long. Others referred to humor as something that assists them in connecting with others" (Jarzab 2004). Jarzab attests that humor "helps us to view the world with perspective," a technique that comes in handy when faced with seemingly insurmountable obstacles like a serious illness or disability. This is a strong-held belief of Patch Adams, a physician who uses clowns and other laughter-inducing techniques to help bring relief to his patients. Surely, then, teens who struggle with adolescence and its attendant pressures could benefit from a little laughter once in a while. "LOL @ Your Library" will help teens practice the art of improvisation and enjoy a few laughs through a workshop styled after the famous television show *Whose Line Is It Anyway?* and a live performance from a local comedy troupe.

How

To break the ice and set the tone for silliness right from the start, hand out red foam clown noses or plastic "Groucho" glasses to your comedian wannabes as they arrive at the program. You might also want to play a laugh track in the background because, after all, laughter is infectious. After everyone has arrived, introduce yourself and ask the teens to introduce themselves as well, explaining why they wanted to attend the workshop. Then, explain a bit about the structure of the workshop so the teens will know what to expect. Now it's time to get started.

A couple of warm-up exercises act as icebreakers for the group, allowing the participants to build trust and camaraderie with each another. The first exercise is called "Free Association" and is probably one with which the participants are already familiar. Standing in a circle, one person shouts out a word. The person to her left then says the first word that comes to his mind, whether or not it is funny or makes sense. Some of the word combinations will be ridiculous, but this is helpful in creating an atmosphere open to absurdity. The warm-up ends when the circle is completed, but the cycle can be repeated if desired.

The next exercise—called "Greetings"—gets the participants interacting with each other a bit more; it also helps them take and interpret cues. As the facilitator, ask the teens to mill around the room shaking hands and greeting each other. Then shout out instructions that end with a qualifier, like "Greet everyone as if they smell bad," "Greet everyone as if you're bored," or "Greet everyone like a long-lost uncle." By the end of this activity, the teens will be more familiar with each other, and hopefully more comfortable with the fast pace of improv.

Next, the teens will participate in a couple of exercises well suited for a workshop because they help novices start developing their improvisation skills. In other words, these are not activities well suited for performance involving audience participation. Those activities, called "handles," will be demonstrated by an improvisation comedy troupe later in the program. The first exercise is called "The Conducted Story." It is similar to "Free Association" in that what one person says affects what the next one says. However, this exercise builds on previous players' responses to make a story rather than just a string of random words. To facilitate this exercise, split the teens into groups of four or five with one person assigned to conducting the story. The first person in each group should start telling a story. When the conductor points at the second person in the group, she should continue the story. The exercise continues as long as the group can keep going. As the facilitator for this exercise, you can give as much or as little direction as you'd like. For example, you could give each group a place to start, like "Tell a story about dogs," or, even more specifically, "Tell a story about an alien invasion." Give free reign, however, to the conductors, who can move from person to person rapidly cutting them off midword, or very slowly, forcing each player to embellish his or her story. This exercise can be repeated a few times, shuffling members of each group around to change the dynamics.

The second exercise is called "The Emotional Symphony" and is similar to the first because it also involves a conductor; however, this exercise explores the use of emotions. Arrange the teens in a semicircle with the conductor in the middle facing her "symphony." When the conductor points at someone, that person must silently demonstrate an emotion. If the conductor raises her arm, the emotion must be heightened. For instance, a participant may decide to portray sadness by pouting, but when the conductor raises her arm, the participant must advance the emotion to a new level, by sniffing, then crying, and so on. Each participant must convey a different emotion as the conductor points at him or her. As the conductor randomly starts to point more rapidly at the different members of the "symphony," the participants will be strengthening their attention skills.

Many other warm-ups and workshop exercises can be explored at Learn Improv (www.learnimprov.com) and the Improv Encyclopedia (www.humanpingpongball.com). You can change or add as many of the activities as you desire, but make sure to have the necessary props and space required to perform the activities you choose. Next, provide an opportunity for the teens to see an improv troupe in action. Improv

Across America (www.improvamerica.com) is a great resource for locating improvisation comedy troupes—many of which travel and have cheap booking fees—in your area. To give the comedy troupe a chance to set up, have the teens enjoy some snacks and browse the books, videos, and magazines you've collected. You could also offer Laffy Taffy® to any teen who volunteers to stand up to tell a joke (rated PG, of course). After this brief intermission, invite the teens to sit back and enjoy the show. Since many of these traveling improv groups are skilled at leading workshops, ask the performers if, after the show, they would be willing to describe to the teens how to execute the same handles they performed on stage. If time permits, the performers could even lead some teens in presenting some of those handles for their peers.

At the end of the program, hand out goody bags of gags like whoopee cushions, disappearing ink, and hand buzzers, to congratulate and thank the teens for participating.

Time, Cost, and Supplies

The warm-ups and exercises described in this chapter do not require any special props or preparation, but if you choose other activities for the workshop, this could change. Also, most comedy troupes come with their own props, but you may have to provide a bell, a stool, and paper and pencils that the audience can use to write down their suggestions. The other supplies you'll need for this program include the following:

Groucho glasses

clown noses

whoopie cushions

disappearing ink

hand buzzers

Laffy Taffy

a laugh track

snacks

Nearly all of these items can be purchased at a minimal cost from suppliers like Oriental Trading or U.S. Toy. Costs for the supplies have been kept to a minimum because the fee for booking a comedy troupe could vary widely. Book the improv group several months in advance, and plan on spending time heavily promoting this program since you wouldn't want to disappoint the comedians with a measly turnout.

Promotion

For an in-house promotional display, feature the phrase "LOL @ Your Library" in large letters over either pictures of people laughing, or one big mouth opened wide in laughter. Decorate the space with classic symbols of comedy, such as a plastic banana peel, sets of chattering toy teeth, and Groucho glasses. Place a sign-up sheet for the improv workshop right next to the display so teens needn't bother taking an extra step to register. Of course, dedicate space in the display for some of the funny titles listed below.

Since this program features paid performers, advertise the family-friendly event through press releases and flyers deposited at local comedy clubs, community theaters, and recreation centers. Contact drama clubs as well as performance arts teachers so they can help you recruit their students. If the comedy troupe you hire has a Web site featuring upcoming appearances, ask if they will list the date, time, and location of your program. This will help promote the program to the troupe's preexisting fan base, which could result in "new blood" at your program.

Collection Connection

Fiction

24 Girls in 7 Days—Alex Bradley (Dutton Juvenile, 2005)

Absolutely Normal Chaos—Sharon Creech (HarperCollins, 1995)

The Adventures of Blue Avenger—Norma Howe (Henry Holt and Company, 1999)

Al Capone Does My Shirts—Gennifer Choldenko (Putnam Juvenile, 2004)

All's Fair in Love, War, and High School—Janette Rallison (Walker Books for Young Readers, 2003)

The Amazing Maurice and His Educated Rodents—Terry Pratchett (HarperCollins, 2001)

Angus, Thongs, and Full-Frontal Snogging (and sequels)—Louise Rennison (HarperCollins, 2000)

Be More Chill—Ned Vizzini (Miramax, 2004)

The Beetle and Me: A Love Story—Karen Romano Young (Greenwillow, 1999)

The Black Book series—Jonah Black (Avon)

Burger Wuss—M. T. Anderson (Candlewick, 2001)

The Cannibals—Cynthia Grant (Roaring Brook Press, 2002)

Confessions of a Shopaholic—Sophie Kinsella (Dial Press Trade Paperbacks, 2001)

Confessions of a Teenage Drama Queen—Dyan Sheldon (Candlewick, 1999)

Confess-o-Rama—Ron Koertge (Scholastic, 1996)

The Earth, My Butt, and Other Big, Round Things—Carolyn Mackler (Candlewick, 2003)

A Fate Totally Worse than Death—Paul Fleischman (Candlewick, 2004)

Flavor of the Week—Tucker Shaw (Hyperion, 2003)

Flipped—Wendelin Van Draanen (Knopf Books for Young Readers, 2001)

Girl 15, Charming but Insane—Sue Limb (Delacorte Books for Young Readers, 2004)

Girl Gives Birth to Own Prom Date—Todd Strasser (Simon and Schuster Children's Publishing, 1996)

The Glass Café—Gary Paulsen (Wendy Lamb Books, 2003)

Hitchhiker's Guide to the Galaxy—Douglas Adams (Del Rey, 1995)

Mates, Dates series—Cathy Hopkins (Simon Pulse)

My Cup Runneth Over: The Life of Angelica Cookson Potts—Cherry Whytock (Simon and Schuster Children's Publishing, 2003)

No More Dead Dogs—Gordon Korman (Hyperion, 2000)

Planet Janet—Dyan Sheldon (Candlewick, 2003)

The Princess Bride—William Goldman (Ballantine Books, 1998)

Rats Saw God—Rob Thomas (Simon and Schuster Children's Publishing, 1996)

The Schwa Was Here—Neal Shusterman (Dutton Juvenile, 2004)

Sleeping Freshmen Never Lie—David Lubar (Dutton Juvenile, 2005)

Son of the Mob—Gordon Korman (Hyperion, 2002)

Squashed—Joan Bauer (Putnam Publishing Group, 2001)

Sunshine Rider: The First Vegetarian Western—Ric Lynden Hardman (Laurel Leaf, 2001)

This Place Has No Atmosphere—Paula Danziger (Paperstar Books, 1999)

Thwonk!—Joan Bauer (Puffin, 2005)

Truth or Dairy—Catherine Clark (Harper Tempest, 2000)

Vampire High—Douglas Rees (Delacorte Books for Young Readers, 2003)

Whistling Toilets—Randy Powell (Farrar, Straus and Giroux, 2001)

The Year My Life Went down the Loo (and sequels)—Katie Maxwell (Dorchester Publishing Company)

Nonfiction

Adam Sandler (*People in the News* series)—Dwayne Epstein (Lucent Books, 2004)

Group Improvisation: The Manual of Ensemble Improv Games—Peter Campbell Gwinn (Meriwether Publishing, 2003)

How Angel Peterson Got His Name—Gary Paulsen (Wendy Lamb Books, 2003)

Improv for Actors—Dan Diggles (Allworth Press, 2004)

Jim Carrey: Fun and Funnier—Nancy Krulik (Simon Spotlight Entertainment, 2000)

King of the Mild Frontier—Chris Crutcher (Greenwillow, 2003)

Live from New York: An Uncensored History of Saturday Night Live, as Told by Its Stars, Writers and Guests—James A. Miller (Little Brown, 2002)

The Second City Almanac of Improvisation—Anne Libera (Northwestern University Press, 2004)

Truth in Comedy—Charna Halpern, Del Close, and Kim Howard Johnson (Meriwether Publishing, 1994)

The Ultimate Improv Book: A Complete Guide to Comedy Improvisation—Edward J. Nevraumont (Meriwether Publishing, 2002)

When Time Is Short and Money Is Tight . . .

Promote Banned Books Week by challenging teens to read banned titles and write short synopses about them to be published on your Web site later.

Hold a bookmark design contest to promote National Library Card Sign-Up Month.

Contact your local home-schoolers' association to invite home-schooled teens to a brown-bag lunch during which new titles can be booktalked.

REFERENCES

Center for the Study of College Student Retention (2005). Retrieved May 5, 2005, from Center for the Study of College Student Retention/Journal of College Student Retention Web site: http://www.cscsr.org/retention_journal.htm.

Grossman, L., Mustafa, N., van Dyk, D., and Kloberdanz, K. (2005). Grow up? Not so fast. *Time*, *165*(4), 42–54.

Jarzab, A. (2004). Attack it with humor and make it as wonderful as you can. *Exceptional Parent*, *34*(4), 38–40.

University of Missouri Career Center (2002). Finding a major or career—MU career center career interests game. Retrieved September 2, 2005, from MU Career Center Web site: http://career.missouri.edu/modules.php?name=News&file=article&sid=146.

U.S. Department of Labor, Bureau of Labor Statistics (2005). College enrollment and work activity of 2004 high school graduates. Retrieved May 5, 2005, from News: Bureau of Labor Statistics Web site: http://www.bls.gov/news.release/hsgec.nr0.htm.

Chapter 10

OCTOBER

The September rush will have died down now that school is in full swing for another year, leaving time for some new programs. "One Book, One Voice" is a program that will entail quite a bit of planning, but ties in nicely with Teen Read Week. A field trip midmonth gets teens out of the library and into a different setting: an art museum. Finally, the end of the month usually brings Halloween to mind, but this year, why not celebrate the Day of the Dead by making pocket shrines and learning a bit about this Mexican custom?

ONE BOOK, ONE VOICE ($$$$) (GRADES 7–12)

Teen Read Week has a new theme each year, spawning a plethora of programs and book lists that are created around that theme. Many of the programs inspired by Teen Read Week are wonderfully creative and certainly fun for teens. Sometimes, though, these programs have little to do with reading. To get back to basics, "One Book, One Voice" is a program that can supplement the other fun activities happening throughout the week or month, or can stand alone if you decide to forego traditional Teen Read Week programming.

The "One Book, One Community" concept was initiated by the Washington Center for the Book in 1998. Since then, the movement has swept the nation. Forty-seven states now have "One Book" events happening in at least one of their communities, with libraries usually spearheading the projects. The concept involves encouraging a community to read a selected title that may have significant social, economical, or educational impact. My library, for example, chose Catherine Ryan Hyde's *Pay It Forward* as the title for its first ever "One Book, One Community" initiative because of its message of philanthropy, neighborliness, and goodwill. Because it is often difficult, however, to choose a book that is both appealing and appropriate for all ages, it may be a good idea to choose a separate title for the youth in your community. Whether or not your library is involved in a community-wide read such as this one, this program is a great way to encourage teen reading.

How

The first, most logical, step for this program is to choose the title you will use. This can be done by committee, including the young adult library staff at your library as well as teachers and parents in your community, or you could narrow the field down to a few titles and let the teens choose which book they want to read. Voting boxes in schools, the library, and around the community would do the trick, or you could create an online poll on your library's Web site. From past experience, I suggest choosing a book that is available in paperback form because this is easier on the budget.

After the book has been selected, it is time to heavily promote the title to your audience. In fact, a large portion of the time involved in this project is tied up with the promotion itself. Therefore, the Promotion section below is fairly extensive, containing several ideas for making this program a success in your community.

When all is said and done, if the promotion ideas described below have done their job, you should have a fairly good-sized audience for a few days of activities designed around the title you and your community of teens have chosen. Book discussions are an obvious activity choice, but you may also want to consider showing the film version of the book (if there is one) and inviting the author to speak at your library. To do this, make initial contact with the author at least six months ahead of the week you have in mind. First, check to see if the author has a Web site; many times authors offer their e-mail addresses on their Web sites, which makes it very easy to get in touch with them. If this is not an available option, determine which publisher the author uses, then check its Web site for contact information. You may have to go through an agent, or write to the publisher itself to inquire about the author's availability. Whichever route you take, be sure to be as specific as possible about your needs, and tactfully inquire into the matter of the author's required honorarium. A sample inquiry letter has been provided for you below. Once you hear back from the author, agent, or publisher, make sure to send a follow-up letter of thanks for agreeing to speak at your library. In this letter, confirm the date and time of the speaking engagement, and let the author know that you will be in touch regarding travel arrangements as the time gets a little closer. Your library or the author's publisher may require a contract; this would be a good time to send that as well. Next, make flight and hotel reservations for the author.

November 7, 2005

Margaret Peterson Haddix
c/o Simon & Schuster Children's Publishing
Publicity Department
1230 Avenue of the Americas
New York, NY 10020

Dear Ms. Haddix:

I am writing to inquire about your availability for a speaking engagement at the Wadsworth Public Library in March of 2006.

Wadsworth teens are huge fans of your books. Our after-school book discussion group for fifth and sixth graders read *Among the Hidden* last year and will be trying *Running Out of Time* this fall.

A panel of Wadsworth teens, teachers and librarians have chosen *Turnabout* as the selection for our first-ever "One Book, One Voice" initiative. Throughout this year, we will be encouraging every area teen to read *Turnabout* in preparation for a week's worth of discussions and activities which we hope will culminate in a visit from you.

Thank you in advance for your consideration. I look forward to hearing from you so that we can further discuss your availability and required honorarium.

Sincerely,

Valerie A. Ott, M.L.I.S.
Teen Services Librarian

The next important task to complete entails ordering multiple copies of the book. Many times, publishers will offer a great discount to libraries hosting author appearances, so check into this option first. However, if your budget will not permit the purchase of multiple copies, you may need to solicit donors for help with this project. If approached early enough in the budget cycle, area schools may be able to chip in financially. You could also ask area businesses to purchase ten to fifteen copies each, which would add up quickly and not be too much of a burden on any one donor. If this is the route you choose, consider placing a label with the donor's name inside. Ideally, it would be nice to have several copies of the book for the library to circulate to those unwilling or unable to purchase it. However, it will be necessary to make the bulk of the books available for teens to have—or purchase, if recouping costs is an issue—in order for the author to sign. Don't forget to purchase a couple of copies of the book in an audio format—even as an MP3—for teens who don't like to read or who have reading difficulties so they can still participate.

Time, Cost, and Supplies

This program is by far the costliest one described in this book. The author's honorarium, combined with marketing and promotion costs, and purchasing multiple copies of the book, add up to a significant chunk of change. If this program seems important to you, however, and you plan for it properly by dedicating a portion of your yearly budget to it, you won't miss the money. Luckily, many young adult authors' honorariums are still in the $2,000 range, making them much more affordable than adult writers. Don't forget to budget for airfare, hotel accommodations, and meals for the author, as well as refreshments you may want to serve at the book discussions.

This program also takes quite a bit of time to plan. As with anything, however, the first time you try it will take the longest. In subsequent years, you will have a model of success to follow, including a marketing and promotion plan. Contact the author and any potential donors at least eight months ahead of time, and start promoting "One Book, One Voice" about two to three months in advance of the events.

Promotion

The sky is the limit when it comes to promoting this program. In order to reach as many teens as possible, you may want to consider several of these ideas:

First, dedicate a spot, a page, or a whole Web site to "One Book, One Voice." The more teen appeal this has, the better, obviously. In other words, don't clutter the space up with discussion questions about the book or anything else that is too scholarly. Consider including an online poll to gauge teens' reaction to the book, a short author bio, and a picture of the cover of the book (make sure to get the publisher's permission for this and any other use of the cover art), as well as information about where to get the book.

Use Bookcrossing (www.bookcrossing.com) for a unique way to pass the word about the program. Bookcrossing is similar to the concept of Found Art! described in Chapter 4 in that it encourages people to read a book, then leave it somewhere for someone else to serendipitously find. Books left for others are assigned unique identification numbers so that they can be tracked. The ID number also allows the person who found the book to learn where it has been and make comments about it on the Bookcrossing Web site. Put a link for Bookcrossing on your "One Book, One Voice" Web page, and encourage your teen participants to either be on the lookout for a copy of the book, or pass on their copy Bookcrossing-style so that others can enjoy it.

Other ideas for promoting the program include

- Cooperate with English and reading teachers to work the book selection into their lesson plans.
- Encourage school library media specialists to promote the title within their buildings.
- Create a blog on the "One Book, One Voice" Web site that poses discussion questions for the teens to respond to; link to an RSS feed of a booktalk of the selected title.
- Place information about the program on schools' Web sites.
- Display a banner on the front of the library.

- Place posters in recreation centers, after-school hangouts, favorite teen restaurants, and bookstores.
- Print bookmarks with the event dates on them.
- Hold an essay contest about one topic of the book; the prize could be dinner with the author.
- Hold a "One Book, One Voice" logo contest.
- Print round stickers that say "I Read It!" to pass out to any teen library customer who checks out or buys the title.

Collection Connection

Normally, this section would contain a list of books to tie in with the program described above. However, because the book your teens choose for this program should be based on your community's makeup and personality, it is difficult to recommend books here. Alternatively, you could opt to see what other communities have chosen by visiting the Library Congress's site for The Center for the Book (www.loc.gov/loc/cfbook/one-book.html). Another resource that lists books meaty enough for discussion is the Multnomah County Library's Talk It Up! Discussion Guide site (http://www.multcolib.org/talk/guides.html). Finally, don't forget the award winners, such as Printz Award and Honor recipients for previous years.

ART TRIP ($) (GRADES 7–10)

Several of the programs contained in this book promote creative expression for artistic teens through avenues such as film (Chapter 1), interior design (Chapter 2), recycled art (Chapter 4), and photography (Chapter 6). But what about those teens who can't draw a straight line, but have an appreciation for art nonetheless? This two-part program is for those who don't consider themselves artistic. Surreal and abstract art are two different art movements of the twentieth century that are perfect for awakening the right side of teens' brains. After introducing these two art forms with brief descriptions and a couple of exercises, a trip to a museum will become a fun outing for solidifying what they've learned, and redefining themselves as artistic—despite what their art teachers may have told them. After all, art truly is in the eye of the beholder.

How

The first part of this program will focus on introducing surreal and abstract art to the teen participants. You may feel more comfortable asking an art teacher for assistance, but since the intended audience for this program is teens who aren't necessarily artistic to begin with, it may be best to lead the program yourself so as not to intimidate them further. (This is assuming that, like me, you are not an artist.) The point of this program, again, is to make art more accessible to those who consider themselves challenged in this area; it is *not* to teach them about such things as form, color, and mood in a stuffy, formal manner. Once the goal of the program has been conveyed and the teens realize that they are not under pressure to create masterpieces, introduce the two art forms to them.

Surrealism is an art form that attempts to balance reality with dreamlike or fantastical elements. Surrealists, inspired by Sigmund Freud's psychoanalytic theories, believed that art could be an expression of our dreaming state, or subconscious. Therefore, the artwork that emerged from this movement often included strangely juxtaposed objects that would not normally appear in real life. Some of the more famous surrealists were Joan Miró, Salvador Dalí, and Rene Magritte.

There are two activities that can be employed at this point to demonstrate surrealism to the teens. The first activity involves the use of dream journals to create surreal art. In Chapter 2, teens tapped into their inner psyches with an informal dream analysis program. The participants at this program were invited to make dream journals, which they could then take home to record common symbols and patterns recurring in their dreams. Invite the participants of "In Your Dreams" to bring their dream journals to your program in order to use their journal entries as fodder for surreal expressions. If some of your program participants did not attend "In Your Dreams," simply invite them to recall a particularly strange dream they've had and jot down the symbols, animals, and colors that appeared in that dream. For instance, at the "In Your Dreams" program I conducted, a teenaged girl recalled a dream she had about floating bananas. This would make a wonderful surrealist painting. After the teens have picked an image from their dream world, have them spend fifteen to twenty minutes drawing what they see with colored pencils or oil pastels on white paper.

Another activity commonly used to demonstrate surrealism is called the "exquisite corpse." According to William Rubin, the exquisite corpse is a technique "[b]ased on an old parlor game . . . played by several people, each of whom would write a phrase on a sheet of paper, fold the paper to conceal part of it, and pass it on to the next player. . . . The technique got its name from results obtained in initial playing. . . . 'The exquisite corpse will drink the young wine'. . . . These poetic fragments were felt to reveal . . . the 'unconscious reality in the personality of the group' . . . [and were] immediately adapted to drawing" (Rubin 1968). Therefore, with sheets of paper folded in fourths, invite groups of four teens to construct an "exquisite corpse." Another way to play this game involves the use of flip chart paper set up on an easel. Turn the easel around so that the group cannot see what is being drawn. Ask for four volunteers to draw a portion of the corpse as you flip up the previous components so that they can't see the figure developing until it's finished. Either way you play this game, the resulting images are sure to have surrealistic qualities. Other activities illustrating surrealism can be found in Joyce Raimondo's book *Imagine That! Activities and Adventures in Surrealism*.

Next, introduce abstract art to the teens. Most people are familiar with this art form as the type of creative expression that invokes comments like "Geez, even *I* could do that!" or "Why is that worth so much money? It looks like a bunch of scribbles!" In fact, abstract art is similar to surrealism because the images rendered are not realistic due to the artists' purposeful distortion of their subjects. Cubism is one form of abstract art that presents recognizable, albeit distorted, images painted from various viewpoints. Other forms of abstract art are much more free-form, and may focus primarily on shapes and colors to evoke feelings. Three well-known abstract artists are Pablo Picasso, Georges Braque, and Jackson Pollack.

Making sun prints is one activity you could use to demonstrate abstract art. Before the program, collect a fairly large assortment of objects from around home and in the library. Your collection could include things like paper clips, keys, bits of string, articles of clothing, leaves or flowers, seashells, pieces of lace, or small figurines. On photosensitive paper, have the teens arrange a selection of the objects in such a way that the objects' outlines will combine to create a new image. With the objects still arranged on the paper, expose the paper to sunlight for a few minutes, then soak the paper in a tray of water to develop the image. The result will be an example of abstract art. Photosensitive paper can be purchased at art supply or craft stores, or from online retailers such as Dick Blick Art Materials (www.dickblick.com) or Porter's Camera Store (www.porters.com).

The idea for this second activity was adapted from one offered by KinderArt® (www.kinderart.com). To illustrate abstract expressionism, read a set of instructions aloud to your teen participants who are armed with markers and paper. The instructions could consist of directives such as "draw three lines from one edge of the paper to the other," "draw six circles of any size," and "fill in three areas of the paper any way you want." After the teens are finished drawing what they heard, ask them to sign their pieces of abstract art, then share them with the group. The variation among the artwork, despite being created from the same set of directions, will illustrate the concept that abstract art often relies on individual perspectives rather than a defined set of rules.

Whether you use all four of these art activities, or just two of them, depends on how much time you have. Whenever you plan on wrapping up this part of the program, though, arrange for a field trip to a local museum in order to view examples of surreal and abstract art. Obviously, if you live in an urban area this will be easier to do than in suburban or rural areas. If going to a museum is impossible, find examples of these two art forms in art books or on the Internet and project them onto a screen or wall for the teens to view as a group. If there is a museum in your area, however, call ahead of time to find out which pieces it houses that are representative of surreal and abstract art. Also, inquire about the locations of these pieces within the museum. The American Association of Museums (www.aam-us. org) is a good source to consult for lists of museums in your state.

At this point, it is important to mention some precautions that should be taken when arranging for a program to take place off-site. First, if your library is situated within walking distance of the museum, it will be easy to arrange for the group to walk there together. If the museum is further away, public transportation is a viable option. Most libraries, however, are probably located fair distances from the nearest art museum, in which case it may be necessary to car pool. In any case, it will be necessary to receive written permission from the teens' parents or guardians before allowing them to participate in an off-site program. Make sure the permission forms have a space for a phone number should an emergency require reaching a teen's parent or guardian.

After arriving at the museum, hand out a photocopied list of the surreal and abstract pieces housed at the museum to be used as a guide for a sort of scavenger hunt. Set the teens loose with a map of the museum so they can locate each piece, and give them plenty of time to locate the surreal and abstract art, as well as explore other areas of the museum they may be interested in seeing. Instruct the group to reconvene at a specific time and place in order to talk about what they saw. You could award small prizes like art supplies or items from the museum's gift shop to those who complete the scavenger hunt.

Time, Cost, and Supplies

This program is easy to plan, and very cost-effective. Three to four hours is all you should need to promote the program, gather the art supplies, round up some art books, and contact the museum. The supplies you will need consist of

colored pencils, oil pastels, or markers

white paper

photosensitive paper

various objects collected from home or the library

flip chart paper with easel (optional)

prizes (optional)

Promotion

One of the most famous examples of surreal art is Magritte's *The Son of Man*, a portrait of a man wearing a suit and a derby hat, with a large, green apple covering most of his face. For an in-house display at your library, re-create this painting along with the caption "Uncover the Mysteries of Art." If you have access to a secure glass case, you may want to enhance the display with art supplies such as an easel, sketch pads, or oil pastels. If your space cannot be locked, however, you could easily cut out one or two painter's palettes from brown construction paper and mimic the small quantities of paint with multicolored, irregularly shaped "splotches." Make sure to pass out flyers promoting this event to art teachers, community recreation centers that may have art classes, art studios, and art supply stores. It may save you some hassle if you design the bottom third of the flyer to be a registration form that requires a parent or guardian's signature granting permission for their teen to take the trip to the museum.

Collection Connection

Fiction (featuring characters who are artists)

Better than Running at Night—Hillary Frank (Houghton Mifflin, 2002)

Bittersweet—Drew Lamm (Clarion Books, 2003)

Buddha Boy—Kathe Koja (Farrar, Straus and Giroux, 2003)

Casa Azul: An Encounter with Frida Kahlo—Laban Carrick Hill (Watson-Guptill Publications, 2005)

Chasing Vermeer—Blue Balliett (Scholastic, 2004)

Dante's Daughter—Kimberley Hueston (Front Street, 2003)

Drawing Lessons—Tracy Mack (Blue Sky Press, 2002)

Freewill—Chris Lynch (HarperCollins, 2001)

Harley Like a Person—Cat Bauer (Winslowhouse International, 2001)

In Summer Light—Zibby O'Neal (Starfire, 1986)

Myrtle of Willendorf—Rebecca O'Connoll (Front Street, 2000)

The Outcasts of 19 Schuyler Place—E. L. Konigsburg (Atheneum, 2004)

Pictures of Hollis Woods—Patricia Reilly Giff (Wendy Lamb Books, 2002)

Saffy's Angel—Hilary McKay (Margaret K. McElderry, 2002)

Shizuko's Daughter—Kyoko Mori (Fawcett, 1994)

Simon Says—Elaine Marie Alphin (Harcourt Children's Books, 2002)

A Single Shard—Linda Sue Park (Clarion Books, 2001)

Smoking Mirror: An Encounter with Paul Gauguin—Douglas Rees (Watson-Guptill Publications, 2005)

Speak—Laurie Halse Anderson (Farrar, Straus and Giroux, 1999)

Spirit Catchers: An Encounter with Georgia O'Keefe—Kathleen V. Kudlinski (Watson-Guptill Publications, 2004)

The True Meaning of Cleavage—Mariah Fredericks (Atheneum, 2003)

The Truth about Forever—Sarah Dessen (Viking Juvenile, 2004)

The Wedding: An Encounter with Jan Van Eyck—Elizabeth M. Rees (Watson-Guptill Publications, 2005)

Nonfiction

Andy Warhol: Prince of Pop—Jan Greenberg (Delacorte Books for Young Readers, 2004)

The Annotated Mona Lisa: A Crash Course in Art History from Prehistoric to PostModern—Carol Strickland (Andrews McMeel Publishing, 1992)

Frida Kahlo and Diego Rivera: Their Lives and Ideas—Carol Sabbeth (Chicago Review Press, 2005)

Getting to Know the World's Greatest Artists series—various authors (Children's Press)

The Mad, Mad, Mad World of Salvador Dali—Angela Wenzel (Prestel Publishing, 2003)

Salvador Dali and the Surrealists: Their Lives and Ideas—Michael Elsohn Ross (Chicago Review Press, 2003)

DAY OF THE DEAD ($$) (GRADES 7–10)

Are you tired of throwing some version of a Halloween party every October? Chances are, if you're sick of candy corn and costume parties, so are your teens. To shake things up a bit, try this program that puts a cultural spin on things, but still maintains the spirit of the season.

Mexico's Day of the Dead (El Dia de los Muertos) is celebrated at the very end of October through the first two days of November. According to Ricardo J. Salvador, this is a festive time rather than a morbid one, despite the macabre elements (Salvador 2003). To observers, it might seem a strange celebration indeed, but when one understands native Mexicans' reverence for the circle of life and their strong connections to family and loved ones, the spirit of the holiday becomes clear. Kathy Cano-Murillo describes the holiday by saying, "In Mexico the concept of dying . . . is respected and acknowledged as part of the wondrous cycle of life. . . . Mexican families and friends are saddened when their loved ones pass on, but they use El Dia de los Muertos as a way to rejoice over their loved one's journey on Earth and the beginning of a new one in the afterlife" (Cano-Murillo 2002). Therefore, throughout this festive time, families gather in cemeteries to have picnics and adorn the grave sites of loved ones with bright flowers, and even offer food, drink, and cigarettes for the spirits of their dearly departed. In their homes, Mexicans assemble shrines filled with memorabilia and their loved ones' favorite things in an effort to entice and welcome the departed souls into the home to be honored and remembered. Many times, communities will also hold street fairs with art booths, food stands, and processions including strolling musicians and lots of people dressed as skeletons. In the end, this holiday is a joyous and somber occasion all at the same time in that it gives Mexicans a chance to receive closure for, and to celebrate, the lives of those dearly missed.

This program will familiarize teens with Mexico's Day of the Dead through a short introduction, with traditional food and music enhancing the atmosphere. The primary activity, however, will consist of making pocket shrines to honor departed spirits.

How

Librarians who work in areas with large Hispanic populations may not need to spend time introducing the concept of the Day of the Dead to the teen participants. However, if necessary, spend five to ten minutes giving a brief overview, showing pictures of the festivities if possible. To set the mood for the program, play some authentic Mexican music in the background.

The majority of the time at this program, though, will be spent making pocket shrines. Let the teens know that, traditionally, shrines are religious monuments created to honor the dead, but that they can also be very whimsical and celebratory—even comical—in nature. Mexicans in particular create colorful, fanciful shrines on the Day of the Dead. Shrines can be very large, but the pocket shrines teens will create at this program can carry an object that will help them remember and honor loved ones, pets, or even famous people who have passed away but have left a mark on their hearts.

First, ask the teens to think of someone they would like to honor with a shrine. Obvious choices would include parents, grandparents, siblings, friends, or neighbors who may have passed away. If a teen is fortunate enough not to have lost a loved one, he or she may have had a special pet to remember. Alternatively, some teens may greatly admire someone famous who has died. For instance, the deaths of John Lennon and Kurt Cobain shocked and saddened many people in the early 1980s and mid-1990s, respectively. Princess Diana is another famous individual whose death moved many to erect makeshift shrines all over the world. To illustrate this point, it may be a good idea to show pictures of Strawberry Fields in New York City, or the Alma Bridge in Paris, where a statue of a golden flame commemorates Princess Di's death. If any of the teen participants have trouble thinking of someone to memorialize with a pocket shrine, encourage them to honor their personal heroes, or anyone who has been a source of inspiration to them. This could include a favored aunt or uncle; an admired writer, actor, band, or musician; an athlete or sports team; or even imaginary figures like Superman or Bugs Bunny. Finally, shrines don't have to honor a person. Other ideas for shrines include

- a special place (the beach, New York City, or one's own home)
- a significant event (a family reunion, a concert, or a memorable vacation)
- a dream or goal (to travel to Paris, to visit every major league baseball stadium, or to attend college)
- a hobby or passion (playing an instrument, writing poetry, or watching horror movies)
- a personal quality (serenity, patience, or courage).

Show the teens examples of the different kinds of shrines to serve as inspiration. To date, pocket shrines haven't really "caught on," but here are three Web sites containing examples:

Aisling's Art Gallery
www.aisling.net/gallery/gallery-shrines.htm

Shrines of Jen Worden
jenworden.com/faves/shrines/index.html

Spinster Spin—Tiny Little Shrine
www.spinsterspin.com/?q=node/24

Regardless of the theme they choose, the teens should think of the shrines as a way to pay homage to something special in their lives through respect, remembrance, and reverence—three concepts that meld nicely with Mexico's Day of the Dead.

Once the teens have thought of a theme for their shrines, allow them some time to brainstorm about what to put in them. Small objects, quotations, and images that relate to their subjects should all be considered. Cano-Murillo suggests using glitter, trinkets, and rhinestones for celebratory projects; velvet, lace, vintage collectibles, and muted colors are best for an elegant or aged look; and, found objects, word clippings and beads work well for eclectic or artsy shrines (Cano-Murillo 2002). In addition, teens can bring items of their own from home; tiny plastic figurines or shells, artificial flowers, or anything else in miniature can be added.

Next, let the teens get to work assembling their shrines, and encourage them to use their creativity and to have fun. Empty Altoid® tins serve nicely as containers for pocket shrines. Instruct the teens to cover the outside (and inside if they desire) with paint, a collage using decoupage medium, fabric scraps and glue, or a combination of all of these techniques. Make sure, though, that they are careful not to get glue on the hinge of the tin as this can prevent it from closing properly. Then, the teens can adorn the outside with an object or two that represents what's being honored inside along with braid, fringe, buttons, or glitter. For the inside, the participants may well be able to create the look they want using objects you've collected, but it may be necessary for them to wait until they get home to finish the project. That way, they can collect more specific objects or trinkets such as, for example, a dried flower saved from a loved one's funeral. To wrap up the program, allow time for the teens to share what they've created with the rest of the group.

Time, Cost, and Supplies

This can be a fairly inexpensive and quick program to pull together. You may want to make a prototype of a shrine to have as a concrete example to show the teens, which could take a little time, depending on how creative you are. Outside of that, however, you should only need to allot time for gathering books and pictures illustrating Mexico's Day of the Dead, and collecting the materials necessary to make the pocket shrines. A list of supplies might include

Altoid tins

glue

decoupage medium

small brushes

metallic paint

fabric scraps or lace

wrapping paper or origami paper

old magazines

scissors

glitter, braid, or string

buttons, shells, or beads

rubber stamps and ink

quotation books

Scrabble letters, postage stamps, postcards, game pieces, dice, doll
    clothes, and shoes

Many of these objects may be readily available lying around your house or library. To find things like small old toys or vintage postcards, consider stopping by an antique or "junk" shop to forage for cheap trinkets. Craft stores often have items like this as well, but prices may be higher there.

Promotion

By using the bright colors of this Mexican celebration, your display is sure to attract attention. Decorate a blank space within your library with two or three hinged cardboard skeletons usually readily available in party supply stores this time of year. Position the skeletons so that they appear to be dancing, and consider fashioning sombreros or maracas for them as well. Then surround the celebratory skeletons with bright paper streamers, three-dimensional crepe fans or spheres, and, if possible, potted marigolds. The phrase "Celebrate Mexico's Day of the Dead" will explain the purpose of the display, and a reserved spot within the display should highlight one or two pocket shrines as examples of the craft project that will take place at the program. Beside the display, consider stacking registration forms, directions for how to make the pocket shrines, and some of the titles mentioned in the section below.

Collection Connection

Fiction (featuring Mexican or Mexican-American characters)

The Beet Fields—Gary Paulsen (Laurel Leaf, 2002)

Border Crossing—Maria Colleen Cruz (Pinata Books, 2003)

Buried Onions—Gary Soto (Harcourt Children's Books, 1997)

CrashBoomLove: A Novel in Verse—Juan Felipe Herrera (University of New Mexico Press, 1999)

Crazy Loco: Stories—David Rice (Puffin, 2003)

Jesse—Gary Soto (Harcourt Children's Books, 1994)

Parrot in the Oven—Victor Martinez (Joanna Cotler, 1996)

Quincenera Means Sweet 15—Veronica Chambers (Hyperion, 2001)

Sammy and Juliana in Hollywood—Benjamin Alire Sbaenz (Cinco Puntos Press, 2004)

Under the Feet of Jesus—Helena Maria Viramontes (Plume, 1996)

Nonfiction

Altered Book Collage—Barbara Matthiessen (Sterling, 2005)

Crafting Personal Shrines: Using Photos, Mementos, and Treasures to Create Artful Displays—Carol Owen (Lark, 2004)

The Days of the Dead: Mexico's Festival of Communion with the Departed—John Greenleigh (Pomegranate Communications, 1998)

Making Shadow Boxes and Shrines—Kathy Cano-Murillo (Rockport Publications, 2002)

Through the Eyes of the Soul, Day of the Dead in Mexico—Mary J. Andrade (La Oferta, 1999)

When Time Is Short and Money Is Tight...

Host a bingo party—but instead of B-I-N-G-O, have the cards spell out C-A-N-D-Y in recognition of Halloween. Use candy corn for the game pieces and give out—you guessed it—candy to the winners.

Hold a pumpkin-carving contest.

Meet in the library after-hours; dim the lights, then share ghost stories and urban legends.

REFERENCES

Cano-Murillo, K. (2002). Making shadow boxes and shrines. Gloucester, MA: Rockport Publishers.

KinderArt (n.d.). A unique drawing experience. Retrieved June 18, 2005, from KinderArt Web site: http://www.kinderart.com/drawing/drawex.shtml.

Rubin, W. (1968). *Dada and surrealist art*. New York: Harry N. Abrams.

Salvador, R. J. (2003). What do Mexicans celebrate on the day of the dead? In *Death and Bereavement in the Americas* (Vol. 2, pp. 75–76). Amityville, NY: Baywood Publishing Company.

Chapter 11

NOVEMBER

November is a time for thankfulness. This month, teens will glimpse slices of history while teaching senior citizens how to revisit their past, in a project called "Living History." Through this intergenerational program, the generation gap may close a bit as a time capsule of personalized histories is developed, fostering teens' appreciation for history and their elders. With the skills teens learn in the HTML workshop that follows, some of those memories may even be able to be digitized into an online collection of local history for your community. Finally, the Anti-Bullying Campaign, inspired by the Mix It Up Day that takes place each November, will help teens become more aware of their differences with each other and hopefully learn to embrace them a bit better.

LIVING HISTORY ($$) (GRADES 7–12)

One of my favorite books of all time is *The Education of Little Tree* by Forrest Carter. In it, Carter tells the story of how he came to live with his Cherokee grandparents after being orphaned when he was 5 years old, and the amazing but simple life he led from that point forward. Through simply told stories and gentle lessons, Little Tree blossoms; his grandparents' steadfast guidance and love is all he needs.

These days, there seems to be a disconnect between generations. Teenagers and senior citizens, in particular, have little in common on the surface, resulting in misunderstanding and a lack of appreciation for one another. To complicate matters, "gone are the days when a family's generations grew up one after another in uninterrupted succession in the same city. . . . Because of this growing trend toward the scattering of families, today's children often grow up without much exposure to their grandparents—or, for that matter, to any elderly people" (Zinn 2002). At the same time, seniors are enjoying longer lives due to advances in health care so that the quality of life in their golden years is vastly better than, say, their own grandparents' was. An intergenerational program, therefore, could have enormous benefits for both teens and seniors. According to a recent article about mixed-age gatherings, intergenerational programs "highlight the wisdom of older family members, while preventing them from becoming marginalized [and] allow teenagers to gain respect for the elderly" (Wilford 2005).

"Living History" is one such program. Over the course of two afternoons, teens will teach seniors specific computer skills while the older adults relate a poignant story from their personal history to create an artifact for a time capsule of sorts. Little Tree understood the importance of such an exercise. He said, "Granma and Granpa wanted me to know of the past, for 'If ye don't know the past, then ye will not have a future. If ye don't know where your people have been, then ye won't know where your people are going'" (Carter 1976).

How

Begin the program with an icebreaker activity. Have each of the participants say their names and ages, then pass out a bowl of M & M candies asking each person to take one. Then, depending on the color they've chosen, each participant should answer a specific question.

- For red, name a defining moment in your generation's history.
- For brown, name an important cultural influence on your generation.
- For light brown, name an important invention in your lifetime.
- For green, name a famous person from your generation.
- For yellow, state what is most important to you.
- For orange, state what you think is most important to older/ younger generations.

Depending on the size of your group, you may choose to pass the bowl of candy around a number of times to give everyone an opportunity to answer a variety of questions.

After the icebreaker, split the group into pairs consisting of one teen and one senior. Allow a few minutes for the pairs to get acquainted, encouraging them to share a little of their backgrounds with one another and to reflect on the icebreaker activity. Next, explain that each pair of participants should create an artifact to be placed into a time capsule at the end of the program. The artifact should consist of a personalized history of a significant moment in the senior's life, along with pictures and memorabilia that illustrate that moment. To create this artifact, the teen participants will help their elder counterparts use the Internet to research some details and provide context for that specific historical snapshot. After interviewing their partners, the teens will also type and print the personalized histories using a word-processing program.

The first afternoon of "Living History" will consist mostly of helping the seniors pick the moment they'd like to preserve in the time capsule, and getting the teens started with the interview process. Some possibilities for the seniors to consider include

- How World War II affected their hometown
- How their family adjusted during the Great Depression
- Where they were the day John F. Kennedy was assassinated
- What school was like when they were teenagers
- What they remember about the day Neil Armstrong walked on the moon
- What teenagers used to do for entertainment
- What their first job was like
- What holidays were like when they were growing up
- What dating was like

Once they have selected a moment in time on which to concentrate, the interview process can begin. Armed with pens and paper for taking notes, the teens should allow their partners to reminisce about their chosen historical moment and attempt to engage them in dialogue about it as well. To prevent the conversation from dragging, however, some questions the teens could ask might be

- How old were you at the time?
- What was your family like? Did you have any siblings?
- Are there any songs you associate with this period in your life?
- Who was president at this time?
- Where did you live at this time?
- What clothes were fashionable?
- What did you like best about this time in your life? What did you like least?
- What were you most frightened of at that age?
- What were you looking forward to at that age?

After the interviews are completed, the "Living History" participants will be finished for the day.

The second day of the program will consist of compiling the information into the artifact that will be placed in the time capsule. The seniors should have been instructed at the end of the first day to bring an object or picture with them on the second day that represents the period in history they've chosen to record. The teens will have been told to type up their partner's recollections and save it as a computer file to be added to later. At this point, the pairs of participants should sit down at computer stations together to begin researching some background material on the Internet. The teens should let their partners control the mouse while instructing them through the process of finding information online. Concepts such as mouse skills, opening an Internet browser, and typing Internet addresses may be new to some of the senior citizens, so the teens should be prepared for this part of the program to move more slowly. Three sites they may want to visit together include the American Memory from the Library of Congress (memory.loc.gov/ammem/), Decades in 20th Century America (www.aclibrary.org/teenroom/decades.asp), and the National Museum of American History (americanhistory.si.edu/index.cfm). Looking at these sites and browsing others they may come across may spark other memories and details for the seniors to add to their personalized histories.

After the personalized histories are complete, they should be printed on archival quality paper, inserted into acid-free binders, and placed in the time capsule along with the objects the seniors brought with them. You could opt to bury the time capsule in the traditional manner, with the caveat that it shouldn't be opened until a specified date in the future. It may be more beneficial to your library and your community, however, if the time capsule is more like a preservation project that can be added to throughout the years and accessed by anyone at any time. In this way, the project could serve to preserve the posterity of your community's local citizens for years to come.

Time, Cost, and Supplies

This program is relatively inexpensive in that the only supplies you will need to purchase are the archival paper and storage binders. In addition, computers will be necessary for the participants to research their chosen memories. Although this program has been described as a two-day affair, you could opt to have it take place over several hours on a Saturday afternoon. All in all, however, "Living History" should not take an exorbitant amount of time to plan after the participants have been recruited (see the Promotion section below).

Promotion

An obvious audience for this program is grandparents and their teen grandchildren. But, as previously stated, there is a need for more mixed-age gatherings because grandparents don't always live near their grandkids. Therefore, this is the perfect program to coordinate in conjunction with your library's outreach department, or your community's senior centers and assisted-living facilities. With the help of these agencies, recruiting seniors to participate in this program should be easy. As for the teen participants, consider enlisting members of your teen advisory council to pair up with seniors for the pilot run of the program. Take pictures of the participants working together, and gather anecdotes and quotations from them to use in promotional pieces for the next time, when you may need to ask teachers or facilitators of after-school programs for help in recruiting new teens. As with many of the programs contained in this book, make sure to alert the media about "Living History" as this project has particular human interest aspects and local appeal.

Collection Connection

Fiction (featuring strong intergenerational relationships)

The Canning Season—Polly Horvath (Farrar, Straus and Giroux, 2003)

Checking on the Moon—Jenny Davis (Laurel Leaf, 1993)

City of the Beasts—Isabel Allende (Rayo, 2002)

Cold Sassy Tree—Olive Burns (Houghton Mifflin, 1984)

Dancing on the Edge—Han Nolan (Harcourt Children's Books, 1997)

The Education of Little Tree—Forrest Carter (University of New Mexico Press, 2001)

Fair Weather—Richard Peck (Dial Books, 2001)

Freak the Mighty—Rodman Philbrick (Scholastic Paperbacks, 2001)

Freewill—Chris Lynch (HarperCollins, 2001)

Gracie's Girl—Ellen Wittlinger (Simon and Schuster Children's Publishing, 2000)

Homecoming—Cynthia Voigt (Atheneum, 1981)

Kit's Wilderness—David Almond (Delacorte Books for Young Readers, 2000)

Lena—Jacqueline Woodson (Laurel Leaf, 2000)

A Long Way from Chicago—Richard Peck (Dial, 1998)

Loose Threads—Laurie Ann Grover (Margaret K. McElderry, 2002)

Marisol and Magdalena: The Sound of Our Sisterhood—Veronica Chambers (Scholastic, 2001)

Ruby Holler—Sharon Creech (Joanna Cotler, 2002)

Rules of the Road—Joan Bauer (Putnam Publishing Group, 1998)

The Same Stuff as Stars—Katherine Paterson (Clarion Books, 2002)

Stand Tall—Joan Bauer (Grosset and Dunlap, 2002)

Strays Like Us—Richard Peck (Puffin, 2000)

Toning the Sweep—Angela Johnson (Orchard Books, 1993)

Walk Two Moons—Sharon Creech (HarperCollins, 1994)

Words of Stone—Kevin Henkes (Greenwillow, 1992)

Yellow Raft in Blue Water—Michael Dorris (Picador, 2003)

Zazoo—Richard Mosher (Clarion Books, 2001)

HTML HOW-TO ($) (GRADES 7–12)

According to a 2005 report by the Pew Internet and American Life Project, "The number of teenagers using the internet has grown 24% in the past four years and 87% of those between the ages of 12 and 17 are online"

(Lenhart 2005). This probably comes as no surprise; today's teens have grown up with e-mail and the Internet. Considering that fact, however, leads one to question whether teens really understand how the Internet works. Certainly some do, and many design their own Web pages and start their own blogs with this seemingly inherent knowledge. Others, however, are likely to take technology for granted because it has been such an integral part of their lives all along. They use computers to communicate, seek information, and play games, but they may not know how it all works. Like prior generations who grew up with television, or radio for that matter, how many of those teenagers really understood how those things operated? Most of us take advantage of the things that make our lives easier, but we don't always have the knowledge about how those inventions work. Why is it, then, that so many adults assume teenagers are any different?

In answer to this question, this program will teach teens the basics of HTML at a hands-on workshop. With the skills they learn, the participants will have the opportunity to design their own personal Web pages to be linked from your library's teen advisory board Web site. A discussion about what makes a good Web site will ensue, giving the teens a chance to voice their opinions about how the library's site appeals—or doesn't appeal—to their age-group.

How

This section is not intended to teach you HTML. Rather, it will point out some of the key concepts your workshop should cover, and direct you to resources that will aid you along the way. That said, don't worry if you don't understand HTML yourself. If this is the case, it would be a good idea to ask someone else to lead the workshop so you could learn right alongside the teen participants. For instance, if you ask your library's technology coordinator for a hand, that individual could teach the workshop and, at the same time, gain some insight into what teens in your community think of the usability and appeal of your library's Web site. He or she might be able to implement some of the teens' suggestions later. If you still wish you had just a basic understanding of HTML before getting started, check out one of these books:

- *HTML for the World Wide Web with XHTML and CSS*—Elizabeth Castro
- *SAMS Teach Yourself HTML 4 in 24 Hours*—Dick Oliver et al.
- *Teach Yourself Visually HTML*—Ruth Maran

Some Web sites to consult include

HTML Goodies
www.htmlgoodies.com/primers/html/article.php/3478131

Introduction to HTML
www.cwru.edu/help/introHTML/toc.html

WEBalley
http://www.weballey.net/

Web Developer's Virtual Library
www.wdvl.com/Authoring/HTML/

To start off, some questioning teens may wonder what the point is in learning HTML when there are programs like Macromedia Dreamweaver and Microsoft Frontpage that will create Web sites without it. The reason many still believe in the importance of learning HTML rather than relying on a Web-authoring software product is that a basic understanding can help one troubleshoot problems with Web pages, or tweak them to a greater degree of precision. HTML is also the nuts and bolts of Javascript, another, more sophisticated, markup language.

Start the workshop with a discussion about what makes a good Web site versus what makes a bad one. Here are some points to cover when helping the teens determine what makes a good Web site:

- Both the content and the design of a Web site are important and should work well together (i.e., a Web site about the Holocaust should not have images of, for example, clowns or balloons).
- The user should quickly be able to tell what the Web site is about.
- The content should be updated regularly, spelled correctly, and should offer some original work rather than just a list of links.
- The Web site should load quickly.
- The Web site should be easily navigable.
- The Web site's design should include "white space" (places for the user's eye to rest) and should be readable (e.g., black text on a white page works much better than lime green text on a yellow page).

There may be other points the teens bring up as this discussion ensues. Allow some time for them to contemplate what problems they have encountered with some sites, and what features they have appreciated. Since a picture is worth a thousand words, illustrate these concepts with a selection of both well-designed and poorly designed Web sites. Some sites that belong in the Web site Hall of Fame include:

www.google.com

www.kidshealth.org

www.ipl.org

Those that belong in the Web site Hall of Shame include:

www.tinawilliford.com/Annoying/Frameset1.html

www.angelfire.com/super/badwebs/main.htm

www.goingclear.org/

After discussing the merits and shortcomings of the above Web sites, turn the teens' attention to your library's Web site. Have them apply the same set of criteria to the site, and allow them time to share their opinions about what could be changed or improved, particularly on the teen services portion of the Web site.

Now it's time for the teens to apply the concepts of good design to their very own Web pages using HTML. As previously stated, you may opt to have someone else teach this portion of the workshop. Since it will be important for the teens to get their hands dirty, so to speak, while learning this new skill, you will likely need to limit the amount of participants so each teen can have his or her own computer on which to work. The time of day at which you offer this workshop will depend on how many computers your library has, and whether or not they are housed in a lab. In other words, if your library has only a few public computer stations for general use, you may have to hold the workshop after-hours. In any case, one nice thing about teaching HTML is that the only software required to create Web sites using this language is Notepad and an Internet browser, both of which are installed on most computers.

The basic idea behind HTML is that it is a type of language that "talks" to the computer's Internet browser to tell it how to display a Web page. HTML, which stands for Hyper Text Markup Language, is made up of a set of codes that include opening and closing tags that tell the computer what to do. For instance, a word enclosed in the opening and closing tags of **and** will be displayed in bold lettering. At this point, share the basic HTML tags with the teens, then show them how to type them up in Notepad. The tags you should be sure the teens learn include

```
<html>
<head>
<title>
<body>
<p> = paragraph
<br> = line break
<ol> = ordered list
<ul> = unordered list
<li> = list item
<a href> = anchor tag used for links
<img src> = image source
<body bgcolor> = body background color
<font color>
```

After demonstrating how to save the files they have created in Notepad and reopen them with the computer's browser, teens will be amazed at how easy it is to create their own site. For the next couple of hours, the instructor should teach teens how to add sophistication to their Web pages with color, headings, and even cascading style sheets (CSS).

By the end of the program, the teens will have learned the basics of HTML and used their new knowledge to create their own personal Web pages that can be linked from your library's teen advisory board page. Try to have a digital camera on hand to take the participants' pictures so that they can use them on their Web pages. With the teens' input and personalization, this portion of the Web site may become more heavily used by the audience you hope to reach.

Time, Cost, and Supplies

This program does require some expensive equipment—specifically, several computer stations and a digital camera. Since your library most likely owns all of this equipment already, however, the costs for this program can be kept to a minimum. Other than some handouts and the materials needed for promotional purposes, there are no supplies required.

Promotion

In a display case or on a blank wall, cleverly describe the program's details using HTML tags created with an Ellison machine, or just in a large font on a computer. The description should look similar to this:

```
<html>
<head>
<title>LEARN HTML</title>
</head>
<body>
Tuesday, November 4 at 4 pm here at Anytown Library. Bring a friend!
Registration at the reference desk is required.
</body>
</html>
```

You could even make this coding look like it's on a computer screen by using the Courier typeface on a black background and drawing a computer monitor around it. Make sure to connect your library's collection to the program by placing books about HTML and Web site design in or near the display.

Collection Connection

Fiction (featuring teens who use the Internet)

Amy—Mary Hooper (Bloomsbury USA Children's Books, 2002)

ChaseR: A Novel in E-Mails—Michael Rosen (Candlewick, 2002)

Confessions of a Boyfriend Stealer (a Blog)—Robynn Clairday (Delacorte Books for Young Readers, 2005)

Firestorm—Jordan Cray (Simon Pulse, 1997)

Heart on My Sleeve—Ellen Wittlinger (Simon and Schuster Children's Publishing, 2004)

The Last Dance—Tim Lahaye (Westbow Press, 2002)

Love, Sara—Mary Beth Lundgren (Henry Holt and Company, 2001)

One of Those Hideous Books Where the Mother Dies—Sonya Sones (Simon and Schuster Children's Publishing, 2004)

Rob&Sara.com—P. J. Peterson and Ivy Ruckman (Delacorte Books for Young Readers, 2004)

Snail Mail No More—Ann Martin and Paula Danzinger (Scholastic, 2000)

Stalker—Jordan Cray (Simon Pulse, 1998)

ttyl—Lauren Myracle (Harry N. Abrams, 2004)

The Year My Life Went down the Loo—Katie Maxwell (Dorchester Publishing Company, 2003)

Year of Secret Assignments—Jaclyn Moriarty (Arthur A. Levine, 2004)

Nonfiction

Dave's Quick 'n' Easy Web Pages: An Introductory Guide to Creating Web Sites—Dave Lindsay (Erin Publications, 2001)

HTML and XHTML: The Definitive Guide—Chuck Musciano (O'Reilly, 2002)

HTML Goodies—Joe Burns (Que, 2002)

Web Pages That Suck: Learn Good Design by Looking at Bad Design—Vincent Flanders (Sybex, Inc., 2002)

ANTI-BULLYING CAMPAIGN ($$$$)
(GRADES 6–12)

All of us have encountered at least one bully in our lifetime, and the experience was likely so unpleasant that it wasn't soon forgotten. Bullies use ridicule, taunts, threats, and sometimes physical violence to intimidate their victims in an effort to make themselves feel more powerful. Sometimes, though, their tactics aren't so obvious. The movie *Mean Girls,* starring Lindsay Lohan, depicts a clique of girls who make those outside of their exclusive group feel like outcasts with subtle put-downs and pressure to conform. But as anyone who has ever attended a middle or high school could tell you, it's just not possible for everyone to fit the same mold—not everyone can be an athlete, or a cheerleader, or a musician, or an artist. Unfortunately, though, these differences are made so painfully clear that one could practically draw lines separating one group from another in the school's cafeteria. Rather than embracing their differences and getting to know all of their peers, teens often only associate with their "own kind."

Each November, Mix It Up at Lunch Day is promoted by the Southern Poverty Law Center and the Study Circles Resource Center. A Web site dedicated to this initiative (www.tolerance.org) offers resources, teen essays, and polls to promote tolerance and to fight hatred. A 2002 Mix It Up survey indicates the need for such a project stating, "A majority of middle and high school students said that schools were 'quick to put people into categories'; 40 percent admitted that they had rejected someone from another group; and one-third said it's hard to become friends with people in different groups" (Southern Poverty Law Center n.d.). The study also indicates that nowhere are these boundaries more clear than in the cafeteria. Therefore, Mix It Up at Lunch Day challenges students to sit with classmates from another social group or clique in an effort to soften those boundaries and, maybe, make some new friends.

No Name-Calling Week (www.nonamecallingweek.org), a similarly themed program, is aimed at a slightly younger demographic (students in fifth through eighth grade) and states this as their mission: "No Name-Calling Week is an annual week of educational activities aimed at ending name-calling of all kinds and providing schools with the tools and inspiration to launch an ongoing dialogue about ways to eliminate bullying in their communities" (No Name-Calling Week 2004). This project was inspired by James Howe's young adult novel *The Misfits*, in which five students who are tired of being bullied run for student council as a political party promising to wipe out name calling.

With over 900 schools participating in Mix It Up at Lunch Day and over 600 schools involved in No Name-Calling Week, it is clear that school administrators have welcomed the concept of educating teens about how to handle bullies, embrace their individuality, and fight stereotyping. Rather than reinvent the wheel, this program details how to help your local schools fight bullying through one of these established campaigns. The experience will kick off with a book discussion about *The Misfits* and will culminate in either Mix It Up at Lunch Day or No Name-Calling Week. After all, the truth is that there are adult bullies, too. By learning how to effectively deal with bullies at a younger age, teens will grow up to be more secure adults.

How

Since this program is so closely tied to school culture, it will be necessary to contact your local school system's administrators to introduce the concept of this program to them and to invite their participation. The first component to this program is to simply encourage administrators to join one of the already-formed campaigns mentioned above. Administrators can register their schools for the No Name-Calling network, or they could appoint teachers in their schools to help promote Mix It Up at Lunch Day through some of the helpful classroom activities listed on its Web site (www.tolerance.org/teach/activities/index.jsp). Put together packets of information about these campaigns and send them to the superintendent and the building principals along with a letter stating your willingness to be involved in the project. Follow up your letters with personal phone calls in an effort to set up face-to-face discussions about this project.

If your local schools agree to participate, it would be ideal to kick off the campaign with a book discussion about *The Misfits*. First, determine how many copies of the book each school would like to have. Although it would be great for each student to receive a copy of the book, this is highly unlikely for budgetary reasons. Therefore, suggest that the school library media specialists coordinate the circulation of multiple copies of the book throughout the student body. To encourage teens to check out a copy, ask the English and reading teachers to offer extra credit to those who read the book and attend a discussion. Then, ask the schools' library media specialists to act as book discussion facilitators. Alternatively, a random sample of students could be chosen as "ambassadors" to receive copies of the book and participate in a book discussion that you lead. A final option would be to have each English or reading teacher read parts of the book aloud in class throughout a period of time, and engage the students in a discussion at the end. In any case, multiple copies of the book will have to be obtained. Simon and Schuster does offer discounts for titles purchased in bulk. To receive a quote, contact the publisher's Special Sales Department at 1-800-456-6798. Another option would be to ask your local bookstore to make a donation.

A list of book discussion topics can be found at Simon and Schuster's Web site. Some of the discussion topics include questions like

- Which characters "celebrate their individuality" more than others?
- Is name calling a natural part of who we are, or is it learned?
- How does the No-Name Party "win" anyway?
- Does *The Misfits* present a realistic portrayal of life in middle school or junior high?
- What do you think of the expression "That's so gay," or "He/she is so gay"? Would your opinion be different if you were gay?
- Is it possible for unpopular kids to be friends with—or go out with—popular kids? If no, what gets in the way of making this possible? (Simon and Schuster n.d.)

A list of classroom activities is also provided on this site, some of which have cross-curricular connections. For example, students in government or civics classes could research the history of political parties in the United States and determine what platform they would choose if they had the opportunity to run for office. History students could learn about the history of name-calling and how it has led to oppression and ostracism throughout the years. One example of the power of name-calling took place during the Salem Witch Trials of the late seventeenth century, during which women were tortured and killed for being called a witch, whether or not they practiced witchcraft. And, of course, English or composition teachers could assign their students essays on the topic of bullying.

Clearly, the possibilities are exciting and endless if the whole school gets involved with this project. One final idea, although perhaps an expensive one, would involve asking either Mr. Howe, or an author of one of the other books about bullying listed below, to make an appearance at the school or your library. Chapter 10 contains more information about how to invite an author to your community.

Time, Cost, and Supplies

This program could be costly, but partnering with your school system will surely alleviate some of the financial burden. Also, there are grants available through Mix It Up (www.tolerance.org/teens/grants.jsp). The largest expense, by far, will be the books. The cost for other supplies—namely, promotional pieces to be used within the schools—could most likely be absorbed by the school. To implement this program properly, though, plan to spend time as well as money. Approach schools near the end of the previous school year to allow plenty of time for organizing and promoting No Name-Calling Week in November; for Mix It Up at Lunch Day in January, approach schools at the beginning of the school year.

Promotion

Although you can promote the good things the schools are doing with a display in your library and through press releases describing your partnership, most of the advertisement to teens will be handled by the administrators, teachers, and school library media specialists involved with the anti-bullying campaign. Your job will be to promote the availability of resources through your library and the two established campaigns in an effort to make the whole program go more smoothly. If, for instance, your local middle school wholeheartedly embraces No Name-Calling Week, it would be very helpful to those involved if you offered pathfinders on different cross-curricular topics related to bullying, harassment, stereotyping, and name calling. Also, make teachers aware of the lesson plans available on the campaigns' Web sites.

To help spread the antibullying message among teens, coordinate a time at your library to make T-shirts using the iron-on logos available through Mix It Up (www.tolerance.org/teens/posters.jsp) or just by designing their own.

Collection Connection

Fiction

Big Mouth and Ugly Girl—Joyce Carol Oates (Harper Tempest, 2003)

Breaking Point—Alex Flinn (Harper Tempest, 2002)

Buddha Boy—Kathe Koja (Farrar, Straus and Giroux, 2003)

Burger Wuss—M. T. Anderson (Candlewick, 2001)

Carrie—Stephen King (Doubleday, 1990)

The Chocolate War—Robert Cormier (Laurel Leaf, 1986)

Freak the Mighty—Rodman Philbrick (Scholastic Paperbacks, 2001)

Give a Boy a Gun—Todd Strasser (Simon Pulse, 2002)

Hit Squad—James Heneghan (Orca Book Publishers, 2003)

Loser—Jerry Spinelli (Joanna Cotler, 2002)

The Lottery—Beth Goobie (Orca Book Publishers, 2002)

The Misfits—James Howe (Atheneum, 2001)

Names Will Never Hurt Me—Jamie Adoff (Dutton Books, 2004)

On the Fringe—Don Gallo, editor (Speak, 2003)

The Pack—Elisa Lynn Carbone (Viking Juvenile, 2003)

Stargirl—Jerry Spinelli (Knopf Books for Young Readers, 2000)

Tangerine—Edward Bloor (Harcourt Children's Books, 1997)

Nonfiction

Everything You Need to Know about Peer Mediation—Nancy Rue (Rosen Publishing Group, 2001)

Mean Chicks, Cliques, and Dirty Tricks: A Real Girl's Guide to Getting through the Day with Smarts and Style—Erika V. Shearin Karres (Adams Media Corporation, 2004)

Odd Girl Speaks Out: Girls Write about Bullies, Cliques, Popularity and Jealousy—Rachel Simmons, editor (Harvest Books, 2004)

Please Stop Laughing at Me—Jodee Blanco (Adams Media Corporation, 2003)

When Time Is Short and Money Is Tight...

Peanut Butter Lovers' Month—Have fun with a bunch of weird activities centered on one of America's favorite condiments (but make sure no one has a peanut allergy first)! Hold a relay race using a peanut and chopsticks; have teens try to enunciate difficult words with peanut butter in their mouths; have a peanut butter tasting where teens try to differentiate between different brands of peanut butter.

At election time, educate teens about the different issues and set up ballot boxes for them to cast their votes; encourage them to suggest creative write-in candidates with a short explanation of why that person would make a good president/mayor/governor.

Have the teens defend their favorite books of the year at a mock Printz Award voting party.

REFERENCES

Carter, F. (1976). *The education of Little Tree*. New York: Delacorte.

Lenhart, A. (2005). Teens and technology: Youth are leading the transition to a fully wired and mobile nation. Retrieved August 26, 2005, from Pew Internet and American Life Project Web site: http://www.pewinternet.org/PPF/r/162/report_display.asp.

No Name-Calling Week (2004). About no name calling week. Retrieved August 19, 2005, from No Name-Calling Week Web site: http://www.nonamecalling week.org/cgi-bin/iowa/all/about/index.html.

Simon and Schuster (n.d.). The misfits teaching guide. Retrieved August 19, 2005, from Simon Says Web site: http://www.simonsays.com/content/content.cfm?sid=33&pid=412406&agid=21.

Southern Poverty Law Center (n.d.). Mix it up FAQ's. Retrieved August 19, 2005, from Mix It Up Web site: http://www.tolerance.org/teens/faqs.jsp.

Wilford, S. (2005). Gathering generations together in the classroom. *Early Childhood Today*, *19*(4), 18–19.

Zinn, L. (2002). What generation gap? *Nursing Homes Long Term Care Management*, *51*(1), 26–31.

Chapter 12

DECEMBER

'Tis the season! The holidays have arrived, and so has the end of the year—and this book! Chances are, your budget has dwindled down to nothing by this time of year, which is why the three programs offered in this chapter require very little cash. Oddly enough, though, two of them deal with money. "Take Stock" will enlighten teens about the basics of investing with a fun, interactive, stock-picking game. Maybe this will inspire some of the teen participants to invest any holiday money they might receive rather than spend it! On the other hand, the "Duct Tape Wallets" program—while on the surface is just a craft program—offers teens the opportunity to talk about the dark side of money and share their thoughts on the anti-consumerism movement. Finally, "Cyber-Safety" aims to teach teens how to safely navigate the Internet by offering advice about chat rooms, as well as teen consumer and Internet scam information.

TAKE STOCK ($) (GRADES 9–12)

"Yeah, yeah," I used to say to my mother, "pay myself first, I know!" Many teens, like me when I was that age, have endured their parents' or grandparents' lectures about the importance of saving a portion of every dollar they make, but how many of them really understand the importance of that advice? To a teenager, the idea of retirement is relegated to the distant future so that the here and now is all that seems important. Many teens probably think they have plenty of time to think about saving money and on one hand, they're right. It's true that younger people have many years ahead of them to work and save money, but it's also true that investments need that long to grow into a nest egg that's actually worth something. I was almost 30 years old before I really grasped the concept of compound interest. I remember seeing a chart (similar to the one in Appendix D) that blew my socks off. If I had saved all of the money my grandmother had systematically gifted to me throughout my late teens and twenties, I would be a millionaire by the time I reached retirement! I kicked myself for a little while, but then my mother gave me a book about investing that assured me all was not lost. My husband and I began to invest more proactively and aggressively (since neither of us were smart enough to do it when we were younger), but now we're on the right track and have sworn to bore our kids to tears with stories about the miracles of compound interest.

The simple fact is that Social Security and company pensions today are not the same systems on which our parents and grandparents so heavily relied. Most of us—and definitely those who are younger—will have to set up individual retirement accounts (IRAs) and become more educated about 401(k) plans in order to comfortably retire and enjoy our golden years. Again, most teens will brush off these warnings with the false sense of security that comes with youth. But, as the Motley Fool says on their Web site (www.fool.com), "This isn't your parents' retirement." The experts at the Motley Fool advise that younger generations should not expect to receive the entire benefit listed in their Social Security statements, and that pensions are a thing of the past. Furthermore, they say, "Of the three legs that may prop up your retirement, your personal savings are what you have the most control over" (Brokamp n.d.). Most financial advisors—not just the Motley Fool—believe that personally directed savings plans and investments are the best ways to achieve financial freedom.

Money Magazine reports, "Generation Y is more concerned about money than their older counterparts...with [s]ixty-six percent of kids between nine and 17 discuss[ing] with their parents how to save money" (Karchmer 2000). This leaves, though, one-third of the 60 million teens who make up Generation Y without anyone teaching them long-term savings strategies. In other words, teens today may be more concerned about money, but many of them have no idea what to do about it. This program will help teens grasp the basic concepts of investing while at the same time making the idea of saving money more appealing through an interactive simulation of the stock market.

How

"Take Stock" is a game that offers teens the opportunity to play the stock market without actually investing money. The stock choices represent real companies, and the prices for them are derived from their actual performance over the past few years. At the beginning of the program, it would probably be a good idea to introduce a few terms and concepts to the participants so they can play the game without feeling confused about unfamiliar financial jargon. Since many people consider economics to be a notoriously dry subject, you may consider asking someone from a bank or investment firm to assist you with this. Although it is entirely possible for you to go it alone, someone with a financial background may be able to impart an energy and enthusiasm for the subject that may otherwise be missing. A few simple definitions for words and phrases such as stock, mutual fund, return, share, bull market, bear market, and blue chip should be all that is necessary to familiarize the teens with the vernacular. To make this a bit more fun, introduce some of the slang used in the investment industry through a short matching quiz (Appendix H). If you need to brush up on some of this vocabulary yourself, visit Investopedia's dictionary (www.investopedia.com/dictionary).

Now that the teens are warmed up, pass out the stock worksheets (Appendix H) and explain the rules of "Take Stock." Each participant will start investing with the same amount of money. You can determine what this amount should be, but $10,000 will be the amount used for the purposes of explaining the game in this chapter. As you will see, there are several stocks listed on the worksheet, and most of them are familiar to teenagers. The reason companies like Coca-Cola and Nintendo are chosen is that these brands are more familiar to teens than, say, a bioengineering company, making it easier and more fun for them to pick stocks representing products they may recognize or have already used. If you decide that companies like Abercrombie & Fitch are not a good fit for your library's demographics, it's very easy to research other companies to provide as replacements using Big Charts (www.bigcharts.com). This Web site offers a ticker-symbol lookup feature and historical quotes for hundreds of companies. The worksheet mentioned above also provides the actual, historical prices of one share of each company's stock at three different times: the end of 2003, June 2004, and the end of 2004. Again, if you would like to update these figures, Big Charts provides historical quotes.

After allowing the teens to browse through the stock options, explain that they must decide how much of their $10,000 they want to invest in each company. One of the rules of this game is that the teens must diversify. In other words, the participants have to purchase at least ten of the fifteen stocks listed instead of investing their entire savings in just one or two of them. Inform inquiring minds that this practice minimizes the risk of losing money, which is the same reason mutual funds, portfolios of well-diversified mixtures of stocks and bonds, are very popular. Once the teens have decided how much money to invest in each company, arm them with calculators and instruct them to divide this amount by the price of one share to determine how many shares they must purchase.

Now, encourage the teens to imagine that life has been fast-forwarded six months. Then, using an overhead projector, a PowerPoint slide, or just another handout, reveal the prices of each company's stock for this point in time. Have the participants fill in these prices on their worksheet. The teens may be pleasantly surprised or dismayed about the changes in stock prices, depending on how they diversified. Now, the teens will have an opportunity to buy, sell, or hold. In other words, they can decide to buy more of one stock, sell one that isn't performing very well, or hold steady to see what happens next. Allow time for the teens to figure the math for any changes they decide to make. When I tried this program, I found it useful to have several volunteers from local banks on hand to help the teens with the math. Although it's not too difficult for the average teen to do on his own, having professionals on hand made the process go more smoothly and minimized interruptions for questions.

Next, reveal the prices of each company's stock for the close of that year and have the teens compute their profits or losses. Invite them to share the results of their first attempt at trading, and follow this up with a short wrap-up discussion led by a banker or a financial advisor that includes tips for playing the stock market. For instance, advise the teens to keep their eye on the news when investing in the stock market. Martha Stewart's company, for example, made one of the largest gains during the time period used for this game because of her conviction and subsequent release from prison. Conversely, Yahoo's stock dropped significantly, probably because of Google's rise to prominence as the world's foremost search engine.

At the end of the program, if you have the money and the inclination, you could offer a prize—a book about investing, for example—to the participant who made the largest profit.

Time, Cost, and Supplies

Contact someone from the financial industry about a month before the program to see if he or she would be willing to give you a hand introducing and wrapping up "Take Stock." Once this task is completed, look over the worksheet to see if you would like to make any changes to it. Photocopy the worksheets, the new pricing sheets, and the vocabulary quiz, then gather pencils and calculators for the teens to use. This program does not have any significant costs associated with it, unless you decide to purchase prizes or refreshments.

Promotion

One way to promote this program is through your library's Web site. An annotated webliography has been included in Appendix H for you to post as a tool, which teens can use as they begin thinking about investing. Promote this collection of sites to schools—particularly to economics teachers who may be willing to offer extra credit to students who attend the program. Within the library, cover a display space with as much green as possible by utilizing fake money and cutting out large, green dollar signs. Attract attention with the phrase "Find Your Fortune," and make sure any flyers promoting the program explain that participants will have the opportunity to play the stock market through a real-life simulation. If you have the money in your budget, consider visiting www.custom fortunecookies.com to have custom fortune cookies made to pass out with school lunches, or to teens in the library. The fortune in the cookie could read "Find Your Fortune," with the date, time, and location of the program printed underneath.

Collection Connection

Nonfiction

Early to Rise: A Young Adult's Guide to Investing—Michael Stahl (Silver Lake Publishing, 2005)

Get in the Game! The Girls' Guide to Money and Investing—Vanessa Summers (Bloomberg Press, 2001)

Growing Money: A Complete (And Completely Updated) Investing Guide for Kids—Gail Karlitz (Turtleback Books, 2001)

The Motley Fool Investment Guide for Teens: Eight Steps to Having More Money than Your Parents Ever Dreamed Of—David Gardner and Tom Gardner (Fireside, 2002)

Street Wise: A Guide for Teen Investors—Janet Bamford (Bloomberg Press, 2000)

Teenvestor: The Practical Investment Guide for Teens and Their Parents—Emmanuel Modu and Andrea Walker (Penguin Putnam, 2002)

Wall Street Wizard: Sound Ideas from a Savvy Teen Investor—Jay Liebowitz (Simon and Schuster Children's Publishing, 2000)

The Young Investor: Projects and Activities for Making Your Money Grow—Katherine R. Bateman (Chicago Review Press, 2001)

DUCT TAPE WALLETS ($) (GRADES 7–10)

There has been a teen trend toward anti-consumerism in recent years. While you may be hard pressed to find a teen not sporting some kind of label, those that purchase secondhand clothing or make their own duds are quick to point it out. They are making their own statement by eschewing commercialism and advertising, and turning their backs on everything considered too mainstream. I had a friend in college who wore a jacket she bought at the Salvation Army for two dollars; it was green with a school bus on it and the name "Donna" embroidered on the front. Even though my friend's name is Susan, she wore that jacket anyway, and I thought she was so unconventionally cool for it. At the same time, advertising agencies are targeting teens now more than ever.

The U.S. Census indicates that this generation—the offspring of the baby boomers—is the largest teen generation in our country's history. Couple that with the fact that many teens have part-time jobs but aren't saddled with many of life's expenses, and the spending potential becomes enormous. According to a recent study conducted by Teen Research Unlimited (TRU), "U.S. teens controlled an estimated $169 billion in disposable income last year [2004]—or $91 per week per teen" (Rosen 2005).

Some teens, though, turn up their noses at this rampant consumerism. This simple and inexpensive craft program will attract those teens who reject the latest fashions, practice recycling and vegetarianism, and wear secondhand shirts with other people's names on them. It can easily be touted as a craft program, but you may attract others with the promise of a discussion on teen tastes and trends, buying habits, and advertising campaigns.

How

This program couldn't be simpler, but it packs a big punch. After buying a few rolls of duct tape, make a prototype to display following the directions for making a wallet available in any of these resources:

3M Scotch® Duct Tape Workshop
www.3m.com/intl/CA/english/centres/home_leisure/duct_tape/dt_wallet.html

The Duck Tape Club
www.ducktapeclub.com/ducktivities/

The Duct Tape Guys': How To Make It Yourself with Duct Tape
www.octanecreative.com/ducttape/howto/

Ductigami: The Art of the Tape by Joe Wilson

Got Tape? Roll Out the Fun with Duct Tape! by Ellie Schiedermayer

Photocopy the directions to use them as handouts before the program, or for the participants to follow at the program. (This should be considered "fair use" according to copyright law, but be sure to cite the source for the directions you provide. If you're unsure, check with the book's publisher to gain permission.) After the teens arrive, show them the prototype you made as an example, and invite them to get started making their own wallets. Encourage them to use markers to decorate the outside, or to put a picture on the front enclosed under some laminate.

While the teens are working on their wallets, start an informal discussion about consumerism. Pass out a quiz about teen products and brand names (Appendix I), then draw their attention to some books on the topic. This may also be an opportune moment to introduce the topic of consumer safety. The "Teen Consumer Scrapbook" (www.atg.wa.gov/teen consumer/) has great information about telemarketing scams, modeling agency rip-offs, and pitfalls to avoid when choosing a cell phone plan. Whether your participants are anti-consumerists or Abercrombie-wearing, cell-phone-carrying consumers, they all can benefit from this information. Finally, you could also play excerpts from Janet Tashjian's *The Gospel According to Larry* on tape or CD as topical entertainment while the teens work on their wallets.

Promotion

To promote this program, consider what segment of the teen population you most want to attract. Teens interested in the anti-consumerism movement may be enticed by using dollar signs under the international "no" symbol (a circle with a cross through it) on posters and flyers. You may also pique the interest of other teens by using this same symbol in conjunction with famous brand names. Try using catchphrases like "Frugal Fashion: Make Your Own Duct Tape Wallet" or "No Money? No Problem! Make Your Own Duct Tape Wallet." On bulletin boards or in display areas, prominently display the books you have on duct tape crafts, but consider gathering resources on budget living, anti-consumerism, and marketing to teens. You could also display facts about advertising to raise teens' awareness of the strategies used to specifically target their age group.

Time, Cost, and Supplies

Other than duct tape, chances are your library already has the supplies necessary for this program. You will need

2–3 rolls of duct tape

scissors

colored permanent markers

magazines to cut out pictures (optional)

a few sheets of laminate (optional)

Clearly, the cost for this craft program is nominal and the time required to prepare for it is also quite reasonable.

Collection Connection

Fiction

Feed—M. T. Anderson (Candlewick, 2002)

Going, Going—Naomi Shihab Nye (Greenwillow, 2005)

The Gospel according to Larry—Janet Tashjian (Henry Holt and Company, 2001)

Jennifer Government—Max Barry (Doubleday, 2003)

So Yesterday—Scott Westerfeld (Razorbill, 2004)

Vote for Larry—Janet Tashjian (Henry Holt and Company, 2004)

Nonfiction

Branded: The Buying and Selling of Teenagers—Alissa Quart (Basic Books, 2004)

Ductigami: The Art of the Tape—Joe Wilson (Boston Mills Press, 1999)

Got Tape? Roll Out the Fun with Duct Tape!—Ellie Schiedermayer (KP Books, 2002)

Made You Look: How Advertising Works and Why You Should Know—Shari Graydon (Annick Press, 2003)

No Logo: No Space, No Choice, No Jobs—Naomi Klein (Picador, 2002)

Teen Consumer Smarts: Shop, Save, and Steer Clear of Scams—Francha Roffé Menhard (Enslow Publishers, 2002)

Why We Buy—Paco Underhill (Simon and Schuster, 2000)

CYBER-SAFETY ($) (GRADES 6–12)

While teenagers of my generation, and many before mine, passed notes surreptitiously in class or made phone calls after school to communicate with friends, teens today are way more technologically "dialed in." This comes as no surprise to teen services librarians, since walking into most public libraries after school reveals scads of teenagers glued to the public computer stations, typing e-mail messages, instant messaging (IMing) their buddies, or playing Runescape. Unfortunately, though, despite their level of comfort with it, teens aren't always smart about safety while using the Internet, making them prime targets for scams, hoaxes, or worse.

For the first time in 2003, the Gallup Poll asked about Internet crime and found that 6 percent of all respondents had either been a victim themselves, or live with a victim of a "computer or Internet-based crime, such as fraud or computer hacking" (Gallup Poll 2003), while using a computer at home. Additionally, according to a yearly survey conducted by the Computer Security Institute (CSI) in coordination with the FBI, "Losses reported per respondent due to unauthorized access crimes was up a huge 580 percent in 2005 over 2004, while theft of proprietary information because of a security breach rose 211 percent" (Keizer 2005). These numbers are high, but as with most types of danger, measures can be taken to help protect us from Internet crime. At this program, teens will learn about four different aspects of Internet safety and gain advice about chat rooms, as well as how to avoid Internet scams and hoaxes.

How

Many police departments nowadays have cyber units dedicated to handling crimes committed over the Internet. Before you spend a lot of time devising materials and an agenda for this program, contact the police in your area to see if someone on staff would be willing to partner with you. If you find a willing volunteer, he or she may already have pamphlets or a presentation prepared that could be the basis of your program. If you discover, however, that you'd like to cover more than what the police department offers, or that you will need to create this program from scratch, there are four main topics to consider.

Protecting Your PC

It makes sense to start this program with a brief introduction to some of the tools used to protect personal computers from viruses, spyware, and the like. After all, it would not make much sense to take extra precautions when shopping or communicating on the Internet if the computer itself is vulnerable to attack. For this portion of the program, consider inviting a staff member from your library's IT department to give a ten-minute tutorial on antivirus software, spyware, ad-ware, pop-up blockers, and cookies. Armed with the knowledge of how these software programs protect computer users from outside attacks, teens will be ready to move on to other safety issues.

Safe Searching

It is very unsettling when an innocent Internet search results in Web sites or images that are unwelcome. More than once, an embarrassed teen has been brave enough to approach me at the library's reference desk to tell me that he or she was conducting a search and accidentally stumbled across some pornographic material that can't be closed out from the screen. To prevent this from happening, the government has tied federal funding to Internet filtering compliance in public libraries. As we all know, however, filters aren't perfect, allowing some objectionable Web sites to seep through the safeguard. To help teens avoid this embarrassing distraction at home or in the library, encourage them to use kid-friendly search and research tools such as the following:

The Awesome Library
www.awesomelibrary.org

Ask Jeeves for Kids
www.ajkids.com

The Internet Public Library for Teens
www.ipl.org/div/teen

Kids Click
www.kidsclick.org

The Librarians' Index to the Internet
www.lii.org

Yahooligans!
www.yahooligans.com

Show some or all of these Web sites to your audience to prove to them that there are sophisticated Web-searching tools other than Google available.

Next, briefly go over some points to remember when evaluating a Web site's content. While entire library and information science courses are taught on this topic, a condensed version will be enough to make teens more aware of a Web site's merits and shortcomings. Pull up a couple of Web sites to compare and contrast them, then point out the things to look for, such as an author, a publishing or "last updated" date, the amount of space devoted to advertisements, and a noticeable bias. A great, albeit extreme, example to use is the vast difference between www.whitehouse.gov/kids and www.whitehouse.org/kids. At first glance, both sites look authoritative; they even have similar links in their menu bars and both sport the presidential seal. But a closer inspection will quickly reveal that the second site is published by a company called Chickenhead, rather than the United States government, and that it contains an obvious bias against the Bush administration. Since it is most likely that a teen conducting research about the White House will be looking for factual information, the spoof site can be disregarded as an inappropriate source for a school assignment.

Spotting a Scam

As has been established in the duct tape program described above, the teenaged demographic consumes a large chunk of the goods and services sold in this country. Many of them use the Internet to shop for electronics, downloadable games, and clothing, increasing their risk of having their identity stolen or getting scammed out of money without ever receiving the product they purchased. The Teen Consumer Scrapbook (www.atg. wa.gov/teenconsumer/index.htm), sponsored by the Washington State attorney general, contains valuable information about the scamming techniques used by sweepstakes companies, CD clubs, modeling agencies, cell phone providers, and credit card companies. Direct teens to this site for tips on how to avoid getting ripped off by recognizing the tactics used by some companies to fool unwitting consumers. Similar tactics are used by companies that target people via unsolicited e-mail messages, or spam. Following are some tips to remember when dealing with unsolicited e-mails:

- Never make a purchase from spam.
- Never reply to spam.
- Never click on links embedded in an e-mail from an unknown source trying to sell you something.
- Never provide personal information such as a social security number via e-mail.
- Be cautious when opening e-mails with subjects such as "Your Bill" or "Your Account Needs Attention" since most reputable companies, such as Amazon.com and eBay, promise not to request personal information via e-mail.
- Avoid get-rich-quick or work-from-home schemes advertised through spam.

When shopping for goods and services over the Internet, it's very common to be bombarded with ads, some more obvious than others. Many companies pay to have their advertisements strategically placed on search result screens, or in pop-ups. Show teens how to recognize an online advertisement, however cleverly disguised, and let them know that clicking on them could open up more unwanted pop-ups that can ultimately compromise the security of one's computer.

The Teen Consumer Scrapbook also deals with issues related to privacy, such as password protection, use of one's social security number, and identity theft. In addition to the helpful information contained on this site, here are some other key things teens should remember when making online purchases:

- Look for a small yellow padlock in the bottom right-hand corner of any site requesting credit card or personal information; this is the symbol for Secure Sockets Layer (SSL), a protocol used to transmit private documents online.
- Look for https:// or s-http:// at the beginning of a Web site address requesting credit card or personal information; the "s" stands for "secure."
- Devise passwords that are made up of numbers, letters, and symbols. The hardest passwords to crack contain symbols typed using the Alt key.
- Don't use the same password for every site requiring a registration.
- Use one credit card—not a debit card linked to a checking account—dedicated solely to online purchases.
- Make sure the shipping charges aren't exorbitant before agreeing to the purchase.
- Carefully read the description of the item you wish to purchase before agreeing to the sale. If you're unsure about the company, check the Better Business Bureau (www.bbb.org) for their rating.
- Shop with companies that also have a physical location, or at least a phone number.

Finding Friends

The Internet can be a great place to meet people, especially for teens who are shy in face-to-face situations. Online communities of people with shared interests, backgrounds, or problems abound on the Internet, using tools such as blogs, message boards, instant messaging, and even games to communicate with each other. It goes without saying, however, that some of these outlets are safer than others. According to Larry Magid of SafeKids.com, "Millions of children engage in chat and instant messaging every day and the overwhelming majority are not victimized" (Magid 2004). But, even though it is not extremely common, there have been several cases of "online enticement," involving teens being lured into meeting an online friend in person, only to find that an adult, or in some cases, a criminal, was behind the screen name. Teens need to have their wits about them when entertaining contact with someone they don't know on the Internet. Since this is a more sensitive safety issue with the potential for far more upsetting consequences, it may be best to have a police officer or other law enforcement official take the lead for this portion of the program.

Chat is one of the most common methods of online communication and is very popular with teens because, unlike e-mail that requires waiting for a response, it provides instant gratification. It is not uncommon for teens to chat with several of their friends at once using, for example, AOL's Instant Messenger. With a law enforcement official's help, make sure teens keep the following important tips in mind when entering a chat room:

- Use a gender-neutral screen name.
- Keep personal information, including your e-mail address, private.
- "Lurk" in a chat room or on a blog before signing up, to learn a little more about the type of people who communicate there.
- Use monitored forums.
- Leave the chat space anytime you feel bullied or uncomfortable.
- Do not send pictures of yourself over the Internet to people other than well-known friends or family members.

There are a number of Web sites committed to the online safety of children and teens. More information about chat rooms, instant messaging, and Internet scams can be found on these sites:

CyberAngels
www.cyberangels.org

Don't Believe the Type
tcs.cybertipline.com/

GetNetWise
www.getnetwise.org

I-Safe America
www.isafe.org

NetSmartz for Teens
www.netsmartz.org/netteens.htm

SafeKids.com
www.safekids.com

Now that the teen participants have been made aware of the potential dangers of the Internet and how to circumvent them, they can enjoy the benefits of online computing with fewer hassles, and happier parents. Award certificates to all of the teens who attended this program as a way of congratulating them for their initiative.

Time, Cost, and Supplies

There are virtually no supplies, and therefore few costs, associated with this program. Promotional materials, award certificates, and a computer with a projector are the only things you will need to conduct this workshop on cyber-safety. If you decide to ask a police officer and a representative from your library's IT department to help with portions of this program, make sure to ask them a couple of months in advance. If you decide to hand out bookmarks or pamphlets listing some of the tips or helpful Web sites mentioned in this section, plan on spending a couple of hours preparing those. Also, make sure to bookmark the Web sites you intend to exhibit for the participants ahead of time.

Promotion

It's quite possible that teens will not sign up for this program on their own accord. Therefore, it may be wise to promote this program to parents instead, inviting them to bring their teens to the program so they can learn together. Alternatively, you could offer the program as a workshop that you take on the road to schools, community centers, or after-school programs. It's still worth the effort, however, to promote this program within the library with a display featuring the phrase "Cyber-Safety for Teens" on a background that looks like cyber-space. Adhere stylized planets and stars—each containing a factoid about computer safety—on top of black paper to get teens thinking about the topic.

Collection Connection

Fiction (featuring teens who use the Internet)

Amy—Mary Hooper (Bloomsbury USA Children's Books, 2002)

ChaseR: A Novel in E-Mails—Michael Rosen (Candlewick, 2002)

Confessions of a Boyfriend Stealer (a Blog)—Robynn Clairday (Delacorte Books for Young Readers, 2005)

Firestorm—Jordan Cray (Simon Pulse, 1997)

Heart on My Sleeve—Ellen Wittlinger (Simon and Schuster Children's Publishing, 2004)

The Last Dance—Tim Lahaye (Westbow Press, 2002)

Love, Sara—Mary Beth Lundgren (Henry Holt and Company, 2001)

One of Those Hideous Books Where the Mother Dies—Sonya Sones (Simon and Schuster Children's Publishing, 2004)

Rob&Sara.com—P. J. Peterson and Ivy Ruckman (Delacorte Books for Young Readers, 2004)

Snail Mail No More—Ann Martin and Paula Danzinger (Scholastic, 2000)

Stalker—Jordan Cray (Simon Pulse, 1998)

ttyl—Lauren Myracle (Harry N. Abrams, 2004)

The Year My Life Went down the Loo—Katie Maxwell (Dorchester Publishing Company, 2003)

Year of Secret Assignments—Jaclyn Moriarty (Arthur A. Levine, 2004)

Nonfiction

Always Use Protection: A Teen's Guide to Safe Computing—Dan Appleman (Apress, 2004)

Blogging for Teens—John W. Gosney (Course Technology PTR, 2004)

Cybersafety: Surfing Safely Online—Joan Vos MacDonald (Enslow Publishers, 2001)

Girl.net: For Girls Who Click—Sarra Manning (Chicken House, 2001)

Katie.com: My Story—Katherine Tarbox (Plume Books, 2001)

When Time Is Short and Money Is Tight ...

Hold a white-elephant swap. Ask teens to wrap a silly, kitschy, or useless item from home, then lay out all the "gifts" on a table. After drawing numbers, the participants should choose gifts in numerical order, then open them in that order. As they open their gags, each participant will have an opportunity to swap their item with someone else's. A variation on this might be a gift swap that involves each teen bringing used items such as books, CDs, and clothing that they no longer need to trade with other teens.

Organize a caroling party (perhaps using diverse types of songs, rather than just Christmas songs), then gather back at the library for hot chocolate and cookies.

Invite your teen advisory council to make a book tree using old, discarded, or donated books.

REFERENCES

Brokamp, R. (n.d.). Five retirement must-knows. Retrieved July 2, 2005, from the Motley Fool Web site: http://www.fool.com/retirement/retirement01.htm.

Gallup Poll (2003). Crime victimization about the same as last year. Retrieved August 10, 2005, from Computer Crime Research Center Web site: http://www.crime-research.org/articles/crime_victim.

Karchmer, J. (2000, March 16). Generation Y savings. *Money Magazine*. Retrieved July 2, 2005, from http://money.cnn.com/2000/03/16/strategies/q_retire_geny/.

Keizer, G. (2005, July 14). Cyber crime rates, losses fall, says survey. *Internet Week*. Retrieved August 10, 2005, from http://internetweek.com/internetbusiness/165702566.

Magid, L. (2004). Help children know the risks of chat rooms. Retrieved September 2, 2005, from SafeKids Web site: http://www.safekids.com/chatdanger.htm.

Rosen, J. (2005). As if! Marketing to older teens. *Publisher's Weekly*, 252(28), 73–75.

CONCLUSION

Sometimes it's hard to determine whether or not what we do as librarians who serve and advocate for teens makes any difference to our audience. Teens are much harder to read than, say, young children, who are less self-conscious and therefore more inclined to show excitement, or even adults, who are more forthright and effusive with praise for a well-run and enjoyable program. Without that immediate feedback and—let's face it—gratification, serving teens can sometimes be a thankless job. For this reason alone, it is my belief that those who serve teens are some of the most enthusiastic, selfless, and dedicated individuals in our profession. What these folks know, however, that others may not, is how rewarding it can be when a program reaches a teen who might be shy, confused, struggling, or insecure. We all know when that happens—we can see it in more relaxed body language or a smile, or in a sudden willingness to seek us out for advice, a good book, or just some after-school small talk. Those moments are encouraging, and help us know when we're on the right track. It is my hope that the programs contained in this book help achieve that sort of success by opening new doors for your teenaged library users and helping them to see what's on the other side.

Appendix A

DREAM JOURNAL ENTRY PAGES

Date: _____   Bedtime: _____ a.m. / p.m.

Pre-sleep Thoughts: _____

_____

_____

_____

Wake Time: _____ a.m. / p.m.

Post-sleep Thoughts: _____

_____

_____

_____

Date: _____   Bedtime: _____ a.m. / p.m.

Pre-sleep Thoughts: _____

_____

_____

_____

Wake Time: _____ a.m. / p.m.

Post-sleep Thoughts: _____

_____

From Teen Programs with Punch: A Month-by-Month Guide by Valerie Ott. Westport, CT: Libraries Unlimited. Copyright © 2006.

Date: _____   Bedtime: _____ a.m. / p.m.

Pre-sleep Thoughts: _____

_____

_____

Wake Time: _____ a.m. / p.m.

Post-sleep Thoughts: _____

_____

_____

Date: _____   Bedtime: _____ a.m. / p.m.

Pre-sleep Thoughts: _____

_____

_____

Wake Time: _____ a.m. / p.m.

Post-sleep Thoughts: _____

_____

_____

DREAM INTERPRETATION QUIZ

1. If the color white features prominently in your dream, you may be feeling

   a. Anxious

   b. Frightened

   c. Hopeful

2. Which animal appears in dreams most often?

   a. Horse

   b. Dog

   c. Cat

3. A dream of being soaked in a rainstorm may signify that you are

   a. Afraid of water

   b. Feeling the need to come clean about something

   c. Guided too easily by your emotions

4. Climbing a hill in your dream may mean that you

   a. Have a problem in your waking life

   b. Like hiking in the outdoors

   c. Neither of the above

5. A dream about your teeth falling out may mean

   a. You need to see the dentist

   b. You are concerned about your appearance

   c. You are anxious about something

6. A dream about a crying baby could mean

   a. You crave attention

   b. You feel stressed out in your waking life

   c. Someone in your life needs help

7. The color red in dreams often symbolizes

   a. Embarrassment

   b. The need to take caution

   c. Love

8. Dreaming about time travel could signify
    a. Your romantic nature
    b. Your desire to escape reality
    c. Both of the above

Answer Key: 1(c); 2(a); 3(c); 4(a); 5(b); 6(a); 7(b); 8(c)

Appendix B

STYLE QUIZ

WHAT'S YOUR STYLE?

1. What is your idea of a great Saturday afternoon?

    a. Taking a long hike

    b. Taking a cooking class

    c. Downloading new music onto your iPod

    d. Going shopping

    e. Practicing yoga

2. Which of these lunches sound most appetizing to you?

    a. A veggie sub with fresh-squeezed lemonade

    b. Gourmet pizza

    c. A croissant sandwich with a cup of cappuccino

    d. Indian curry

    e. A salad and green tea

3. Which movie would you most like to watch?

 a. *The Notebook*

 b. Anything that's old and black and white

 c. *I, Robot*

 d. A *National Geographic* special on the Amazon rainforest

 e. I don't have a TV

4. What color palette are you attracted to?

 a. Keep it simple: khaki and white

 b. Bright colors like red, orange, and purple

 c. Metallics like sleek silver and electric blue

 d. Nature's colors like blue, brown, and green

 e. Anything that coordinates well

5. Which word would your best friend use to describe you?

 a. Crazy

 b. Stylish

 c. Calm

 d. Down to earth

 e. Trendy

6. Which of these places would you most like to live in?

 a. A loft in downtown Seattle

 b. A penthouse overlooking Central Park

 c. A small cottage on the beach

 d. In various hotel rooms—I want to travel as much as possible

 e. A cabin in the woods

7. Which of these pieces of furniture would you love to have in your bedroom?

 a. A soft, comfy chair to read in

 b. An Asian-style armoire

 c. A sleek metal desk

 d. A canopy bed

 e. Nothing—I like a lot of space

8. What do you consider the most important function of your bedroom?

   a. Sleeping

   b. Listening to music or surfing the net

   c. Reading or studying

   d. Daydreaming

   e. Relaxing

SCORING

1. a—1; b—2; c—3; d—4; e—5
2. a—1; b—3; c—4; d—2; e—5
3. a—1; b—4; c—3; d—2; e—5
4. a—5; b—2; c—3; d—1; e—4
5. a—2; b—4; c—5; d—1; e—3
6. a—3; b—4; c—1; d—2; e—5
7. a—1; b—2; c—3; d—4; e—5
8. a—5; b—3; c—1; d—2; e—4

MOSTLY 1s: CASUAL

Your goal is to be comfortable in your room. Lots of soft pillows and blankets, plus comfy chairs to curl up in are your idea of coziness. You like color, but nothing too bright or glaring. Wooden or whitewashed antique furniture decorated with personal mementos and photographs appeal to you.

MOSTLY 2s: EXOTIC

You have a flair for the exotic and are the first of your friends to accept a dare. You are attracted to bold, bright colors and items inspired by faraway places. Items like Chinese lanterns or African artifacts appeal to your sense of adventure.

MOSTLY 3s: CONTEMPORARY

You are trendy and up-to-date on all the latest gadgets. Your sense of style is defined by sleek, clean-lined furniture without a lot of frills or ruffles. Colors like blue, gray, white, and black catch your eye, but you're not opposed to other colors as long as they don't compete with one another. You are more concerned with function rather than form.

MOSTLY 4s: TRADITIONAL

You have classic style and are attracted to anything well designed. Color is your friend, but you like your palette to be well coordinated and not too flashy. Your tastes often run on the formal or expensive side.

MOSTLY 5s: MINIMALIST

You are more interested in achieving calm and order than a high-style look. You are attracted to open, airy spaces with soothing colors—or no color at all—and very few decorations cluttering up your room. Your motto is "less is more."

Appendix C

❖❖❖ ❖❖❖ ❖❖❖

MUSICAL TASTES QUESTIONNAIRE

Circle the number that corresponds to how strongly you feel about each statement (1 is the least strong; 5 is the strongest)

1.	I like music that is reflective	1	2	3	4	5
2.	I like music that has a good beat	1	2	3	4	5
3.	I like music that makes me feel energetic	1	2	3	4	5
4.	I like music that has an edge to it	1	2	3	4	5
5.	I like music that makes me feel contemplative	1	2	3	4	5
6.	I like music with aggressive lyrics	1	2	3	4	5
7.	I like music that is simple and fun	1	2	3	4	5

If you scored high for questions 1 and 5, you might consider

Classical, Blues, Jazz, or Folk music

From Teen Programs with Punch: A Month-by-Month Guide by Valerie Ott. Westport, CT: Libraries Unlimited. Copyright © 2006.

If you scored high for questions 2 and 3, you might consider

Hip-Hop, Rap, Funk, Soul, or Electronic music

If you scored high for questions 4 and 6, you might consider

Alternative, Rock, or Heavy Metal music

If you scored high for question 7, you might consider

Pop, Religious, Country, or Soundtrack music

Appendix D

REAL WORLD OPTION SHEETS*

*All of the materials for this program are adapted versions of the materials used by the Medina County Extension of the Ohio State University.

BANK STATION MATERIALS

Checking Account Ledger

Description of transaction	Payment	Deposit	Balance

Savings Account Ledger

Description of transaction	Payment	Deposit	Balance

Taxes (in dollars) Withheld for Uncle Sam–Single Family Household

Monthly salary	You only	You & 1 child	You & 2 children	You & 3 children	Refund for each additional child
750–1,000	172	141	111	98	30
1,001–1,250	244	213	183	150	30
1,251–1,500	310	279	249	216	30
1,501–1,750	376	345	315	282	30
1,751–2,000	442	411	381	349	30
2,001–2,250	514	483	453	421	30
2,251–2,500	610	554	520	487	55
2,501–2,750	707	651	596	553	55
2,751–3,000	805	749	694	635	55
3,001–3,250	903	846	791	732	55
3,251–3,500	1,011	954	899	840	55
3,501–3,750	1,108	1,051	996	938	55
3,751–4,000	1,205	1,149	1,094	1,036	55
4,001–4,250	1,314	1,257	1,202	1,144	55
4,251–4,500	1,414	1,355	1,300	1,241	55
4,501–4,750	1,518	1,457	1,397	1,339	55
4,751–5,000	1,624	1,561	1,500	1,436	55

Occupations

Occupation	Education required	Annual salary	Monthly gross income
Jeweler	High school	$26,260	$2,188
Machinist	Technical training	$32,573	$2,714
Baker	High school	$15,750	$1,312
Metal processor	High school	$24,565	$2,047
Farmer	Technical training	$43,470	$3,623
Waiter/Waitress	Dropout	$14,144	$1,179
Dry cleaning employee	Dropout	$10,400	$867
Retail salesperson	Dropout	$17,700	$1,475
Pilot	College	$47,970	$3,998
Truck driver	Dropout	$33,218	$2,768
Auto manufacturer	High school	$44,096	$3,675
Welder	Technical training	$25,200	$2,100
Meat cutter	High school	$16,800	$1,400
Textile worker	High school	$18,900	$1,575
Security guard	High school	$19,950	$1,662
Hair stylist	Technical training	$18,000	$1,500
Police officer	Technical training	$30,450	$2,538
Gas station attendant	Dropout	$12,000	$1,000
Railway worker	High school	$28,350	$2,363
Dentist	College	$123,210	$10,268
Veterinary assistant	Technical training	$22,950	$1,913
X-ray technician	Technical training	$38,970	$3,248
Physical therapist	College	$40,000	$3,333
Teacher	College	$29,850	$2,488
Lawyer	College	$60,000	$5,000
Nurse-RN	College	$34,000	$2,833
Dental assistant	Technical training	$27,248	$2,271
Nurses aide	High school	$19,947	$1,662
Social worker	College	$33,150	$2,763

(continued)

Occupations (continued)

Occupation	Education required	Annual salary	Monthly gross income
Psychologist	College	$38,560	$3,213
Computer analyst	College	$45,000	$3,750
Chef	High school	$20,509	$1,709
Chiropractor	College	$44,140	$3,678
Optometrist	College	$62,030	$5,169
Bus driver	High school	$21,861	$1,822
Legal assistant	College	$30,020	$2,502
Fast-food worker	Dropout	$14,310	$1,193
Administrative assistant	High school	$22,280	$1,857
Radio DJ	College	$20,613	$1,718

Family Sizes

No Children	2 Children 6-year-old girl 3-year-old girl	No Children	3 Children 6-year-old girl 4-year-old boy 1-year-old girl
1 Child 2-year-old boy	2 Children 8-year-old girl 6-year-old girl	1 Child 8-year-old girl	1 Child 6-year-old boy
No Children	No Children	2 Children 4-year-old boy 2-year-old girl	1 Child 2-year-old boy
1 Child 6-year-old boy	1 Child 4-year-old girl	3 Children 7-year-old girl 5-year-old boy 3-year-old boy	2 Children 5-year-old girl 3-year-old girl
1 Child 5-year-old girl	1 Child 7-year-old girl	2 Children 4-year-old girl 8-month-old boy	2 Children 5-year-old boy 2-year-old boy
1 Child 6-month-old boy	No Children	2 Children 5-year-old twin girls	2 Children 7-year-old boy 5-year-old boy
No Children	1 Child 4-year-old girl	2 Children 7-year-old boy 2-year-old boy	No Children
2 Children 5-year-old boy 3-year-old girl	2 Children 6-year-old girl 3-year-old girl	2 Children 5-year-old girl 1-year-old boy	2 Children 8-year-old boy 1-year-old girl
5 Children 9-year-old boy 7-year-old boy 5-year-old boy 2-year-old twin boys	2 Children 4-year-old girl 1-year-old girl	3 Children 7-year-old girl 5-year-old girl 3-year-old boy	4 Children 8-year-old twin boys 6-year-old boy 2-year-old girl
1 Child 8-year-old girl	1 Child 2-year-old boy	No Children	2 Children 7-year-old girl 2-month-old girl

REAL ESTATE STATION MATERIALS

Purchase Options

Choices	Market value*	Cost per month	Taxes per month	Insurance	Total cost per month
House A—single story; 25 years old; 1000 sq. feet; 3 bedrooms; 1 bath; small lot	$60,000	$500	$44.75	$17.92	$563
House B—two story; 50 years old; 1800 sq. feet; dining room; 3 bedrooms; 2 bath; small lot	$80,000	$680	$59.67	$20.41	$760
House C—two story; 3 years old; 2100 sq. feet; 3 bedrooms; 2 bath; 1.5 garage; 5 acres; storage building	$115,750	$950	$86.33	$31.91	$1068

*Costs based on current market prices and figured on 20 percent down payment at 8 percent interest for thirty years.

Rental Options

Choices	Cost per month	Renter's insurance per month	Total monthly rental expenses
Apartment A—1 bedroom; located in town; parking on street; no pets	$350	$11.17	$361.17
Apartment B—2 bedrooms; newly redecorated; patio; A/C; quiet neighborhood; no pets; 24-hour maintenance service; common laundry facilities	$500	$11.17	$511.17
Apartment C—2 bedrooms; nice lawn and deck; dishwasher; pets OK	$700	$11.17	$711.17

GROCERY STORE STATION MATERIALS

Grocery Shopping Plans

Family size	Thrifty plan	Low-cost plan	Moderate plan	Liberal plan
Single	$129	$164	$203	$253
Family of 2 adults	$284	$361	$446	$556
Family of 4 (2 children, 2 adults)	$400	$490	$640	$770
Additional children (add figure onto the "Family of 2" amount)				
1–5 years old	$80	$100	$123	$148
6–11 years old	$118	$151	$192	$224
12–18 years old	$125	$161	$198	$235

Source: U.S. Department of Agriculture, "Cost of food at home at four levels, U.S. Average, September 2003."

Note: The costs for each plan were figured based on the assumption that food for all meals and snacks will be purchased at the store and prepared at home.

CAR DEALERSHIP STATION MATERIALS

Car Choices

Choices	Cost*	Cost per month	Insurance	Tax & license fee	Gas & upkeep	Total cost per month
1998 Chevy Cavalier— 2-door coupe; automatic transmission; A/C; cruise control; AM/FM cassette	$11,995	$245	$68.17	$15.31	$40	$368.48
1998 Chevy S-10—small truck; automatic transmission; A/C; slide rear window; AM/FM cassette	$12,500	$255	$59.00	$12.36	$40	$366.36
1998 Chevy Lumina— 4-door sedan; automatic transmission; A/C; CD player; power trunk opener	$16,065	$330	$62.00	$15.50	$40	$447.50
1998 Chevy Camero— 2-door sports car; automatic transmission; A/C; CD player	$21,000	$430	$77.09	$25.94	$40	$573.03
Public Transportation	$6.00 round-trip	$120 (x 20 rides)	$0	$0	$0	$120.00

*Costs figured at 8 percent interest, no money down, sixty-month loan.

CHILD CARE STATION MATERIALS

Child Care Costs

Provider	Age of child	Monthly cost
Real World Day Care	Infant (birth to 2 years; in diapers)	$495* (Includes breakfast, lunch, and two snacks for a ten-hour day)
	Preschool	$428
	Kindergarten	$390
	After-school care	$234
TLC Babysitters	Any age	$3/hour per child**

*For each additional hour, add $5; for additional children, take 10 percent off the total cost per month.

**For each additional child, add $0.50 to the hourly rate.

HEALTH CARE STATION MATERIALS

Medical Options

Features of plan	Employee + one—costs per month	Employee + family—costs per month
Choice A $1,250 deductible; insurance pays 80% after deductible; no eye exams	$203	$264.08
Choice B $5 co-pay for office visits; $7 co-pay for prescriptions; $5 co-pay for eye exams; no deductible	$225	$290

Dental Options

Features of plan	Employee + one—costs per month	Employee + family—costs per month
Choice A Insurance pays 80% for any dentist	$17	$26
Choice B Insurance pays 80%; insurance company picks dentist	$15	$24

UTILITY STATION MATERIALS

Basic Monthly Necessities

Type of service	Monthly cost
Gas/Electric	$100
Water/Sewer	$31
Trash pickup	$25
Telephone	$35

Optional Features

Type of service	Monthly cost
Basic cable	$50
Cell phone	$30
Long distance plan	$25

SHOPPING CENTER STATION MATERIALS

Clothing Options

Gross income	Cost per month*	For each additional child
Above $4,200	$250	$90
$3,800–$4,100	$200	$80
$3,400–$3,700	$190	$70
$3,000–$3,300	$180	$60
$2,500–$2,900	$130	$50
$2,100–$2,400	$120	$40
$1,700–$2,000	$100	$30
Below $1,600	$70	$20

Source: Bureau of Labor Statistics, Consumer Expenditure Survey, 1995.

*Clothing purchases vary by individual tastes and professional needs. The above costs are based on 5 percent–6 percent of gross income.

Furniture Options

Type of furniture	Total cost	On 3-year payment plan
High quality—includes 1 bedroom suite, 1 twin bed, kitchen table and chairs, living room suite	$5,000	$194 per month
Moderately priced—includes 1 bedroom suite, 1 twin bed, kitchen table and chairs, living room suite	$2,500	$97 per month
Low priced—1 bedroom suite, kitchen table and chairs, couch, 1 chair	$1,500	$58 per month

Additional Options

Option	Total cost	On 3-year payment plan
Television	$400	$12 per month
DVD player	$130	$4 per month
Stereo	$150	$4.50 per month
Home computer	$800	$24 per month

Laundry Options

Own washer and dryer	$39.00 per month for 3 years
Laundromat	$36.00 per month (based on 24 loads/month at $1.50 each)

CHANCE STATION MATERIALS

Pay the newspaper bill for this month. Deduct $15.

Your best friend is getting married and you plan on hosting a shower. Deduct $50 for food and decorations.

You win $50 worth of free groceries. Return to the grocery store to receive your refund.

Your car needs an oil change. Pay $20.

You need a jump-start for your car battery. Pay a $20 service charge to the towing service.

Happy Halloween! Purchase $15 worth of candy for the trick-or-treaters.

Time to register your child for camp. Pay $20. If you don't have children, draw another card.

Cousin Jane and her two kids drop in unexpectedly for the weekend. Increase your grocery bill by $40.

You have a cavity that needs to be filled. Pay $50.

Happy Holidays! You receive a gift of $25.

Your TV goes on the blink. Pay a $30 deposit toward the repair bill.

Your bank statement arrives. You made a subtraction error this month. Deduct $20.

Homeowner: Your water heater dies. Pay $75 for a down payment on a new one. If you rent, draw another card.

You inherit $5,000 from Aunt Effie.

Buy a Mother's Day gift for your mom. Pay $15.

There's a white sale at J. C. Penney's. Pay $40 for two new sets of sheets and towels.

Buy a Father's Day gift for your dad. Pay $15.

The church is having a building drive. Donate $20.

Your niece is selling Girl Scout cookies. Pay $12.

Your vacuum cleaner died. Make a $50 down payment on a new one.

Your child needs a new pair of soccer cleats. Pay $40. No children? Pick another card.

Your pet needs shots. Deduct $20.

(continued)

(continued)

You receive a free kitten.
Deduct $10 for food and litter.

You hit a pothole and have a flat tire.
Pay $10 to have it patched.

It's time to pay your CD of the month
club dues.
Deduct $15.

You were caught speeding on the highway.
Pay $75 for the ticket.

You purchased a new DVD.
Pay $20.

Your school loan is due.
Pay $100.

It's your grandmother's 75th birthday.
Pay $25 for her gift.

You break your arm roller-blading.
Pay the emergency room fee of $100.

Surprise! You find an extra $20 in your
coat pocket from last winter.

You illegally parked next to a fire hydrant.
Pay $10 parking ticket.

Postage is due on a package you
received.
Pay $10.

You go to the movies to see the new
Harry Potter flick.
Pay $20.

You receive a tax return.
Add $200 to your account.

Your co-workers are pooling their
money to pay for a get-well-soon
bouquet for your boss. Contribute $10.

You bounced a check
last month.
Pay $50 in fees.

A friend takes you out to eat.
Add $10 to your account.

Your credit card bill arrived.
Subtract $40.

You found a lost wallet and
receive a $100 reward!

Happy Birthday!
Add $50.

You had a car accident and
have to pay the $250
deductible.

You are invited to a wedding.
Pay $30 for a gift.

You need a haircut.
Pay $15.

A new store has a grand
opening. You win a $50 gift
certificate.
Add this to your entertainment
budget.

You've made some extra
money on eBay!
Add $75 to your account.

It's tax time! Pay your tax
professional $50 to prepare
your return.

Your friend had a baby and
you were there to take pictures.
Pay $10 for film development.

You get a bad case of the flu.
Pay $15 for cold medications.

You're out of shampoo,
toothpaste, and toilet paper.
Pay $10 at the drugstore.

MAD MONEY STATION MATERIALS

Entertainment Options

Movie (includes popcorn)	$15 each person
Video rental	$3.50
Concert tickets	$35 each person
Tickets for professional sporting event	$20 each person
Lunch Out	$5
Dinner Out	$30
Party (includes food, beverage, decorations)	$100
Mini-vacation for two (3-day, 2-night getaway includes hotel, meals, car transportation)	$450
Full vacation for two (7-day, 6-night vacation includes hotel, meals, air transportation)	$1500

Charitable Giving Guide

Yearly income	% income	Amount per year	Yearly income	% income	Amount per year
$5,000	.40	$20.00	$95,000	2.2	$2,090.00
$7,000	.45	$31.50	$100,000	2.3	$2,300.00
$10,000	.52	$52.00	$105,000	2.3	$2,415.00
$12,000	.56	$67.20	$107,054	2.34	$2,500.00
$15,000	.62	$93.00	$120,000	2.40	$2,880.00
$17,000	.68	$115.60	$125,000	2.40	$3,000.00
$20,000	.80	$160.00	$140,000	2.50	$3,500.00
$22,000	.87	$191.40	$150,000	2.50	$3,750.00
$25,000	.96	$240.00	$160,000	2.60	$4,160.00
$27,000	1.04	$280.80	$170,000	2.60	$4,420.00
$30,000	1.16	$348.00	$180,000	2.70	$4,860.00
$35,000	1.4	$490.00	$183,868	2.72	$5,000.00
$40,000	1.53	$612.00	$190,000	2.80	$5,130.00
$45,000	1.68	$756.00	$200,000	2.80	$5,600.00
$50,000	1.80	$900.00	$210,000	2.90	$5,880.00
$55,000	1.90	$1,045.00	$220,000	2.90	$6,380.00
$60,000	1.98	$1,188.00	$250,000	3.0	$7,500.00
$65,000	1.98	$1,287.00	$300,000	3.25	$9,750.00
$70,000	2.0	$1,400.00	$306,336	3.27	$10,000.00
$75,000	2.0	$1,500.00	$400,000	3.5	$14,000.00
$80,000	2.1	$1,680.00	$500,000	3.75	$18,750.00
$85,000	2.1	$1,785.00	$750,000	4.0	$30,000.00
$90,000	2.2	$1,980.00	$1,000,000	5.0	$50,000.00

Examples of Charities

American Cancer Society	Doctors without Borders
American Red Cross	Habitat for Humanity
Amnesty International	Humane Society
Big Brothers/Big Sisters	Ronald McDonald House
Children's Miracle Network	United Way
Church	World Wildlife Fund

Dream Savings Options

Dream*	Amount necessary	Savings per month**
Retire early *Retire a millionaire at age 55!*	$1,000,000	$200
See the seven Wonders of the World *Go by plane, boat, bicycle, camel, canoe,* *or limo to see the wonders in first-class style.*	$200,000	$80
Box seats for pro sports team *License a twelve-person private skybox booth* *with food and beverage service for one season.*	$200,000	$80
Private fishing cabin in Montana *Enjoy six months of solitude while fishing* *from the dock of this remote cabin. Use of* *float plane included.*	$100,000	$40
Golf around the world *You and three friends will take a first-class,* *five-star resort tour to play the twenty best golf* *courses in the world.*	$50,000	$20
Cannes Film Festival *Party with the stars! Tour France, plus* *one week in Cannes to rub elbows* *with celebrities.*	$50,000	$20
Private yacht cruise of the Mediterranean *You and twelve friends will visit small harbors* *in Italy, France, and Greece for one month.*	$10,000	$4
African photo safari *Go on a wildlife safari photographing the most* *exotic animals in the world. Enjoy five-star luxury* *at the most exclusive camps.*	$10,000	$4

*Credit: *Cashflow 101* by *Rich Dad, Poor Dad* (Robert Kiyosaki).

**Based on 10 percent interest gained over a thirty-seven-year period (assuming one
will start saving at age 18).

Compound Interest Chart

Age	Kim invests (dollars)	Growth (10% per year)	Tom invests (dollars)	Growth (10% per year)
22	1,000	1,100	0	0
23	1,000	2,310	0	0
24	1,000	3,641	0	0
25	1,000	5,105	0	0
26	1,000	6,716	0	0
27	1,000	8,487	0	0
28	1,000	10,436	0	0
29	1,000	12,579	0	0
30	0	13,837	1,000	1,100
31	0	15,221	1,000	2,310
32	0	16,743	1,000	3,641
33	0	18,418	1,000	5,105
34	0	20,259	1,000	6,716
35	0	22,285	1,000	8,487
36	0	24,514	1,000	10,436
37	0	26,965	1,000	12,579
38	0	29,662	1,000	14,937
39	0	32,628	1,000	17,531
40	0	35,891	1,000	20,384
41	0	39,480	1,000	23,523
42	0	43,428	1,000	26,975
43	0	47,771	1,000	30,772
44	0	52,548	1,000	34,950
45	0	57,802	1,000	39,545
46	0	63,583	1,000	44,599
47	0	69,941	1,000	50,159
48	0	76,935	1,000	56,275
49	0	84,628	1,000	63,002
50	0	93,091	1,000	70,403
51	0	102,400	1,000	78,548
52	0	112,640	1,000	87,497

(continued)

53	0	123,904	1,000	97,347
54	0	136,295	1,000	108,182
55	0	149,924	1,000	120,100
56	0	164,917	1,000	133,210
57	0	181,409	1,000	147,631
58	0	199,549	1,000	163,494
59	0	219,504	1,000	180,943
60	0	241,455	1,000	200,138
61	0	265,600	1,000	221,252
62	0	292,160	1,000	244,477
63	0	321,376	1,000	270,024
64	0	353,514	1,000	298,127
65	0	388,865	1,000	329,039
	Value at retirement	$388,865	Value at retirement	$329,039
	Less total contributions	$8,000	Less total contributions	$35,000
	Net earnings	$380,865	Net earnings	$294,039

Note: Kim invested $8,000 ($1,000 per year) from the time she was 22 until the time she was 30. Tom invested $35,000 ($1,000 per year) from the time he was 30 until the time he was 65 ... *And Tom never caught up!*

Appendix E

SCHEDULING SPREADSHEET

Day	Time	School	Grade	Teacher	Staff
Example	12–12:40	Anytown Middle School	8	Ms. Getz	Me, Becky
Monday					
Tuesday					
Wednesday					
Thursday					
Friday					

From Teen Programs with Punch: A Month-by-Month Guide by Valerie Ott. Westport, CT: Libraries Unlimited. Copyright © 2006.

Appendix F

CAREER WORD SEARCH

```
H E B J L A C X Z H W R L Y Y G V X T V P U E W V C Q W K B M K R O G A S P I D
Y H R E Z X Y M W D E A E T S Q S S R G H L T M E N Z Q Q Y L O N M F M H Z N V
N H M U K Q U U W N W E Q N K X I P Y W U R W R T Q N M W G T G N F D O D P W P
R E E N I G N E N Y R R E L G M Y R E P O L E V E D B E W C N T R H T P T U N M
Z Q R D B S V A E Z W K L F E I E Q T T R F Z G R N U B A U X Y C O C L W K Q G
Q U S L U H L R Q X C T M H U P S Y C H O L O G I S T F D I Q A G Z H A K W H H
B G M R C P U Z F U F N C K B X C E B F K B Y K N K O K X U X R J Z P K O H E Q
V O X A Y G C H A Z X G K C T D V C D L J L O B A N C C P O A Q F Z N S M C Y I
I O A T M Y V E D V W G X X Q L C F I N L U F K R K Q U I P P J O Y M W X N D Y
T E R E E J Q V B H J N T E C M W C G T O Z S Q I V X G H A I D X N W N Z E T N
A A X E T G S J M P L H V M G N O B X W S I M F A P M E Q W L Q N G G F B G N N
A R C H I T E C T I U C L E P F L O R I S T Y S K G H U F F K R O F K Q W Y M Z
K X D L A K X L G J J J S U N M L N B F U F A B A L T O C H E F P R E L Z A W Q
B H A T E P E I T N Y K T E D O P T J J Y A X R B F H E A D B Z S E K W S P H G
G A B V E M E I I I Y E E O V H Z V U H S R O J M O O K I F Y T A N V E D C B F
S S N F U H R L A Y R W R K R Z O J N T O P F V H T L X A J V S X G M V R L O O
W O J T A X L V T P M X P E C J N T N R B S B F I S E M R V D I D I J O C A V C
B Q R T P S U W R N J N H Q D B J Q Z K V A U J I P U H T U Q L T S K T F Z Z I
S X D I P S P O O L A H Z F C M C B J N O E S S T N D K I Z I A R E F S B T J L
M Y P K X D G Y U U Q T Z C R U J V D Q J J D B A A R Z S C Q N N D V V Y I J J
S Z V Y R R G V X D J H N E K K Z E V J M K W Z R C N I T A F R X C A M M H N M
G Z S E A P A T Y W O C F U L Y W K O S L G P C F I L Q T S I U X I D D T Z K E
M N N M S J P K W S N G V J O X D H Z G T V K I R R L I J M W O I H Y K J A L H
R O M V M M H I F W S S G I S C R R N A J Y W W M F R I X D Y J I P O O T W I M
L E Q P D J M M K Z W E E L F Z C R V I Z Z P J X C P N B R O H Q A W N U B T K
R S Q H K L T O E Q V M C C D Q L A R R L C Q H N I Z I H R U O C R Y Z Q B P T
P W O C D V C H E T H H Y R C B A I X T A J Z M J C M T G R A Q D G V X Z Y Y N
C E M Q N R D K I D E G A P M J P F R V M E I O I S S S I Q L R C O Y T Z V A O
Q C N U O X T J E C Z I P L N Q T L Q Z B R T M H G Q C R I T D I U M B D I K J
M Y B M G K O J T Z B R N N A A D N U P R Z Q Q S I M W C H I B G A T N C Z J B
V U F D G X V T E W U H M P I R Q I B H B H X R J H T Y H O Y O H D N I O W A O
B N U W H S X T G F N X U X C Y I S G Y X B D N T X Q R A C H D R J T Z W I C D
Y Y D O C F F T H K J B G M I R J J F S H B W D S E J D Z L Q L B I L G V J T L
T D I B U P M I V F L T N R S W O B L I J M Y Y X F A B V O L E L P I G S I O F
S G A O U W X V G I Z K I D U I S N G C R E T I R W G C K G A O H M P T O F L E
Z G N O I V Z Z C A L K D O M Y P Q B I U O M F E Y Z C H P P N S T O H X F I K
J B V Q Q R U I H F N W T K S I N U L A J Q T W P Z Y Y R E Z H A M S B H H P W
H P G K O P S I E N A D V N G G F M F N U N A K C G A E V B R V L F X U J K Q R
N O Q U F T N R Y B I I X U R F B H N U G B H J A R D E V Q H Y X K A N Z Z N X
```

ACCOUNTANT	FLORIST	PHOTOGRAPHER
ACTOR	GRAPHIC	PHYSICIAN
ARCHITECT	DESIGNER	PILOT
ARTIST	INVESTMENT	POLITICIAN
CHEF	BANKER	PSYCHOLOGIST
CHEMIST	JOURNALIST	PUBLICIST
COACH	LAWYER	SOCIAL WORKER
COMPUTER	LIBRARIAN	TEACHER
PROGRAMMER	LOBBYIST	VETERINARIAN
ENGINEER	MUSICIAN	WEB DEVELOPER
FASHION DESIGNER	PARTY PLANNER	WRITER

CAREER WORD SEARCH SOLUTION

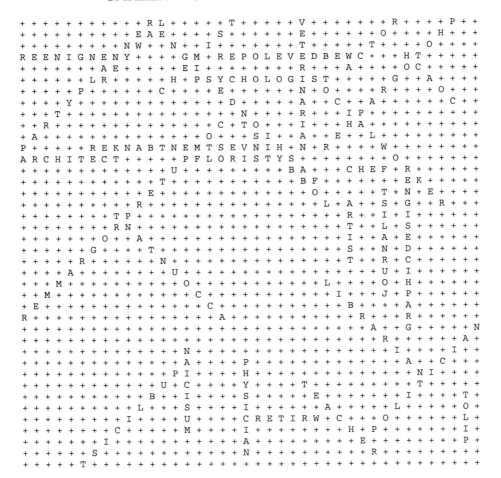

Appendix G

SCAVENGER HUNT
CLUE SHEETS

FOR GUYS

1. What year did women receive the right to vote? Look up "voting" in the *World Book Encyclopedia* to find out. **(U)**

2. If a girl asked you to pick up a "cosmo" from the store, what would you buy? Find this in the library. **(R)**

3. Using the *Encyclopedia of Family Health*, answer this question: True or False—Women get more migraine headaches than men. **(A)**

4. This woman led the "Underground Railroad," which helped slaves during the Reconstruction make their way to free states. Use one of the library's biographical databases to find out which year she was born. (Hint: "Google" this clue first if you don't know the name of this person.) **(G)**

5. Using the catalog, locate the book *Little Women*. Who is the author? **(S)**

---

6. Using the catalog, locate the book titled *The Only Astrology Book You'll Ever Need*. Which sign of the zodiac is symbolized by a woman? **(#)**

---

7. Locate the classic chic-flick about cheerleading, starring Kirsten Dunst. **(E)**

---

8. Which has less carbs? A McDonald's Filet-o-Fish or a McChicken? Use the *Corrine T. Netzer Encyclopedia of Food Values* located in the reference section to find out. **(Y)**

---

9. What was the color of Van Morrison's girl's eyes? (Hint: Use the catalog to locate a CD by this artist, then scan through the song's titles for the answer.) **(!)**

---

10. Using the database called *The Britannica Student Encyclopedia*, find out which French fashion designer is famous for the "little black dress." **(1)**

Answers: (1) 1920; (2) *Cosmopolitan* magazine; (3) True; (4) Harriet Tubman—1820; (5) Louisa May Alcott; (6) Virgo; (7) *Bring It On*; (8) McChicken; (9) Brown; (10) Coco Chanel

FOR GIRLS

1. Using the library's catalog, determine which classic comedy act made a movie called *I'm a Monkey's Uncle*. Locate this movie. **(I)**

2. Find a Dewey decimal number for a book about the animal Indiana Jones is most afraid of. **(L)**

3. Carson Kressley talks about men's clothing in his book *Off the Cuff*. What should a "pocket square" be made of? **(R)**

4. Which martial art was Bruce Lee famous for? Use one of the library's biographical databases to find out. **(R)**

5. Using the catalog, locate the book called *Football Made Simple: A Spectator's Guide*. How many yards is a team penalized for "roughing the kicker?" **(!)**

6. Just who is Alfred E. Neuman? Locate the latest issue of *Mad Magazine* to find out. **(G)**

7. Use the *Celebrity Directory* in the reference section to find the address of the actor famous for playing Billy Madison. **(L)**

8. Who was the NASCAR Rookie of the Year in 1979? Use the *World Almanac and Book of Facts* located in the reference section to find out. **(U)**

9. Which year was the Ford Mustang introduced? Use the library's database called *Discovering Collection—History* to find out. **(E)**

10. Look up Mount Everest in the *World Book Encyclopedia* to find out the name of the first man to reach this mountain's summit. **(S)**

Answers: (1) The Three Stooges; (2) Snakes—597 or 598; (3) Silk; (4) Kung fu; (5) 15 yards; (6) The freckle-faced character on the cover of every issue of *Mad*; (7) Adam Sandler—9150 Wilshire Blvd, 350, Beverly Hills, CA 90212; (8) Dale Earnhardt; (9) 1964; (10) Sir Edmund Hillary

Appendix H

INVESTMENT BUZZWORD QUIZ*

Match the buzzword or phrase with its correct definition.

1. Lipstick Indicator

a. The generation of middle-aged people who are pressured to support aging parents and growing children.

2. Aspirin Count Theory

b. An expression used to describe a very bad investment that causes an investor to lose everything he or she has invested.

3. Goldilocks Economy

c. Any investment strategy that is classified as extremely high risk.

4. Casino Finance

d. A slang technical analysis term referring to a rounding bottom in a stock's price pattern.

*All of these definitions came from www.investopedia.com/dictionary.

From Teen Programs with Punch: A Month-by-Month Guide by Valerie Ott. Westport, CT: Libraries Unlimited. Copyright © 2006.

5. Turkey	e. The act of a large buyer scooping up huge quantities of a stock.
6. Cockroach Theory	f. A slang term used to describe a perfect stock or investment.
7. J.Lo	g. A term referring to the U.S. economy of the mid- to late-1990s. It was "not too hot, not too cold, but just right."
8. Back Up the Truck	h. A jump in the price of stocks that often occurs the week between Christmas and New Year.
9. Losing Your Shirt	i. Slang for an investment that yields disappointing results.
10. Bo Derek	j. A theory that says purchases for less expensive indulgences tend to increase during times of economic uncertainty.
11. Sandwich Generation	k. A market theory that states bad news tends to be released in bunches.
12. Santa Claus Rally	l. The term for the belief that as stock prices fall, more and more people need pain relievers to get through the day.

Answers: (1) j; (2) l; (3) g; (4) c; (5) i; (6) k; (7) d; (8) e; (9) b; (10) f; (11) a; (12) h

Stock Worksheet

Stock symbol	PPS* on 12/31/03	# Shares to buy	$ Invested 1/1/04	PPS on 6/30/04	# Shares invested	$ Invested 6/30/04	# Shares to buy/ sell/hold	PPS on 6/30/04	$ Invested 6/30/04	PPS on 12/31/04	# Shares invested	Total $ invested	Total loss/ profit
Example	36.55	27	$986.85	42.35	27	$1,143.45	Buy 3	42.35	1,270.50	12.25	30	367.50	−619.35
COKE	52.86												
GPS	23.21												
MSFT	27.37												
NKE	68.46												
TGT	38.40												
MSO	9.85												
ANF	24.71												
TWX	17.99												
VZ	35.08												
SNE	34.67												
PEP	46.62												
MCD	24.83												
NINTF	93.31												
NXTL	28.06												
YHOO	45.03												

*PPS = Price per share

Stock symbol	Company	Industry
COKE	Coca-Cola Bottling Co.	Beverages (nonalcoholic)
GPS	Gap, Inc.	Retail (apparel)
MSFT	Microsoft Corp.	Software and programming
NKE	Nike, Inc.	Footwear
TGT	Target Corp.	Retail (department discount)
MSO	Martha Stewart Omnimedia	Periodical publishers; home furnishings
ANF	Abercrombie & Fitch Co.	Retail (apparel)
TWX	Time Warner Inc.	Motion picture and video production; cable and other pay television services; television broadcasting
VZ	Verizon Communications	Communications
SNE	Sony Corp.	Audio and video equipment
PEP	PepsiCo, Inc.	Beverages (nonalcoholic)
MCD	McDonald's Corp.	Restaurants
NINTF	Nintendo Ltd.	Computer gaming
NXTL	Nextel Communications	Communications
YHOO	Yahoo! Inc.	Information retrieval services; computer integrated systems design

Stock symbol	PPS on 6/30/04	PPS on 12/31/04
COKE	57.77	57.05
GPS	24.25	21.12
MSFT	28.56	26.72
NKE	75.75	90.69
TGT	42.47	51.93
MSO	9.00	29.02
ANF	38.75	46.95
TWX	17.58	19.45
VZ	36.19	40.51
SNE	38.05	38.96
PEP	53.88	52.20
MCD	26.00	32.06
NINTF	115.94	125.60
NXTL	26.66	30.01
YHOO	36.40	37.68

WEBLIOGRAPHY

The 411 on Social Security 4 Teens
www.ssa.gov/ny/exploring-index.htm
    Answers your questions about what social security is and how it can help you in the future.

2020 Green
www.2020green.com/greenst/login/login.jsp
    Absolutely wonderful site created by ING that takes you through the steps to financial success, from getting a job all the way to tracking investments, with interactive activities, games, and tons of helpful tools and information, all in a user-friendly format. Really can't say enough about this site!

Escape from Knab
www.escapefromknab.com
    A fun exercise in saving and investments; after crashing on an alien planet, you must earn and/or save enough money to buy a $10,000 ticket back to Earth.

It All Adds Up
www.italladdsup.org/
    By choosing a profile, you'll learn how easy it is to get bogged down with credit card debt, even if you plan on making a great salary. This site also lets you calculate the costs of college and for buying a used car, in addition to offering other games and exercises that demonstrate how "it all adds up."

Junior Achievement
www.ja.org
    Learn how to join JA and let other teens' success be your inspiration!

National Teen Resource Board
www.ntrbonline.org
    This sophisticated site contains thirty tips to becoming rich, project ideas that lead to financial success, and money games and quizzes.

Reality Check
www.jumpstartcoalition.org/madmoney/pgv_money_rc_main.html
    Take a quiz based on how you want to live to see how much you need to earn.

Sense and Dollars
senseanddollars.thinkport.org/
    Smart site on earning, spending, and saving money; includes games on how to live on your own, saving for the prom, and shopping with credit.

Someday Soon
www.somedaysoon.brooklynpubliclibrary.org

If you've ever dreamed of starting your own business, this site's for you. Get help for starting, growing, and running a business from marketing and finance, to taxes and publicity.

Teen Consumer Scrapbook
www.atg.wa.gov/teenconsumer
Don't get ripped off! This site gives the scoop on music clubs, fake product and Internet scams, telemarketing, car repair, health club memberships, and more.

Teens & Their Money
www.fool.com/teens/teens.htm
Use this not-so-foolish advice from the wise-cracking team of two brothers, the Motley Fool, to get ahead of the game!

Understanding Taxes
www.irs.gov/app/understandingTaxes/jsp/s_student_home.jsp
Why is my paycheck so much less than I thought it would be? This is an online 'zine for understanding taxes.

YoungBiz
http://www.youngbiz.com
Your guide to business, careers, investing, and especially entrepreneurship, with real success stories.

Young Money Magazine
http://www.youngmoney.com
Monthly articles on timely topics, many written by teens.

Zillions Investment Clubs
http://www.zillions.org/Features/Invest/invest03.html
Tells stories of four different investment clubs started by teens and gives ideas for how to start your own.

Appendix I

BRANDED! QUIZ

1. Which of these companies is the oldest?
   a. Cracker Jack
   b. Coca-Cola
   c. Wrigley's

2. Which of these companies is identified by an embroidered crocodile?
   a. Lacoste
   b. Ralph Lauren
   c. Coco Chanel

3. Whose slogan is "I'm lovin' it"?
   a. L'Oreal
   b. McDonald's
   c. Pillsbury

4. Fill in the blank of this famous slogan: "Pardon me. Do you have any _____?"

   a. Heinz ketchup

   b. Grey Poupon

   c. A-1 sauce

5. Which company owns Frito Lay, Tropicana, Quaker Oats, and Gatorade?

   a. Pepsi Co.

   b. Budweiser

   c. Coca-Cola

6. Where are you most likely to find the Billabong brand?

   a. At the beach

   b. On an airplane

   c. In a school

7. Which clothing brand's simple logo consists of the company name on a navy blue square?

   a. Nautica

   b. American Eagle

   c. The Gap

8. What brand is Michael Jordan most associated with?

   a. Gatorade

   b. Nike

   c. Champion

9. Which credit card company is famous for their "priceless" commercials?

   a. Visa

   b. MasterCard

   c. American Express

10. Which German car manufacturer makes The Beetle?

    a. Audi

    b. BMW

    c. Volkswagen

11. Which cell phone company asks "Can you hear me now?"

   a. Verizon

   b. Nokia

   c. T-Mobile

12. Which broadcasting company uses a peacock for their logo?

   a. CBS

   b. ABC

   c. NBC

Answers: (1) b; (2) a; (3) b; (4) b; (5) a; (6) a; (7) c; (8) b; (9) b; (10) c; (11) a; (12) c

INDEX

Photograph by Kathy Stauffer

About the Author

VALERIE A. OTT is the Manager of the Reference Department at Wadsworth Public Library where she was Teen Services Librarian for four years. She is on the Action Council of the Young Adult Services Division of the Ohio Library Council, and is a member of ALA as well as YALSA, for which she serves on the Communications Task Force. Ott has been editor for YALS, YALSA's quarterly journal and is a monthly reviewer for *VOYA* and *Kirkus Reviews*. She lives in Cuyahoga Falls, Ohio, with her husband, Eric.